LIFE

Amit Lodha is an IPS officer currently serving as the inspector general of Magadh Range, Gaya, Bihar. Over the course of his career, he has been part of a number of successful police operations, including the arrest of gangsters and the rescue of kidnapped victims. He has been awarded the prestigious President's Police Medal for gallantry, the President's Police Medal for Meritorious Service, the Utkrisht Seva Medal and the internal security medal for his work.

He has also headed the Border Security Force (BSF) in the border region of Rajasthan. Together with Akshay Kumar, he played a key role in establishing Bharatkeveer.gov.in, a web portal to support the families of the martyrs of the Central Armed Police Force (CAPF).

BY THE SAME AUTHOR

Bihar Diaries

S. HUSSAIN ZAIDI PRESENTS

LIFE IN THE UNIFORM

Adventures *of* an IPS Officer in Bihar

Foreword by
Amish Tripathi

AMIT LODHA

**BLUE
SALT**

EBURY
PRESS

An imprint of Penguin Random House

EBURY PRESS

USA | Canada | UK | Ireland | Australia
New Zealand | India | South Africa | China

Ebury Press is part of the Penguin Random House group of companies
whose addresses can be found at global.penguinrandomhouse.com

Published by Penguin Random House India Pvt. Ltd
7th Floor, Infinity Tower C, DLF Cyber City,
Gurgaon 122 002, Haryana, India

Penguin
Random House
India

First published in Ebury Press by Penguin Random House India and
Blue Salt Media 2021

ISBN 9780143450597

Typeset in Adobe Garamond Pro by Manipal Technologies Limited, Manipal
Printed at Thomson Press India Ltd, New Delhi

www.penguin.co.in

MIX
Paper
FSC   FSC® C010615

For my family. You are the reason for every happiness in my life!

Contents

Foreword

My brother-in-law, the late Himanshu Roy, was an IPS officer. Through him, I have met many IPS officers over the years. I have never met one who was not patriotic. There's something about those in uniform—their commitment to the nation is so strong. I have always been impressed by their skills: high IQ and EQ, commitment, supreme instincts and pragmatism. But rarely have I met an IPS officer who is also a master storyteller. Himanshuji was one such officer. And my friend Amit Lodha is another.

I've known Amit for a few years now. Every time we meet, he has the most interesting and enthralling stories to tell me about his work. Sometimes it is about a case that he has managed to close, thanks to his ingenious method or clever questioning, but my favourites are the ones he follows his instinct on, even though they sometimes point in another direction.

Whenever Amit tells me about his work, his passion is obvious. What strikes me is that he doesn't think of it as a job but, rather, as a way of life. And this is something that I find in all IPS officers I know, including my late brother-in-law. I think this is a quality that is instilled in officers right from their academy days and in the early years of their career. Amit began his career in Bihar, and I know how fond he is of the time he spent in different postings in that kaleidoscopic state. His anecdotes, which he has recounted here in *Life in the Uniform,* come alive with the delightful culture and people of the state, and he shows us how policing can lead to serious but also hilarious situations. I'm so glad everybody now has a chance to share in the wonder of Amit's stories. This book is a must-read!

—Amish Tripathi

Introduction

Policing is a difficult job. But writing a book is even tougher, at least for me. I've always wanted to write a book—it was on my bucket list—but never did I imagine that my first book would be so loved by readers. I am humbled by the fact that *Bihar Diaries* could change the general perspective that people in India have about policemen in our country. I am glad that my book could contribute to projecting the police force and its work in a positive light.

Truth be told, after the success of *Bihar Diaries*, I was happy to just be known as an author. The thought of writing another book never occurred to me. But I kept getting an overwhelming number of mails and messages from readers on social media and on other platforms to pen another book on the police. I felt privileged that they wanted me to share more stories from my life as a policeman.

This book is about my journey as an IPS officer. I have truthfully recounted my experiences that helped me become both a better police officer and a better human being. I have had a lot of adventures along the way and, luckily, have been able to learn from them. I am nowhere close to the legends the IPS boasts, nor am I old enough to write an autobiography, but I am hopeful that this memoir of sorts will give the readers a better insight into the life of an IPS officer. Young civil servants, particularly those in the IPS, might find a lesson or two in the chapters. I have deliberately chosen not to write about sensational cases or encounters with criminals. Nor have I gone into the technicalities of policing. Luck has played a major role in quite a few of my 'successes'—but, then, the harder you work, the luckier you get.

There is a lot of irreverent humour in this book, as, unlike my job, I don't take myself very seriously.

The book largely describes my work as a superintendent of police, a post every young IPS officer dreams of holding. I have written extensively about my posting in Nalanda, my first district. The first posting is like a first love—you always remember it, whether you succeed or fail.

One of my DIGs always used to tell me, 'You know, Amit, if the SP of a district is good, the DIG has nothing to do. And if the SP is bad, the DIG can do nothing.'

I hope this book plays a role, however small, in bringing out the best in every police officer.

I am proud to don the police uniform every day. Whatever I am today is because of it.

Jai Hind!

Prologue

Bihar Mein Aapka Swagat Hain

'*Main naukri chhod doonga*. I'll quit my job if I am insulted,' I kept thinking as I made my way to Buddha Marg to meet a former minister. I was new in Bihar and had heard a lot of officers narrate incidents of people being humiliated by the politician—how they had been kept standing outside for hours and how some of them were even asked to prepare *khaini*, the local tobacco.

'*Saheb* is in the garden. He heard that you have joined as ASP Patna, so he wanted to meet you,' said Mahesh Babu, the politician's PA, ushering me into the bungalow.

'If I am not treated well, I will not take it lying down— I will quit immediately,' I kept repeating in my head as I walked across the sprawling lawns. A few cows mooed from the shed. I wondered who kept a cowshed right next to a garden. Beside the shed was a basketball court for 'chhota saheb's' practice. Apparently, the politician's son was a reasonably good basketball player. But was he being groomed to be an athlete or to take over his father's political team in future?

At the end of the lawn, I saw the former minister sitting on a rattan chair, his legs resting on the table in front of him. He was wearing a lungi and a vest, which showed off a million strands of hair protruding from his back and shoulders.

I braced myself for some kind of jibe, but was in for a surprise.

'*Aaiye, aaiye, Lodha Saheb. Bihar mein aapka swagat hain.* Welcome to Bihar. I have heard that you are an IIT-ian. Your father-in-law is an ADG in Rajasthan, isn't he?' said the politician in a sweet Bhojpuri accent.

It looked like he had done his homework on me.

'Will you have some lime juice?' he asked as he got up from his chair.

I nodded.

I was taken aback by his civility. He was behaving nothing like the man I had heard all those horror stories about. 'He seems quite decent,' I mused.

He yawned widely and suddenly undid his lungi, exposing the red *langot,* or loincloth, he was wearing. He proceeded to rub his hairy back with his lungi and then nonchalantly wrapped it back on! I was shocked and squeezed my eyes shut. All my ideas about the man's 'decency' vanished with the little stunt with the lungi.

I still don't know if he had actually been feeling itchy or if he had done it to deliberately unnerve me.

'*Aap Madam se mile hain*? Have you met Madam? *Madam hi aajkal minister hain.* Madam is the minister nowadays,' the former minister asked as he pointed to a lady squatting in the cowshed. The woman stopped milking the cows, got up and tidied her saree.

'*Namaste*, SP Saheb,' she said meekly.

'Jai Hind, Madam, I am still an ASP,' I replied, as I raised my hand slowly to salute her. The minister didn't seem flummoxed by the fact that she had mistaken my rank, and Madam went back to milking the cows without any further conversation.

Over the next year, I would learn just how much power she really wielded. There would be many instances when I would see her commanding senior police officers with an air of absolute authority, 'Arre, *dekhiye*, SP Saheb . . . Take strict action in this case.'

It is true. *Kursi sab sikha deti hain*—the chair teaches you everything.

My stay in Bihar would teach me a lot, not just about the former minister, who was essentially a good man, but also a lot about managing people. Also that all the stories about the politician's misbehaviour with officials were rumours. Now when I think of those memories, I laugh at the idea that I could even have thought about quitting the IPS, a career I have grown to cherish so much, just because I thought I would be insulted.

As I left the bungalow, I felt lighter. It felt like it was the start of something, the beginning of an adventure. I thought about what it had taken to become an IPS officer and what a rollercoaster ride it had been until then.

1

You Get Only What You Want in Life

'*Lodha, tera kya hoga*? What will become of you?' asked my friend Tarun Tyagi.

'*Haan yaar, mujhe bhi lagtaa hain tera life mein sahi katega.* Yes, even I think you will get screwed in life,' added Jagdeep Pahwa.

'*Yaar, Amit, thoda toh serious ho ja.* Be a little serious. Your CGPA is so bad, your grades are so low—no company is going to hire you,' Gulati said.

'And you are thinking of becoming an IPS officer. Don't you know almost a million people appear for the UPSC exam and only a few hundred get selected, particularly for the IAS and the IPS? I don't think you can succeed unless you work hard,' Tarun said.

'Listen, dude, we are your friends. We genuinely hope you become an IPS officer, we know it's your dream. But you need to be serious about your career—you can't get into the IPS like this,' Gulati said.

'*Jo bhi ho*, whatever happens, we will always be there for you. You know that, buddy, don't you?' said all my friends in unison.

I sat quietly in my room after they left. I thought about the mess my life was. IIT was over and all my friends had been offered excellent jobs in MNCs or were going to prestigious universities such as Princeton and Harvard.

I was the only one in my group who had not got a job yet. My CGPA was a low 6.2 on 10, since I had largely got Cs and occasionally Ds in almost all the courses over the past four years at IIT. I had gone to IIT as one of the toppers from my school, only to realize that I was competing with toppers from all over the country. Moreover, I had appeared for engineering entrance exams, as I had done well in math throughout my school life. But being good at math is entirely different from having an interest in engineering, as I was to later realize.

Not only was my academic performance pathetic, my confidence was at an all-time low too. I felt like a complete loser in every way. I had no option but to go back to my house to prepare for the UPSC exams. My parents had a tough time explaining my staying at home after graduation to all our relatives and neighbours.

'*Amit abhi civil services ki tayyari kar raha hain*. Amit is preparing for the civil-service exams,' my parents would say, avoiding the topic of my placement after college.

* * *

'*Amit, kitna patla ho gaya hain! Beta, parathe pe ghee aur lagaa le, dimaag bhi tez chalega.* How thin you have become! Son, put some more ghee on the paratha, your mind will also work faster,' my *maasi*s used to say lovingly. Soon, this love started showing on my body. I used to play squash regularly when I was in IIT, and the hostel food was almost unpalatable, so I was naturally fit. But in Jaipur there was no squash— only lots of delicious food. From a lean 63 kg my weight ballooned to 79 kg.

I couldn't concentrate on my studies either, finding it difficult to focus for even half an hour. Every thirty minutes, my mind would wander to thoughts of food. And what better way to give in to my cravings than opening a pack of bhujia and eating spoonfuls of it?

I would do anything to distract myself from studies. I would switch on the TV and immediately tune in to a sports channel, even if it was showing an old match. I was a huge fan of Sachin Tendulkar. If he was batting, I would promise myself I would watch just a few overs of his batting. Those few overs would often turn into twenty or thirty.

I also played a collection of sad songs on the tape recorder while studying. One can imagine how my understanding of the Constitution and economics was clouded by my love for the soulful rendition of *Zindagi Ka Safar* by Kishore Kumar.

Whenever I attempted a question and failed to solve it, I would immediately dial a friend's number. I would make small talk for a long time and then ask, '*Yaar, tere ko ye savaal aata hain?* Do you know how to solve this problem? I'll come over to your house right away, you can help me.'

And off I would go. There I'd discuss all the things under the sun except that question.

'*Naveen, tune* Hum Aapke Hai Koun *dekhi hain*? Have you watched *Hum Aapke Hai Koun*? *Madhuri Dixit ekdum zabardast lag rahi hain*. Madhuri Dixit is looking stunning.'

I'd spend a few hours and go back home without finding out the answer to my question.

I also had a tendency to keep looking at myself in the mirror and try to style my hair. It's a different matter that my efforts did not elicit any response from the opposite sex.

In short, I was doing everything to ensure that I failed the civil-service exams. I had programmed myself for failure. It was as though I was trying to run away from success.

The prelims were around the corner, just a few months away. Sensing my impending disaster, I got even more irritable.

'*Aap logo ki wajah se main padh nahin pa raha hoon.* I am not being able to study because of you people. You are disturbing me so much,' I would complain to my family.

'What are we doing? You are the one who starts watching TV after studying for twenty minutes. And you talk on the phone for hours,' they would retort, equally irritated with my behaviour.

I started meeting palm readers and astrologers to ask about my fate. Ever since my terrible four years at IIT, I had started thinking I was the unluckiest person in the world. '*Kaafi bada havan karana padega. Saare griho mein dosh hain.* A big havan will have to be done. All the planets are aligned against your success.' Even the pandit was sceptical about my chances in the civil services and that, too, after charging a bomb for making such a lousy prediction. At least he could have lied and made me happy!

* * *

As the exams loomed closer, I continued sailing aimlessly.

Nearly everyone had given up hope of me succeeding at anything. Except my brother Nikky.

'You were so good in school—you were quite a brilliant student, really. So what if you didn't do well at IIT? You had no interest in engineering. You can crack the UPSC; this is your destiny. I firmly believe you can do this, you just need to take charge of your life,' he told me.

Then one day my friend from IIT, Yashish Dahiya, who went on to found Policybazaar.com, met me when he was visiting Jaipur.

I cribbed about all the things that were going wrong in my life and rued my luck. 'Yashish, *life mein hum jo chahte hain woh kahaan milta hain?* When do we ever get what we want in life?' I said in my typical depressing manner.

Without any hesitation, Yashish replied, '*Nahin, Amit, wahi milta hain jo hum chahte hain*. No, we get only what we want in life.'

During the rest of the conversation, I just kept thinking about this one thing Yashish had said. For the rest of the day, it kept repeating in my head and made me reflect deeply on my life. I looked back at all that had happened in the past few years—during my time at IIT and after that, since I had left and started preparing for the exams.

'What the hell am I doing with my life? And why do I keep thinking so negatively? If I think I am a loser, I will always remain a loser.'

It was a thought that stayed in my mind.

I could see now what I had been running away from for months—years, actually. The battle was within. I had become my worst enemy. I had to overcome my fears and my doubts, and start believing in myself.

The pep talks by Nikky and Yashish had reinvigorated me. Sometimes a small conversation can be a game changer. A moment of epiphany needs but a small trigger. You do not always need a guru or self-help books. And you certainly don't need to go to an astrologer. All the answers and solutions to your problems lie within.

'From today, I will think positively. I want to become an IPS officer, so I will become an IPS officer,' I promised myself.

That was the beginning of it all. To keep myself away from distractions, I moved to my Nana's house. My Nana and Nani lived by themselves. Nana, being a bureaucrat himself, had always wanted me to join the civil services. Nani was an extremely pious woman.

'*Mann lagaa ke padhna, zaroor hoyega*. Study diligently, you will get through,' Nana told me lovingly. Of course I wanted to study with my heart, but it was more important to use my brains. Effectively and efficiently.

Since the syllabus for UPSC is as vast as an ocean, it is impossible to be perfect at everything in it. I went through the question papers of the past ten years, made a data bank of the most common questions and started studying systematically.

I also brought order to my life.

I started sleeping by 11 p.m. and waking up at 7 a.m. My body initially resisted, because I was used to sleeping at 2 a.m. and waking up at 11 a.m., way past breakfast time, but soon, I started getting up early without requiring any alarm. I realized that starting early in the day definitely helped me concentrate better.

I started having light meals—just two chapatis and some vegetables—and stopped eating junk food completely. So there was no more bhujia, no pakodas. My stomach stopped growling in just two days.

In the evening, I went swimming for two hours. I lost about 15 kg in six months.

At night, just before sleeping, I would visualize myself in the uniform of an IPS officer. And every morning, I got to work to realize my dream.

I marvelled at the power of the mind. I easily adapted to the lifestyle changes and started feeling much better, both physically and mentally.

I stopped calling my friends and started believing in myself. 'If they can solve the problems, so can I.'

I had failed math at IIT, but I took it up as one of the optional subjects for the CSE mains. I wanted to prove to myself that I could overcome my failures.

In the beginning, it took six to seven attempts to solve a problem, but it gradually came down to one or two with practice. I started becoming more and more confident with time.

To stop wasting my time trying to settle my hair, I got rid of the problem. I shaved off my hair and stopped shaving my beard. In a few months, I started looking like a monk who had no Ferrari to sell but was at peace with himself. I stopped looking for external validation from my friends and other people. My only focus was studies and self-improvement. Soon, my face started exuding an inner calm.

The best part of the year-long preparation was the absolute silence I enjoyed both on the outside and within myself. Since Nana and Nani were the only people in the house and busy with each other's company, I became quieter and quieter. I realized that being silent solved almost all my problems. I no longer had any arguments with my family members who visited Nana's house once in a while. Everyone was surprised at the change in my attitude.

When it was time to take the exams, I appeared confidently for all the papers. I was positive about the results as I had done my best.

* * *

'*Amit, UPSC ka result aaya hain newspaper mein.* The UPSC results are out in the newspapers. *Dekh zara.* Check,' Nana said. Tension was writ large on his face but I was remarkably cool. I checked and found my roll number in the list of successful candidates. Though I had landed a decent rank, I knew that I wouldn't make the IPS. But I would get my next choice—the CBI. I had already added the CBI as one of my top choices in the form submitted to the UPSC, as I found the CBI similar to the IPS in terms of the nature of work.

I was not disappointed at not getting through the IPS on this attempt. My change in habit had brought about a change in demeanour as well. I was at peace with myself. Also, getting selected for the civil services was a big thing in itself. I had been unemployed and not done well at IIT. At least my parents could now tell the aunties in the neighbourhood that I had a '*sarkari*' job.

Later, I came to know that I had scored exceptional marks in all subjects, particularly in math and the personality test. I was happy to have done so well at math after failing it in IIT. I wish I had applied myself as diligently at IIT too. Surprisingly, it was essay writing that had let me down. I had a lot of confidence in my writing skills but the examiner obviously didn't think so. As I realized, even a few marks could make a huge difference in rank and cost you a chance at the service you were aiming for.

I appeared for the exams again while training at the CBI Academy, Ghaziabad. The rigorous schedule hardly gave me time to study properly. Truth be told, even I had become a bit casual since starting the job. And my earlier attempt at the civil-service exams had drained me. Unfortunately, my personality was again drifting to its earlier form, probably because I was 'employed' then. My schedule was still all right but I had lost interest in studying hard again.

* * *

'The interview results are about to come out,' Prashant said. He and a few other CBI batchmates had also appeared for the CSE again.

'*Arre yaar, mera toh chance kam hi hain*. My chances are low,' I replied.

Since I had not worked hard this time, I was not expecting an interview call. But I was wrong. I was surprised to receive an interview call soon after. But I did not do anything special to prepare for the interview except read the newspapers, as I was not confident I would be selected.

* * *

My interview board had three very stern-looking gentlemen, but the chairman of the board was a genial person from Nagaland. His friendly demeanour put me at ease.

'So, can you tell me about the Exim policy?' asked a member of the board.

I replied with a stammer, 'Er . . . Sorry, sir. I don't know much about economics.'

The next question was about India's relations with China. I again fumbled.

'Should India also have the presidential system of elections, as the US does?' asked the chairman with a big smile. He thought that such an easy question would help me gain some confidence.

I do not know what happened to me that day but my mind went blank. I was hardly able to answer any question satisfactorily. I remember saying sorry at least nine times during the interview. I was very disappointed with myself. I had made a mess of the personality test, that too after doing exceedingly well on it just a year ago. Before leaving, I went to the chairman and whispered, 'Sir, I am very sorry. I did not prepare well for the interview, maybe because of my busy schedule at the CBI.'

Normally, this kind of behaviour is not appreciated at all, but the chairman graciously smiled and said, 'It's all right. Best of luck!'

* * *

After a few days, Prashant, Manish and a few other CBI batchmates came to my room again.

'The civil-service results will be announced today. We are going to the UPSC office in Delhi to check. Are you coming?

'*Nahin, doston, mera toh koi scene nahin hain. Tum log jao.* No, friends, I have no chance of getting selected. You go,' I said dejectedly.

I was alone at the CBI Academy. I waited for my friends to return. I knew I wouldn't get through but nevertheless called a few of my friends to check their results. I dialled my friend Ajay Chauhan. His brother picked up the phone and sounded elated.

'*Ajay toh nahin hain.* Ajay is not here. He has gone to the temple to thank the Almighty. After all, he has made the eleventh rank,' he said.

I hung up. I felt a little jealous of Ajay's success.

'I should have studied seriously,' I cursed myself.

I then called Saajid, another friend.

'*Meri rank 135 aayi hain.* My rank is 135. I am hopeful of getting the IPS,' he said, sounding happy.

Now I was crestfallen.

'All my friends will be joining the elite IAS and IPS, except me,' I thought.

'*Tu itna dukhi kyun hain?* Why are you so low?' Saajid asked.

I remained quiet.

'*IPS toh tujhe zaroor mil jayega.* You will get through the IPS for sure. Your rank is better than mine,' he said, with a hint of surprise in his voice.

'What? Are you serious? Have I been selected?' I said with utter shock.

'Why would I joke with you, that too about your career?' Saajid replied.

I immediately called home, my heart beating really fast.

'Beta, congratulations! You have made us proud,' said my mother joyfully.

'Your IIT friends Tarun and Anuj checked your result. They did not have your CBI Academy number, so they called me,' she continued.

I was thrilled beyond imagination. I did not know how to react to the news. I started jumping around and dancing. Then I started running around in the academy campus to look for someone to share my happiness with, but there was no one except a few guards. So I just shook hands with them and hugged them. They were bewildered!

My CBI batchmates returned late in the evening from Delhi. Manish and Bharti had also qualified for the IPS. They were quite happy, but Prashant was upset with me.

'*Yaar, tum kitne bade actor ho*. You are such a big actor. You said you wouldn't get even an interview call and now you have got through the IPS. Joking with friends is not a good thing,' said Prashant, who had, unfortunately, not made it.

I just smiled and hugged him.

I checked my marks later and found that I had done very well in the mains again. I had got great marks in essay writing too this time. My hard work for the first attempt had probably reflected in my performance in the exams.

I had got average marks in the interview, which pushed my rank down. Nevertheless, I was extremely thankful to the chairman for being magnanimous in spite of my disastrous performance. The chairman had probably liked my honesty!

My dream had come true. I was soon going to wear the uniform of an IPS officer. I felt truly blessed.

2

The Third Most Handsome Guy!

It was a wonderful feeling to set foot inside the fantastic Lal Bahadur Shastri National Academy of Administration for our foundation course. The academy was nestled in the beautiful hills of Mussoorie, blanketed by clouds. It all looked even prettier to me because of the pride and joy I felt at being part of the elite civil services of India. My friend Manish Kharbikar and I were among the first to reach the academy. We saw the lovely tennis courts there and promptly started playing a match. In the evening, many of our batchmates from various services such as the IAS, the IFS, the IRS and the IRTS reached the campus. We talked like long-lost friends, though we had met for the first time. The bonhomie was palpable and we were all smiles, but Manish came up to me with a sullen face.

'*Dost, mujhse galti ho gayi hain.* Friend, I have made a mistake,' he said.

'*Kya ho gaya?* What happened?' I asked in surprise.

'The course director, Tarun Sridhar, had asked all the probationers to assemble for the course briefing. Only the two of us were missing. He saw me coming from the tennis court and fired me for not being present for the briefing. He asked me the name of my tennis partner. I got tense and blurted out your name. I am sorry!' explained Manish, feeling guilty that he had betrayed me.

An hour later, I had a terse memo from Sridhar Sir in my locker. The memo sought an explanation for my absence during the briefing. I was the first probationer of the 1998 batch to get a 'love letter' from the faculty! I had no excuse and promptly accepted my inadvertent mistake. It's a habit I have maintained throughout my career. If ever I feel I have made a mistake on the job, I accept it with equanimity, so I can learn from it and move on.

The remaining three months in Mussoorie were a lot of fun. We had interesting lectures from eminent people; we also had a plethora of activities, ranging from photography classes to trekking in the Himalayas. It was a privilege to make friends with my batchmates, all of whom came from diverse backgrounds and were each brilliant in their own way. But some of these future bureaucrats had a mean sense of humour.

One night, Pankaj Thakur and a few of my other batchmates came to my room. Pankaj or PKT, as we called him, was in a particularly naughty mood.

'Amit, yaar, you are quite popular with the ladies of our batch. Maybe it's because of your good looks,' he said.

'PKT, don't try this joke on me,' I said laughing.

Suddenly, our batchmate Varun Sandhu entered the room. He had been desperate to get his cadre changed. According to the government rules, if both husband and wife belonged to an all-India service, they could either go to each other's cadre or opt for a third cadre, subject to certain conditions. So Varun was also looking for a suitable match. Moreover, he was quite vain about his looks. He had been trying to impress our female batchmates but had had no success so far.

Sensing an opportunity to play a prank, I immediately said, 'Arre, Varun, do you know our female batchmates had a survey of the most handsome guys in our batch? You are third on the list. I am so disappointed that I wasn't even mentioned on the list,' I said woefully. I looked at Pankaj and the others, and winked at them.

'Really? *Sach keh rahe ho?* Are you telling the truth?' asked Varun, with a twinkle in his eye.

'Of course, Amitabh has been declared the most good-looking, Vikram is second and you are third,' added Pankaj, nodding back at me. The other guys joined in, congratulating Varun on his newfound popularity with the girls.

'*Mujhe toh lagtaa hi tha ki main good-looking hoon.* I always knew I am good-looking. In fact, I was surprised I wasn't getting any attention from the girls. *Par aaj dil khush ho gaya.* Today I am very happy!' said Varun elatedly.

'Yaar, this calls for a celebration. Let us all go to Ganga Dhaba and have some parathas,' I announced.

'Of course. *Party toh banti hain.* This definitely calls for a party,' said Varun. So off we went to Ganga Dhaba and stuffed ourselves with delicious parathas, all paid for by Varun.

The next time I met a few women from our batch, I told them about the prank we had played on Varun.

'*Accha, akele hi party kar li.* Oh, so you had a party without us,' complained Manisha.

'You can have your share tomorrow. Just continue with the prank,' I told her.

The next day, a bevy of our female batchmates congratulated Varun on being so good-looking.

'Varun, we voted for you as one of the most handsome guys in our batch. *Ek treat toh banti hain.* We deserve a treat from you,' all of them said.

'You know, quite a few ladies are interested in you,' Natasha chimed in. 'You are in demand, particularly with the ladies who want to get their cadres changed.'

Varun's cheeks turned pink and he started grinning from ear to ear.

'Yeah, sure. Anything for you ladies,' he said happily.

For the next three days, almost the entire batch enjoyed a feast paid for by Varun. In fact, I accompanied two or three groups to eat more parathas!

* * *

I had a feeling that Varun would discover the truth sooner or later. And it finally happened. One night, he came thundering into my room.

'Amit, you fraud! You lied to me. I have made a fool of myself. Pankaj Thakur has told me everything.'

I knew I had been caught, but I quickly regained my composure.

'Yaar, Varun, come with me,' I said, leading him by the hand to the bathroom and making him stand in front of the mirror.

'Look at yourself. Are you not handsome? Tell me, am I lying?' I said angrily.

'*Yaar, hoon toh main handsome.* I am quite handsome, really,' said Varun, lovingly gazing at himself in the mirror.

'Pankaj Thakur is jealous of you. You have actually been voted as the third most handsome guy in our batch. In fact, I am surprised that you have not been declared as the most handsome guy in the batch. *Tera sachcha dost hoon main.* I am your true friend. Come, let us go to Ganga Dhaba again to have some parathas. And I will also have Maggi today.'

'Sure, dost! *Bachna ae haseeno, lo main aa gaya!* Watch out, pretty women, here I come!' said Varun, putting his arm around my shoulder.

3

No Pay, No Holiday

I had a week off before I had to go for training to Sardar Vallabhbhai Patel National Police Academy in Hyderabad. My mother chose that week to have a serious conversation with me.

'*Beta, ab tumhari naukri lag gayi hain, tum settle ho jao.* Son, now you have a job, you should settle down,' my mother, like the millions of other Indian mothers in the 1990s, told me.

She had already found a girl for me to 'settle down' with. The first time I met the lovely Tanu, I was bowled over by her simplicity. I, who had never spoken to a girl until I was in college, was about to get married! I was engaged before I set off for my training.

* * *

The IPS probationers of our batch reached Hyderabad late in December 1999. A few officers and constables from the national police academy (NPA) lined us up and took us to the academy in police buses. The sense of discipline that would be a constant in our lives was already apparent.

As the massive gates of Sardar Vallabhbhai Patel National Police Academy loomed up in front of me, my heart started beating faster. So this was the place where I would turn into an officer and a gentleman!

The bus moved slowly through the sprawling campus, giving us a glimpse of its huge gymnasium, the riding grounds, the football field and the parade ground. I was awestruck by the majestic infrastructure and the beautiful campus.

The moment we alighted from the bus, we were asked by the chief drill instructor (CDI) to report outside the mess. The CDI looked incredibly fit—sinewy and well muscled in his uniform. Years of experience training IPS officers had certainly lent him an aura.

'*Kal subah 6.15 pe sab fall-in honge.* All of you will fall in at 6.15 tomorrow morning. All the gentlemen should shave properly. Ladies will keep their hair tied. Attendance will be taken here. If anyone is found absent, they will have an extra period, and strict disciplinary action will be taken against them,' he announced.

Most of us woke up with great difficulty the next morning. Even in Mussoorie we had PT, but we used to bunk it regularly. One of our batchmates gave proxy attendance for at least ten of us. But here at the NPA, there would be an extra class if we missed it.

During our training later, even when I had severe pain from ankylosing spondylitis, a condition I suffered from, I would try to attend all the periods, unless the excruciating pain left me totally immobile. Doing those tough drills through the pain definitely helped me during many a crisis in my career. Policing is a job where you don't have the luxury of working online. Even if you are in pain you have to be in the field—you can't face a hostile mob or fight terrorists from the confines of your office.

* * *

I put on my uniform and looked at myself proudly in the mirror. It was a surreal feeling—I was actually in a police uniform with 'IPS' on my shoulders! I touched my nameplate and the badges. I was living my dream!

The next day, looking smart in our uniform, we assembled outside the mess, where the CDI was waiting for us. He split us up into squads named 'Puma', 'Tiger', 'Cheetah', etc. It was a different matter that we could never roar, only meow in the NPA.

'We will start with light PT exercises and then practise drill. After that, we will have some classes of unarmed combat,' the CDI announced.

'After your indoor classes, we will assemble again in the evening for horse riding and weapons training. And then we will have games. *Koi shaq?* Any questions?' he asked, looking at all of us.

We were shell-shocked. This was going to be sheer torture.

'*Sir, nahane dhone ka time kab hoga?* When will we get time for our bath?' asked Dayal Gangwar, my squad mate.

'*Time nikalna seekho.* Learn to make time. It will help you in your career,' thundered our assistant director, outdoor, Atul Karwal, an IPS officer known for his fitness. He went on to climb Mount Everest in 2008.

'I am in charge of your outdoor activities. Apart from basic training such as PT, parade and shooting, you will also learn rock climbing, jungle warfare and horse riding, among other things. As IPS officers, you are supposed to be fighting fit,' he said.

Before joining the NPA, the only body part that most of us had exercised was the brain, during our preparation for the CSE. Soon, Karwal made us discover other body parts that we never even knew existed! After the strict regimen every day, we would be numb and sore. However, the body and mind soon adapted to life at the NPA. Before we knew it, we were rather enjoying the sweet pain of the drills and exercises.

* * *

To have a first-hand experience of night patrolling, each of us was sent to a specific area of Hyderabad. The constable assigned to me was an archetypal policeman, with a big paunch and a tired face. Both of us would walk through the streets of Hyderabad at night, keeping vigil, lest any untoward incident happen in that area. One night, after walking continuously for almost six hours, my knees started hurting badly. I was exhausted, but being an 'IPS officer', I had to lead by example and not sit down unless the constable did so first.

'You must be tired standing for so long. Why don't you sit down?' I asked the constable, hoping he would accept my generous offer.

'*Main toh pichhle tees saalo se khada hoon.* I have been standing for the past thirty years. *Saheb, aap baith jao, aap thak gaye honge.* Sir, please sit down, you must be tired,' replied the constable affectionately. I smiled at him. The constables and junior officers always took care of their senior officers. I promised myself that I would also stand by them.

It was the first of many times that I would realize that our policemen, particularly the constables, kept awake entire nights so we could sleep peacefully.

* * *

A few days later, Kejriwal Sir, one of our instructors, took us for a 14-km-long route march early in the morning. On the way, a number of schoolchildren waved at and saluted us. We felt proud and realized that people always looked up to the police.

After the march, we went directly to the office of the DGP, Andhra Pradesh. After a few introductions, the DG started his speech, which was like a lullaby for us. It was with great difficulty that we managed to keep awake. We were all cursing Kejriwal Sir for getting us so tired. Then, suddenly, Kalpana Nayak, a batchmate, pointed to the front row. Kejriwal Sir himself had dozed off! He was sleeping soundly, quite oblivious to his surroundings. The auditorium in the office complex was now full of giggles. Reddy Sir, AD (ID), was really embarrassed and kept poking Kejriwal Sir to wake him up. Kejriwal Sir, however, would open his eyes for a moment and go back to sleep again. Finally Reddy Sir had to shake Kejriwal Sir, who came out of his stupor rather violently. He looked quite embarrassed himself.

As a face-saving measure, he quickly feigned scribbling something on a piece of paper and asked a completely meaningless question to the DG. The poor DG had no answer, as he was not expecting such an inane question from such a senior officer. Relieved that he had made his wakefulness visible, Kejriwal Sir promptly went back to sleep again. This was a green signal for all of us. Without wasting a moment, we too gave in to the tranquillity and peace of deep sleep. The entire auditorium was now eerily calm, except for the soft hum of snores. The DG sadly finished his speech all too soon.

* * *

A special team led by K. Vijay Kumar, IPS, who later went on to end the reign of the notorious brigand Veerappan, came to the NPA to train us to become expert marksmen. Every one of us held a firearm for the first time. We ran our hands down the smooth surface of the guns, felt their weight and enjoyed striking different poses with them, as we had seen in *James Bond* movies.

'The pistol, or any gun, will be your friend and your saviour when you are down and out. So learn to respect it, treat it as an extension of your hand,' explained Vijay Kumar Sir.

The team taught us the different grips, how to assemble any gun and how to hold our breath while shooting. We soon realized that it was only superstar Rajnikanth who could shoot ten people with one bullet in movies, for we were missing quite a few shots in real life.

Only our dear friend Dinesh Yadav was hitting the bull's eye with remarkable consistency. The instructor was very impressed with him.

'*Dekhiye, in saheb ke jaise fire karte hain.* Look, you should fire like this sahib,' said the instructor to all of us. Suddenly, Yadav turned to the instructor, with the gun pointing straight at him and finger on the trigger, and asked innocently, 'Sir, my pistol is not working. Is something wrong?'

I have never seen a person as terrified as the instructor was in that moment. His face was so contorted with fear that he could not even open his mouth to speak. He was sweating. Luckily, the gun did not fire and any mishap was avoided.

* * *

Pinaki Bose, from our squad, was a country bumpkin in the truest sense. He was the most uncouth, unruly and undisciplined person in the batch. At a crucial moment, when all of us were standing still and concentrating on our respective targets, Pinaki started shaking and moving awkwardly.

'*Saheb, ye kya Bharatanatyam kar rahe ho?* What is this Bharatanatyam you are doing?' the instructor scolded him.

'Sir, I want to go to the latrine—I did not pass my stool in the morning. I can't control my bowels any more,' Pinaki replied shyly.

The instructor blasted him for not being regular with his morning ablutions.

'Sir, I was in the latrine, halfway through, when the whistle blew for falling in. So I pulled up my shorts and ran down,' pat came the reply.

The instructor had nothing more to say.

* * *

The rock-climbing module organized by the experts of the ITBP made everyone realize the value of life. Dangling from the heights of the NPA rocks, almost all of us were afraid. But our batchmate Amrit Raj was doing the difficult stomach-rappelling quite easily, much to our surprise. Soon, we discovered his secret. He would simply close his eyes and get down as soon as possible. When he neared the base, he literally jumped down for his life. After every rappelling session, he thanked god, saying, 'At least I'll live for a few more hours.'

We also had to piggyback, where we had to carry a fellow on our back all the way down the rock face. We were divided into pairs.

Jairam Meena, our thinnest batchmate, barely 56 kg, went to the ITBP trainers and said, '*Sir, main naukri chhod raha hoon.* I am resigning from the IPS.'

'Why?' asked the shocked trainer.

'Sir, you have made Rajul Shukla my partner. I simply can't lift him. Just look at him.'

The trainer turned to look at Rajul, all of 110 kg, sitting on a rock, gobbling down some bananas. Jairam was promptly exempted from the piggyback drill on humanitarian grounds.

* * *

A few days later, all of us were asked to climb our mess building using the drain pipes. Rajul somehow managed to get till the parapet of the second floor, with a lot of guidance from the instructors. But then the poor guy got stuck—he could neither go down nor up, as he simply could not lift his body!

Sheepishly, he asked the ITBP instructor, '*Sir, ab main kya karoon?* What do I do?'

Nonchalantly, the, instructor replied, '*Chai peeyo, saheb. Abhi mangate hain.* Have tea. I will just get it served.' The entire squad started laughing, as Rajul hung on for dear life. Finally, six of us were called to haul him up. It really required a Herculean effort from all of us to pull him over the parapet!

* * *

Amrit always looked as if he had all the problems in the world. One day, as a concerned friend, I asked him why he always looked so melancholic. Amrit broke down.

'Yaar, it's Ragini who is causing me so much tension,' he said.

Although I had zero experience in matters related to the opposite sex, I started doing what every Indian enjoys—give free advice! I started giving him all kinds of fundas on how to deal with girls and heartbreak.

'Yaar, Ragini is not a girl—it is a horse that I am trying to ride. I have already been thrown off twice and now I am really scared to ride it,' said Amrit.

I was speechless.

A horse immediately knows if a rider can mount it. The horse plays all kind of tricks to throw off an inexperienced rider. It is a sight to see petrified riders hang on for dear life with their arms around the horse's neck.

'Sir, what is the point of learning horse riding?' we asked the riding ustad.

'Mounting a horse and riding it gives you confidence, so you can handle any situation, however out of control it seems. It will help you evolve as a policeman,' he replied.

'And, of course, you learn how to ride a horse—what else?' he finished.

* * *

We went to CSWT, Indore, for advanced weapons training. One day, the ustad told us about grenades and their explosive power. The instructor lobbed two to three grenades around 25 yards from us for a demonstration. They exploded with massive force.

'*Grenade bada khatarnak hota hain.* A grenade is a dangerous thing. Once you remove the pin and throw it, it will explode in about four seconds,' he said, holding one up.

'I'll show you the technique to throw a grenade. You need to rotate your arm like Kapil Dev does,' he continued.

The ustad lifted his arm to throw the grenade but it slipped and fell from his hand to the ground.

All of us panicked. The grenade would burst in four seconds, we had been told. We would all die! We ran for our lives. There was utter chaos. People bumped into each other, collided with trees, fell into thorny bushes. Krishna Prakash, who was a great sprinter, ran 400 metres non-stop at breakneck speed.

He'd have probably broken the world record for sprinting if someone were recording this. Some of us, like me, fell to the ground and waited for our end to come, expecting the grenade to burst at any moment. All of a sudden, we heard loud laughter. It was the ustad. He was doubled up laughing.

'*Ye toh dead grenade tha practice ke liye.* It was a dead grenade for practice. It won't explode. Ha ha ha!'

The ustad had fooled all of us. We also started laughing, a little embarrassed at first but then out of sheer relief. Every one of us still remembers that moment of our lives—the feeling of waiting for death, a feeling we would experience a few times in our career.

* * *

Apart from riding, swimming was another test that many of us dreaded. To pass the test, we had to swim a length of 50 metres and jump from a 3-metre diving board.

Vineet Mathur from our batch was known for his flamboyance and fake American accent. He came in style for the test. He was wearing a fluorescent green costume, with matching goggles and a stylish swimming cap. The only problem was that he didn't know how to swim. He came up with a novel idea. He inhaled as much air as he could, closed his eyes and jumped into the pool. He had just started 'swimming' when he ran out of breath. The poor guy panicked. His body gave way and he started shouting for help in chaste Hindi, forgetting his American accent.

'*Bachao, bachao! Main doob raha hoon!* Help, help! I'm drowning!' yelped Vineet, terrified.

Vineet started flailing and gulped a mouthful of water. I am sure he was wondering why no ustad had jumped in to save him.

But then his feet touched the floor of the pool and he realized he could stand in the water. He had not even crossed the shallow end of the pool!

We all had a hearty laugh, but it wasn't long before the mood turned glum. Our AD, OD, Karwal Sir had taken us to the outskirts of Hyderabad for a jungle-survival module organized with the help of CRPF commandos, in the early morning of a Sunday.

'*Kya yaar! Ek hi Sunday milta hain.* We get only one Sunday. Karwal Sir can't let us rest even for one day!' complained Harmeet Singh, the popular sardar of our batch.

'*Aur woh bhi is jungle mein!* That, too, in this jungle,' added Amish. 'We are thirsty and famished. *Haalat kharab ho rahi hain.* We are in trouble.'

'Isn't Sunday declared a holiday by the government? We are not supposed to work today. I'll check the rules and go to court, if required,' said 'Baba', who had earned this sobriquet for all the unsolicited advice, or 'gyan', he would regularly give his batchmates.

All of us chimed in with our outrage at being given only one Sunday and cribbed that we didn't deserve to have it taken away. It was the one day we looked forward to. It was the only day we could go out to eat to escape the mess food or watch a movie, but most of us simply caught up on our sleep. For us, snatching away our Sunday was the worst torture possible.

We had just crawled across a stream as part of our exercise, when I saw a wireless set lying abandoned by a tree. The ustad, or instructor, had probably gone to answer the call of nature and left the wireless set there. Always the prankster, I picked up the wireless set and thundered, trying to modulate my voice to sound like Karwal Sir's, '*Aaj ke exercises yahin khatam hote hain.* All of today's exercises have been concluded. Please assemble all the officer trainees.' The other ustads heard this command and were rather surprised by the sudden end to the exercises. But it was Karwal Sir, and they had to follow orders.

My batchmates were delighted to see the buses lined up for us and hurried towards them, only to see Karwal Sir glaring at us from the jungle's entry point.

'It's a shame that all of you are behaving like juveniles. Just imagine what an impression you have made on the CRPF commandos! Are you fit to lead them in the future?' Karwal Sir asked us.

'Sir, it was a Sunday . . . ' meekly said Vishal, one of the best probationers among us.

'Vishal, you have joined the IPS. It's not a routine office job. There are no Sundays and no holidays for a policeman. Remember, you will celebrate your Holi, but one day later, when everyone in town has played with colours safely and peacefully,' he continued, choking with emotion.

We could see that policing was not just a job but a passion. We realized our mistake and felt apologetic. I, particularly, was very embarrassed for my stupid prank. As I was about to turn around, Karwal Sir shouted at me, 'And Amit Lodha, don't you ever mimic or make fun of your senior again. Imagine your subordinates doing the same with you.'

I did not dare look Karwal Sir in the eye and went back to my exercises with renewed zeal.

* * *

While we were all going through the rigours of numerous physical activities, our faculty gave us even more stress. As IPS officers, we were supposed to be proficient at law, the forensic sciences and other subjects. It was a different matter that we found it extremely difficult to remain awake during our classes. To keep us from falling asleep, our director came up with some great ideas. He got the ACs removed from our lecture rooms. He also deputed a marshal to sit in on our classes to note down the names of the people who were caught sleeping. The marshal soon stopped writing down our names as all of us would be found sleeping in one class or the other.

Soon it was time for our first exam. Hardly anyone had prepared for it, as we never got the time to study, owing to our busy schedules. We all caught hold of our more studious batchmates, promised them treats, cajoled them and even threatened them with dire consequences if they didn't help us study. After all, we had to pass the exam. Unfortunately, even the toppers didn't know anything. The moment the first exam began, glances were exchanged and signals for answers were flashed. In fact, there was absolute 'lawlessness' during the law exam! And a number of us went into 'cadaveric spasms' during the forensic-science test.

There were some exams, such as police telecom, computers and motor mechanism, where the marks scored were not important and we only had to pass. No one took them seriously—we didn't understand a word of these subjects. We found a way out for these too. We pestered the computer laboratory assistant to leak the paper to us. Even under immense pressure, he refused to leak the paper but gave us a question bank instead. The exam questions were to come from it. Now, the problem was the answers to those questions. We barged into the computer assistant's room again. He let out the secret— all the multiple-choice questions had only one correct answer—'d'. The next day, as soon as we got the question paper, without even thinking twice, we circled all the d's as the answers to all questions. We were out of the exam hall in five minutes!

The results was also declared equally fast. All of us had failed!

We realized there were no shortcuts in policing. We would always have little or no time but we would have to deliver each time—no matter the situation. It was an important lesson. Eventually, we all became more attentive in class, studied hard and did well in the subsequent exams.

We realized that the foundation course in Mussoorie and the training at the NPA were two different worlds altogether. Mussoorie was about learning new things and interacting with brilliant minds in a relaxed atmosphere. Training at the NPA involved studying subjects related to policing and, of course, a gruelling physical regimen. We almost had a 'paid holiday' in Mussoorie. At the NPA, there was no pay left after all our expenses. And, of course, there were no holidays.

In the rigmarole of the strict training at the NPA, we found our own ways of laughing at ourselves. It was good training for the times ahead, when we would have to find ways to maintain our sanity in our stressful line of work as policemen and policewomen.

4

Vholtage

'*Arre, apna samaan check kar lo, Bihar aane wala hain.* Check your stuff, Bihar is about to come,' shouted a co-passenger as he checked the chain around his luggage. I was bewildered at the sudden commotion in the compartment.

'*Bhaiyya*, it's better to be careful. Incidents of theft and even robbery are quite frequent here. Miscreants wait at the border. When the train slows down, they board it, thinking they'll find baggage to run off with,' said another passenger.

I did not have any chains to secure mine and Tanu's luggage, so I just pulled out my suitcases and sat on them. I also started rehearsing in my head everything I had learnt about unarmed combat at the NPA. I sincerely hoped that I would not make a spectacle of myself in front of my wife. We had been married just a week.

'Don't worry. *Kuch nahin hoga.* Nothing will happen. Anyway we don't have any valuables,' said Tanu, sensing my worry.

In a few hours, the train reached Jhoomri Talaiya without any event. I sighed in relief! I had finally reached Bihar, my *karambhoomi*, my place of work. Tanu and I did not know a soul there. We had no relatives or friends there, yet we felt a sense of peace. Little did we know that it was the beginning of one of the best years of our lives.

* * *

As IPS probationers, we were to receive training on how to conduct policing in Bihar, at the Police Training College (PTC), Hazaribagh. We were five batchmates starting our new lives together in Bihar from the PTC. When Tanu and I got there, we were welcomed at the PTC mess by a portly constable in a lungi and a vest.

He ushered us to our sparsely furnished room and handed us candles, matchboxes and mosquito coils. 'Why are you giving us these?' I asked, rather annoyed.

'*Huzoor, light ka koi ataa pataa nahin hain.* There is no surety of electricity here. So you will require candles at night. And the coil will ward off the mosquitoes,' replied the constable. I looked at Tanu, hoping she didn't want to run away. 'Listen, I have married you for life. Come what may, I will always be with you,' she said.

The PTC was the exact opposite of the NPA, though the new Bihar Police Academy at Rajgir is world-class. Our training staff was undertrained and, moreover, the college's resources were limited and the infrastructure was in a shambles.

* * *

It was quite cold in Hazaribagh, so I bought a blower for our room. It was a small rectangular blower and would have been effective had the voltage not been so erratic.

'*Chun, iski red light toh jal rahi hain.* The red light is on. But I can't feel any heat. Is it working?' said Tanu, keeping her hands in front of the blower.

'*Huzoor, SP saheb ke wahaan le jaaiye test karne ke liye.* Take the blower to the SP's accommodation to test it. *Wahaan accha vholtage milega.* You will get good "vholtage" there,' suggested the portly constable, when he came to check on us later.

'*Par blower toh humein yahaan apne room mein chalana hain.* But we have to use the blower here in our room. What will we do taking it to the SP's house?' asked Tanu.

'Tanu, let us at least test if the blower is working. Anyway we have to call on the SP,' I said.

* * *

The SP and his wife warmly welcomed us. After we had talked for a while, I hesitatingly brought up the topic of testing the blower. Madam readily agreed. The blower did not work at their house either.

'*Kya kare, voltage bahut kam hain.* What to do, the voltage is very low,' said Madam.

'Then let us switch on the generator,' said the SP.

The blower whirred into life when the generator was switched on.

Tanu smiled at me. '*Chalo, blower theek toh hain.* At least the blower is all right,' she said.

I was disappointed that we could not use the blower in our room as we did not have any generator in the PTC hostel. But I was happy that the electricity department was providing everyone with equally low voltage. It was being impartial to all—the SP and the probationer both.

'You can use it in Ranchi, where you are going for your district training. The voltage is better there,' said the SP.

* * *

A few days later, the SP sent all the IPS probationers to a police station to have a chance to observe the interrogation techniques of the police.

'You will learn how to investigate a crime. The SHO has detained a suspect in a burglary case. It should be quite a novel experience for all of you,' the SP said.

We reached the dimly lit police station and were ushered straight to the chamber of the SHO. The SHO, or Bada Babu, as he was called in Bihar, introduced himself and proudly took us to the lock-up.

'Sir, this is a suspect I picked up on information from my source. He is quite disparate but I will find out the truth from him,' he said, pointing to a frail man hunched in a corner of the lock-up.

'Disparate? What does that mean?' asked Ratan, a fellow probationer.

'Arre, the SHO means "desperate", not "disparate". This is how they pronounce it in Bihar. They also use "vhetener" for "veteran". You will understand the lingo in a few months,' explained our batchmate Praveen, who was a Bihari himself.

Bada Babu picked up his lathi and rapped it against the grill of the lock-up.

'*Bataa, tune hi chori ki hain, na?* Tell me, you are the thief, aren't you?' asked the SHO menacingly.

'*Nahin, sir.* No, sir,' the helpless person replied. The SHO asked a few more times but the man denied his involvement in the burglary each time. The SHO was getting frustrated and embarrassed. After all, he was being snubbed in front of IPS probationers, who would be his future bosses.

Without further ado, the SHO started giving the poor man police 'treatment'. After ten minutes of interrogation, the man 'confessed' to his crime. The SHO looked at us jubilantly. '*Dekha, saheb, maan gaya.* See, sir, he confessed,' said the SHO.

'After this kind of interrogation, anyone would confess to a crime,' said Ramulu, one of my five batchmates.

This was the first time I had visited a police station in my life and witnessed an interrogation. I promised myself that I would try my best to properly investigate a crime and be humane in my approach to criminals.

5

Saat Khoon Maaf

Ranchi was the second-largest city in undivided Bihar. It was quite cosmopolitan, largely because of the presence of a number of big mining and steel companies.

After my basic training at PTC Hazaribagh, I was to undergo my probation in Ranchi. I was tense and excited in equal measure as I embarked upon my career as a policeman. I put on my tunic and crossbelt, and went to call on my trainer, the SSP Ranchi, Jaishankar Prasad. I entered his room with great trepidation. In our time, seniors and juniors didn't really mingle, and seniors were not particularly 'friendly' during such interactions. Today, a probationer immediately sends a friend request to his trainer on Facebook.

My trainer hardly looked at me when I introduced myself. He was busy as the local elections were about to take place soon, and he had to prepare for them.

After a very brief introduction, I mumbled, 'Sir, I have no experience of policing. I hope to learn a lot from you.'

'What is there to teach in policing? You just need to have common sense and be logical. And, of course, your intentions need to be right. The rest will all fall into place,' said Sir, continuing with his work.

'*Probationer ko saat khoon maaf hain.* As a probationer, you can be forgiven for mostly everything. So you have a licence to work freely. If you make any bona fide mistake, we will have your back.' He ended the conversation and dismissed me.

I sincerely hoped that I would not require any 'maafi' for even a single 'khoon'.

I saluted and left.

Everyone outside the SSP's office looked at me as if I were an alien. I soon realized that Bihar was an 'informal' cadre, where the old colonial customs, such as calling in proper formal attire such as a tunic, were not followed.

* * *

'Sir, can I get a vehicle?' I requested the rural SP, who was also looking after the motor transport, or MT, of Ranchi Police.

'*Arre, pehle ke zamaane mein toh SP ke paas ek hi Jeep hoti thi. Kuch log toh cycle pe bhi jaate the.* In earlier times, even the SP had only one Jeep. Some people even used cycles. And you are asking for a vehicle during your training?' snarled the SP rural.

I wondered how I would travel during my training. Would I have to catch an auto every time I had to report to a scene of crime or otherwise?

Luckily, the MT sergeant found a novel solution for me.

'Sir, we don't have any vehicles to spare as of now. *Par aap dog squad ki Jeep le lo.* But you can take the dog-squad Jeep.'

The police dog had died recently and it would be sometime before we got another. So I could use the vehicle till that happened. I was glad to have a vehicle, at least.

The dog-squad Jeep had a special compartment for the dog, just behind the driver's seat. I would sit in my glorious tunic next to this compartment. But I didn't mind. As a policeman, one had to make the best of the limited resources one had.

6

Indian Style

'Sir, I'm Amit Lodha, IPS probationer. I have come to call on you,' I said as I saluted the DIG and stood at attention.

'Ah, a young officer! Good to see you,' said Negi Sir, in his anglicized accent.

'Arre, I had told you to get me a new sanitizer. And why are the pens not arranged according to colour?' he shouted at his orderly. He seemed to be quite particular about small things. I would later find out that he had obsessive-compulsive disorder, or OCD.

'Did you know my predecessor, DIG Chopra?' he asked.

'Unfortunately no, sir. I had no interaction with Chopra Sir, as he was transferred before I came to Ranchi,' I replied.

'You are lucky. You don't know what all nonsense he had done during his short tenure. Come, sit in the car. I'll show you what a catastrophe he has brought upon the post of DIG.'

I sat silently in the car, wondering what acts of omission or commission Chopra Sir would have done. I thought we were on our way to some crime scene, but our car entered the sprawling bungalow of the DIG instead.

'Come, come with me,' said Negi Sir, as he grabbed my wrist and literally dragged me along.

We entered his house and walked through multiple rooms of the colonial bungalow until he threw open the doors of his bathroom. Why was he taking me straight to the bathroom? Now I was feeling really worried for my own safety!

'You see what Chopra has done! He has put an Indian-style lavatory instead of a Western-style commode. You know how troublesome that is? The PWD will take some time to change this because they are not getting the particular model of commode I want,' Negi Sir grumbled as he pointed towards the loo.

I was shocked beyond words. I had heard about jealousy and rivalry among batchmates but this was a whole new level of discontentment.

'You know, Mr Rajiv Mohan could not succeed in becoming DGP Bihar, so he was made DG Sports, or DG Khel Kood. Some days we might have a DG Khel and DG Kood. This is the state of affairs at the top level!' Negi Sir continued to grumble.

There are many people who keep looking at the civil list to check their seniority, and harbour dreams of reaching the top echelons of the service. To further their own dreams, officers often come up with machinations to disrupt the rise of their colleagues. They look for skeletons in the closet when an officer is being considered for a coveted post. This problem is a little more acute in the police force because of the pyramidal hierarchy. Everyone vies for only a few coveted posts. But, ultimately, nothing matters except your hard work and destiny. One can manage a few posts here and there, but, in the long run, strength of character, integrity and leadership qualities define who you are.

I managed to listen to my senior's complaints with a straight face and left a little later. I kept quiet on my way back in the car, but suddenly it all got to me and I burst out laughing. My driver ignored me and continued driving with a deadpan expression.

7

Bihar Bandh

'Tomorrow is Bihar *bandh*, we must prepare for any eventuality,' said the SSP. He had called an emergency meeting to discuss potential law-and-order problems during the bandh.

'My office will issue an order stating everyone's duty. You should all reach your assigned areas on time,' he continued.

I listened with rapt attention. A bandh! That would be a learning experience.

I reached Khookri Guest House and saw Tanu waiting for me.

'Hari has made aloo parwal again. I know you hate it. Let us go out to a restaurant,' she said.

'Tanu, I'm in the mood for some really good home-cooked food. I am yearning for it. But none of this aloo parwal and chane ki daal. Why do all government guest houses make the same thing every day—aloo parwal and chane ki dal?'

'*Toh kya kare?* What do we do?' Tanu asked.

Suddenly she snapped her fingers.

'Let us go to DM Sir's house to call on him. *Kuch snacks toh kam se kam khila hi denge.* At least we will be served some snacks,' she said.

Now there was a big smile on her face. We jumped into our dog-squad Jeep and drove to DM Sulkhan Singh's house.

We were ushered in by an orderly. Both of us were awestruck by the majestic drawing room. The British sure knew how to live royally. But alas, at the expense of our country's money.

Sulkhan Sir and Mini Ma'am were gracious hosts.

'*Kuch loge aap?* Do you want some snacks?' Ma'am asked.

'*Nahin, nahin, Ma'am.* No, no, there's no need,' said Tanu, trying to act formal.

Sensing that Ma'am might withdraw her generous offer, I subtly pinched Tanu.

She looked at me and got the hint.

'Okay, Ma'am, if you insist,' we said in unison.

We devoured everything served to us. Sir and Ma'am could see that we were missing our homes.

'*Amit and Tanu, jab bhi mann ho, aa jaya karo.* Come over whenever you feel like. This is your house too,' said Ma'am as she saw us off.

We took them up on their offer and, over the next few months, visited them frequently. Mini Ma'am and Sir always indulged us lovingly.

When we returned to our guest house, we found a typical sarkari envelope pushed under our door.

'What is it?' asked Tanu with a curious expression on her face.

'It's the SSP's order for deployment during the Bihar bandh. I have to go to Lal Bagh Chowk tomorrow at 6 a.m.,' I said as I read the contents of the letter.

'Shit, it's already 11.30 p.m. Let me catch up on some sleep,' I said grumpily. 'I'll set the alarm for 5.15 a.m. I wish I had known earlier.'

'*Police ki naukri mein aisa khoob hoga.* This will happen often on the police job,' Tanu said, looking at me.

Since there was no time to inform my driver Basant, I drove the Jeep myself and reached Lal Bagh Chowk at the scheduled time. It was freezing in the morning but my teeth were chattering because of tension. I had only read about bandhs in the newspapers and been impacted as a citizen, but this was the first time I was going to witness it up close as a policeman. I was expecting a posse of policemen at my place of duty but there was no one.

Even at 6.30 a.m., there was not a soul in sight. I was getting jittery now. Had I read the order wrong? I checked and rechecked the SSP's order. I was at the right place at the right designated time. I decided to go to the nearby police outpost.

I was a bit nervous. Though I was now an IPS officer, I still did not how to speak to policemen. Maybe it was a subconscious fear of the police. I remembered what the SP Hazaribagh had once told me, 'The best part of being a policeman is that you don't fear the police.'

I tried to muster up confidence and entered the small, dingy room of the outpost. There was a lone constable sitting next to a dimly lit lantern. He took some time to take in my ranks and got up to salute me.

'*Koi force nahin aayi kya?* Has no force arrived yet? I have been assigned to keep an eye out during the Bihar bandh,' I said, deliberately using a serious tone to impress the constable.

'*Saheb, itna subah thoda hi koi aayega?* Who will come so early in the morning? The people who organize the bandh take their own sweet time to gather,' said the constable.

'*Woh sab bhi chai-nashta lekar aate hain.* They also get their own tea and breakfast when they come. And, moreover, they need the public to see the bandh happening. Who will be here right now?'

I shrugged.

'Then when should I come back?'

'*Sir, aap dus baje se pehle mat aaiyega.* Don't come before 10 a.m. That is the time the shops will open. *Dukan khulegi tabhi toh bandh karenge.* Only if the shops open can they close them again. Only then will the bandh be a success,' the constable continued with his pearls of wisdom.

I went back to the guest house and snuggled up next to Tanu.

'*Kya hua?* Bihar Bandh cancelled?' she asked, surprised to see me back so early.

'Next time, I will coordinate with the organizers of the bandh. Only then will I reach my appointed place for duty,' I replied.

Later, with some experience, I realized that for certain events and functions, one should reach only after everything is in order and the concerned people have reached the venue. This holds particularly true for events where one is invited as the chief guest. I have been to events where the auditoriums were vacant and even the organizers were missing at the designated time.

Whether it is a chief guest or a bandh organizer, everyone in our country likes to be fashionably late!

8

Hi, I Am Sachin!

'Amit, I'm the SP Jamshedpur. A cricket match between India and South Africa is scheduled to be held there this Friday. I have requested the DG to send you and some other probationers to Jamshedpur,' said Suneet Sir.

'You will have an experience of crowd control in such situations. Go with your wife if she is in town. She will like Jamshedpur—it's a beautiful city,' he added before hanging up.

I was excited. This would be a unique experience and, if I was lucky, I could even meet some of the players on the Indian team. It was only later that I realized that the top officials, particularly the SP and the DM, have ample opportunities to meet celebrities, film stars and sportsmen, but usually avoid meeting them. That's because they are too busy with administrative work and policing. Moreover, most bureaucrats, particularly the SP and the DM, do not want to been seen in public with celebrities, lest people make unsavoury comments. I remember when Shilpa Shetty had come to Patna to perform at a function. The SSP Patna reluctantly went to attend the event after countless requests from the organizers. Everything was going well until Shilpa started dancing to her famous song *Main Aayi Hoon UP, Bihar Lootne*. The moment the song started, the SSP got a call from one of the *thana*s.

'*Sir, bahut badi ghatna ho gayi hain.* A major incident has taken place. *Baraatiyon ki poori bus ko loot liya hain.* A bus full of people going to attend a marriage party has been looted,' said the SHO.

The SSP cussed and immediately left the venue. The next day, all the newspapers splashed headlines such as, '*Patna mein loot ho rahi hain, SSP dekh rahe hain UP Bihar lootne ka tamasha* (While there are loots happening in Patna, the SSP is watching the fun).' It was a different matter that the SSP and his team arrested all the robbers the same night after a six-hour operation. The newspapers conveniently left that out.

* * *

After reaching Jamshedpur, I went to the stadium to assess the security arrangements. I understood my area of responsibility and briefed the constabulary assigned to me.

'There should be no problem as such. After all, it's just a cricket match,' I thought.

The next day, the scenario was completely different. There was mayhem in the stadium, which was filled to capacity. It was not every day that the Indian cricket team visited a small town such as Jamshedpur. Things seemed to be under control, even though the crowd was exuberant.

But suddenly, during the match, the Indian batting collapsed and we knew we would lose. After the match, the crowd went berserk. People started ransacking the stadium and throwing water bottles, bricks and even plastic chairs at the hapless policemen.

I did not initially know how to react. The crowd was at a height, in the stands, and we were on the grounds. I looked at a few hooligans and decided to chase them out but one of the havildars told me, '*Sir, jaane dijiye. Janta ko gussa aa raha hain ki India haar gayi. Thodi der mein shaant ho jayenge.* Let it go. The public is angry because India has lost. They will be quiet in some time.'

And he was right. Everything turned normal as the crowd dispersed soon after. Sometimes it is best to act with patience in a law-and-order situation.

Later, Tanu and I were invited to a dinner hosted for both the teams. We were delighted to meet all the players and sports stars we had so far seen only on TV. I had quite an enriching conversation with Rahul Dravid and Anil Kumble, both of them otherwise engineers. And the best moment came when we suddenly bumped into the Master Blaster.

'Hi, my name is Sachin. May I have your introduction?' said Sachin Tendulkar, extending his hand. I was struck by his humility. Truly great men really do not need to show any attitude.

'Yes, yes, I know you. The entire world knows you,' I said, excited as a child. Sachin and I talked about cricket and a few other things animatedly.

'Sachin, how do you bear the burden of expectations of millions of Indians? I mean, you are so young . . . ' I said.

'I cherish it, frankly. This is the responsibility I have chosen for myself. It is not that someone has forced me to play cricket for the nation,' he replied genuinely.

Sachin was almost my age and very mature, probably because he had been shouldering the expectations of the entire nation and playing a key role in the team for quite some time.

It was an important lesson for me. As an IPS officer, I had to do the same thing—take responsibility at a young age, stand by my colleagues and lead from the front. The IPS was something I had chosen. I had to follow the high standards of the service by displaying exemplary character and imbibing the ethos of the IPS. I had to live up to the expectations of the people.

We also met the South African team, though we were not too happy as they had beaten our team.

The South Africans were jovial blokes who knew how to celebrate a victory. They were laughing and joking around with everyone and looking completely relaxed and happy.

'We wish we were also treated as demigods in our country,' Hansie Cronje joked with my wife.

Just two days later, his name was mentioned in a betting scandal that shocked the entire cricket world. The match in Jamshedpur was the last he ever played.

9

Gupt Soochna

'That is your problem. You should have married a little late. *Shaadi thoda late karna tha*,' said SSP Jaishankar without batting an eyelid.

'But Sir, that thana does not have any place to live in. You can post me to the most remote police station in the country for my training, but I will be grateful if there is at least a decent place on the thana premises for me and my wife to live in,' I requested sheepishly, feeling embarrassed.

'Amit, you should learn to live in tough conditions. The life of a police officer is not comfortable. This is your training period, so you should know how the policemen, your jawans, survive in adverse situations with meagre resources. If I don't train you hard now, you will have a difficult time later,' replied the SSP.

'And stop travelling in that dog-squad Jeep. I'll arrange a Gypsy for you. I will also give you a bodyguard, as you are going for active field duty,' he said

I didn't say anything more and left the room, a little dejected. I was to undergo three months of training at a rural police station and learn the work of the officer in charge of Bero thana. This was a very important part of my probation.

'Tanu, I will go and have a look at the police station. If I find an okay accommodation, you can come over. Else you can go back to Jaipur. There is no point staying alone in Ranchi for three months,' I told Tanu when I reached the guest house.

'Arre baba, we will live together everywhere. We will live in that place like it is Switzerland,' said Tanu, looking at me lovingly.

I hugged her and started for Bero, the village where I was to be posted. It was about 90 km from Ranchi.

After an arduous two-hour journey, I reached the Bero police station. The building seemed to be a haunted structure, its thatched roof just somehow staying in place. I was surprised to see the munshi and other staff working under a tree, all their *dak*, or correspondence, and paperwork kept outside on the desks. I also saw a man tied to one of the trees.

The entire staff stood at attention.

'Sir, *pranaam*. Welcome to Bero PS,' said the munshi, trying to find his beret.

'Why are you sitting outside? Who's this guy? Why have you tied him to a tree?'

I fired a volley of questions at him, trying to make an impression on the staff.

'*Huzoor, chhat na jaane kab dhah jaaye.* We never know when the roof gives way. Not only are we trying to save our own lives, but we are also trying to protect the criminals from coming in harm's way. Who wants a case of custodial death? *Isliye iss criminal ko bi baahar baandh diya hain.* So we have tied even the criminal up outside,' replied the munshi nonchalantly.

'Pranaam, Sir.' The poor 'criminal' got up and did a namaste to me, grinning and showing his brown khaini-stained teeth.

I could not help but smile at the civil welcome.

A few moments later, the officer in charge entered the premises in his ramshackle Jeep.

'Sir, there was an accident nearby and I had gone to get the injured admitted to the primary health centre. The injured should be fine soon,' said the SI, Hari Shankar.

'Let us take a round of the campus,' I said. To be honest, I was also concerned about the room where I was supposed to stay for the next three months.

'*Hum rahenge kahaan, Bada Babu?* Where will I stay?' I asked the SHO.

'Sir, there is no place in the thana, but, luckily, just about 200 metres away, there is an abandoned PWD inspection room. You can take a look,' said Hari Shankar earnestly.

The inspection room was one of the most dilapidated structures I had ever seen. Its walls gave off a pungent smell because of seepage and dampness. The paint had started to crack as the water had seeped in through many places during the heavy rains. The bathroom was an ecosystem in itself—a number of frogs and lizards were having a field day snacking on the variety of insects there, and two large Dalda cans were placed inside.

'Sir, there is no water supply. *Toh chapakal se paani bharwa lenge.* We'll get these Dalda cans filled from the hand pump,' said the munshi.

All my plans of living in a 'Switzerland-like' abode drowned in those two Dalda cans.

I signed a few papers and formally took over as the officer in charge of the Bero police station. I then called Tanu from the thana's landline.

'Tanu, it'll be better if you go to Jaipur for some time. I'll be busy with work. This is the time to get down to brass tacks and learning the functioning of the police,' I said, deliberately not telling her about the deplorable condition of our 'honeymoon suite'.

Very reluctantly, she went to Jaipur.

* * *

I wanted to carve a niche for myself in the police force.

I sat in the thana building and rummaged through the files, constantly worrying about the roof falling down on my head. I did think about moving under the tree but that would not suit an IPS officer, I mused.

'*Saheb, khana thanda ho raha hain.* Your food is getting cold,' said Shripal, my bodyguard.

I went to the PWD inspection room, my new accommodation, to eat lunch. A constable poured water from one of the cans while I washed my hands.

I sat inside the room under the fan's, which was rotating so slowly that I could see each of its blades individually.

'Why don't you increase the fan's speed?' I asked the constable.

'*Sir, yahi maximum speed hain. Jab kabhi light aati hain, bholtage hi kam aata hain yahaan.* This is the maximum speed. Even when there is electricity, the voltage is very low,' replied the constable, putting my thali on the table.

The thali had dal and parwal. And the three thickest rotis I had ever seen.

'*Itni moti roti!* Such a thick roti!' I exclaimed.

'*Arre, saheb, police ki naukri mein kab agla khana milega kisko pataa.* In our jobs, who knows when we'll see our next meal? We don't have any fixed schedule for lunch and dinner, unlike most people,' said Bholanath, a portly constable.

'*Isliye, sir, hum ek baar mein hi subah bharpet kha lete hain.* That is why we eat as much as possible in the morning to fill us up,' added Khalid, another constable.

I looked at him and smiled. Almost all policemen have very erratic lifestyles. There is no fixed time for sleeping, eating or exercising. No wonder this lifestyle plays havoc with their health and often becomes the reason for many policemen to be out of shape.

Now that I was a cop, I realized my schedule would be similar.

'*Khale, nahin toh baad mein bhookh lagegi.* Eat, or you will feel hungry later,' I told myself and tried to eat as much as possible. It was difficult to bite through the thick rotis, though, and I hated the parwal sabzi.

* * *

I started out in my Gypsy for the night patrol. The roads were pitch-dark, with almost no traffic.

'*Saheb, yahi se laut jaate hain.* Let us turnaround from here. *Aage Naxal ka khatra hain.* There is a Naxal scare ahead,' said the driver, Khalid.

'Why should we be scared of Naxalites? We should at least patrol till the limits of our jurisdiction,' I said.

'*Sir, isme koi bahaduri nahin hain.* There is no bravery in this. The Naxals can lay landmines on these desolate tracks and easily ambush us. And now I will tell you another problem where your police training cannot help you at all,' Khalid continued.

'*Raat ko yahaan haathiyon ka poora jhund ghoomta hain.* A whole herd of elephants wanders this stretch at night,' said Khalid.

I did not argue any more. The NPA had certainly not taught us to tackle wild elephants. Khalid turned the Gypsy around.

We checked a few shops and the local petrol pump, and returned to the thana at 2 a.m.

Life was slow in Bero. Initially I got frustrated and looked for any excuse to go to Ranchi. But after a few weeks, I realized that I had to start treating it as a learning opportunity. I knew I had to keep my chin up and be a responsible officer, no matter how small the jurisdiction under me was. So I stopped giving in to every whim to go to Ranchi and tried to do my best in Bero.

* * *

One day, I opened the post and was particularly intrigued by a letter marked 'Gupt Soochna', or 'secret information'.

The letter mentioned an address where I could find a cache of arms looted by the Naxals.

'*Huzoor, aapse bahut umeed hain.* We have very high hopes from you—a young, honest IPS officer,' the last line of the letter said.

I called Hari Shankar and told him about the letter. 'Sir, this village is quite far off. There isn't even any pukka road to the village. *Bahut nadi-naale hain.* You will have to cross a number of streams to get there. This must be fake information. People know that an IPS officer has joined, so they are sending such letters,' he said.

'You just get everyone ready to go there,' I ordered.

'This guy Hari Shankar is a shirker. He does not want to work. Who knows, I might actually unearth a Naxal den and find some looted weapons,' I muttered to myself.

The journey to the village was exhausting. Hari Shankar was right. It took us almost three hours to reach the village.

My uniform and shoes were badly soiled after crossing all those streams and walking in the mud. We started looking for the address mentioned when we reached the village.

'*Sir, yahi ghar hain.* This is the house,' said an old woman sitting outside a hut on her charpoy.

I wondered how she knew what we were looking for.

'*Isi ghar mein Naxal hatiyar chhupate hain.* This is where the Naxals hide their weapons. Arrest the owner, Ram Dhari Oraon,' she said.

I signalled to my men to cock their weapons and cover each other. In typical Bollywood style, I kicked open the door of the decrepit house, only to see a family eating lunch inside.

All the members got up, looking terrified.

'*Saheb, hum kya kiye hain?*' asked a worried man, with folded hands.

'*Hari Shankar, kona kona chhan lo.* Check every nook and cranny,' I ordered.

The police team and I searched the small house for half an hour but did not get anything.

Finally, the house owner, Ram Dhari, meekly said, '*Humko fasaane ki koshish hain.* Somebody is trying to set me up.'

I knew he was right. I instinctively suspected the old woman who had been sitting outside. She lived in the adjoining house.

'*Maaji, yahaan toh kuch nahin mila.* We did not find anything here. Were you the one who sent the letter to the police?' I asked

'*Haan, maine bheja tha. Ye jo naariyal ke ped dekh rahe ho, woh naariyal mere upar kabhi bhi gir sakte hain.* I had sent the letter. These coconuts you see on the trees can fall on me any time. I have told Ram Dhari to cut down the trees so many times but he doesn't listen. *Main mar gayi toh?* What if I die?' she replied indignantly.

I felt like pulling out my hair.

'So you called the police all the way just to arrest Ram Dhari because he didn't cut down the coconut trees? It was your way of getting even with him?' I asked angrily.

'*Toh aur kya karti? Police se hi toh log darte hain.* What else could I do? People are only scared of the police,' she said with a smile.

I signalled to all my men to return. I could not look them in the eye. I was too embarrassed.

'*Sir, koi baat nahin.* It's all right. In future, be careful before you react to any "gupt soochna",' said Hari Shankar sarcastically.

I did not react but resolved to act on future information only after thoroughly verifying it. 'What if out of ten such letters, one is right?' I thought.

I stuck to this principle, and it certainly helped me in many of my successes later in my career.

10

The Massage

'*Saheb kaise hain?* How is Sir?' asked Tanu. She was calling the Bero police station from her house in Jaipur.

'*Memsaheb, Sir theek nahin hain.* Sir is not exactly well. It's not easy living in a village without a continuous supply of electricity. He is not eating properly. *Bahut weight loss ho gaya hain.* And the worst part is that he does not have any company,' replied my bodyguard Shripal.

'*Accha? Tum dhyaan rakhna Sir ka.* You take care of Sir,' said a worried Tanu.

Three days later, Tanu was at the Bero police station.

I was shocked to see her.

'Tanu, how come you are here? You did not even tell me!' I said as I hugged her.

I saw a few of my men looking at us. Feeling a little embarrassed, I let go of her.

'How can I stay without you? This our life. We will always be together,' she said with her thousand-watt smile.

Without any fuss, she put her luggage in our 'honeymoon suite'. She was totally at ease with the biodiversity in the bathroom.

I wondered how she would be comfortable without a fan that functioned properly, cable TV or a phone.

* * *

I came back from the police station to see Tanu drenched in sweat, trying to make rotis on a stove.

'*Aapke liye pyaaz ki sabzi banaai hain.* I have made onion sabzi for you,' she said with a big smile.

I saw the burnt rotis and the pyaaz ki sabzi and was reminded of a scene from the romantic blockbuster of our times, *Qayamat Se Qayamat Tak*. The heroine, Juhi Chawla, tries to cook for Aamir Khan but ends up burning everything. Tanu's rotis were certainly better!

The electric supply was quite erratic in Bero. One time there was no electricity at all for eleven days! We would eat our dinner before sunset or have a candlelight dinner with insects buzzing around us.

At night, I started taking Tanu with me for the patrol. We frequently stopped at the only PCO in Bero to make calls to our parents in Jaipur. We would wait until 11 p.m. for the call rates to drop before calling. Even at that time, it was difficult to get through. Even after dialling several times, the recorded message would say, 'All lines on this route are busy. Please dial after some time.' Tanu and I would pass the time discussing the simple things in life and cracking jokes at our situation. We thoroughly enjoyed each other's company.

* * *

One night, much after we had returned from patrolling and gone to bed, I heard a loud knock on my door. I checked my watch groggily. It was 4.30 a.m.

'Sir, *Naxals ne Narkopi gaon mein hamla kar diya hain.* Naxals have attacked Narkopi village. They have burnt half a dozen houses and beaten up two people,' said a visibly tense Hari Shankar.

I sensed the urgency of the situation and immediately got dressed. The Naxals always sought to directly challenge state authority. They attacked in large numbers, had sophisticated weapons and were well acquainted with the jungles of Bero.

I reached the police station and frantically dialled all my seniors' numbers.

'Oh, oh, okay . . . We will send some force,' said one of my seniors.

I had no experience dealing with Naxal attacks. My first thought was to go to the place where the attack had taken place.

'Hari Shankar, let us move towards Narkopi,' I said.

'*Sir, force aa jaane dijiye. Ab toh jo hona tha ho gaya.* Let us wait for the force. Whatever had to happen has already happened,' he replied.

I waited until 7.30 a.m. but no force arrived. I started getting restless.

'Hari Shankar, how long will we keep waiting? This is the first time a major incident has taken place under my watch. The SSP and the DIG will question my commitment. Let us go now,' I said, my voice betraying my frustration.

'Sir, I understand your predicament. But as someone more experienced than you, it's my duty to tell you that we should not venture into the Naxal heartland with such little force. At least let our circle inspector reach. He's the nearest to us,' Hari Shankar reasoned with me.

At that very moment, I saw Inspector Diwakar Prasad's Jeep entering the premises. Heaving a sigh of relief, I immediately asked all the available men to jump into the Gypsy and head for Narkopi.

I constantly kept asking for reinforcements on the wireless set, only to be told that they were on their way.

I had no cellphone and, in any case, the network was quite rudimentary then. I just hoped that the Naxals were not catching my frequency and overhearing my messages.

We reached Narkopi in about two-and-a-half hours. We could see the burnt houses from a distance and a lot of angry villagers. The agitated villagers were shouting slogans against the administration. They had also stopped the Hatia Express train on the tracks.

As I walked along the railway track, a few passengers poked their heads out of the windows.

'*Sir, please batao kitni der lagegi?* Please let us know how much time it will take,' asked a passenger.

'*Sir, humko kuch hoga toh nahin? Hum surakshit hain na?* We won't be harmed, right? We are safe, aren't we?' said another.

'*Bhaiyya, please train chalwao. Garmi mein bura haal ho raha hain.* Please get the train moving. The heat is unbearable,' said a sweat-drenched woman who was fanning her child with her pallu.

Hundreds of passengers were suffering. I had to get the train moving again.

I looked at the mob sitting menacingly on the tracks. I don't know how I gathered the courage to talk to them. Inspector Prasad and Hari Shankar gestured at me to stop but I had already walked ahead.

'Please, I request you. Kindly let the train go. The children are getting hungry. There are old people too. What is their fault?' I pleaded with the mob.

The fiery crowd was taken aback as they had not anticipated someone approaching them. Luckily for me, for some reason the people seemed to calm down.

'*Bhaiyya, meri baat suno, please.* Please listen to me. Let the train go,' I said again, looking at the man in front of me.

Inspector Prasad and Hari Shankar kept their hands ready on their pistols. Should they shoot in case the mob attacked me? Or should they ensure their own safety? As policemen, we're often in such situations. One wrong step can change a situation for the worse in a matter of seconds. And there's no way to prepare for them. All we can do is assess, trust our gut and always try to do the right thing.

'*Jab tak mukhya mantri nahin aayenge, hum iss patri se nahin uthenge.* We will not get up from the tracks until the chief minister arrives,' shouted someone from the hundreds of people gathered there.

'Haan, haan, we will get up only when the chief minister meets us,' the others joined in.

A mob often provides voice to the nameless, faceless people. Someone who does not dare to speak in his day-to-day existence can suddenly assume a lot of power in a group.

I knew the chief minister would not come to meet the crowd. Patna was quite a distance from Ranchi.

'*CM saheb toh nahin aa sakte.* The CM cannot come,' I said.

'*Toh phir SSP ya DM ko toh bulao.* Then call the SSP or the DM,' shouted the people.

I was a bit relieved but did not show it. The mob, of course, knew that the CM wouldn't come. I realized they considered the SP and the DM important too—for them they were part of the sarkar—the government.

'I have told the SSP and the DM. They are on their way,' I replied. Hari Shankar did not look too happy with my answer.

'*Train toh nahin chalegi.* The train will not leave. We will wait for the SSP and the DM.' The crowd did not budge.

'*Aisa kariye, aap log mujhe bandhak banaa lo.* I'll tell you what, hold me as hostage until the senior officers come,' I said without thinking.

As soon as I had said it out loud, I realized it sounded foolish. We were just ten policemen facing a crowd of over a hundred people.

'*Bada boodbak ASP hain ye.* This ASP is so foolish,' guffawed somebody from the crowd.

'But he is sincere. *Bilkool butroo hain.* He is a kid,' said another.

'*Je baat toh hain.* That's true. I like him,' said a young man. I think he connected with me because we looked to be the same age.

'*Chalo*, let go of the train. *Jab tak SP ya DM saheb nahin aa jaate, tab tak ASP Saheb se hi thoda gap karte hain, thoda batiyate hain.* Until the SP and the DM come, let's chat with ASP Saheb,' said an elderly man, apparently the leader of the mob.

The people started getting up from the tracks.

'*SP Saheb, aap yahin apni Gypsy par baith jaiye. Hum aise hi baat kar lenge.* You can sit on the Gypsy. We can talk like this,' said the elderly man.

I heaved a sigh of relief. At least the train would be allowed to leave after so many hours.

Emboldened by the public's sudden warmth, I perched myself on the bonnet of my Gypsy. The crowd squatted in front of me. I started talking about my struggles as a student, the training I had had as an IPS officer and other interesting experiences. The people seemed to be quite intrigued by my stories. The youngsters in particular started asking me questions. Even my fellow policemen were amused. They all listened with rapt attention.

Soon somebody came with tea. Some snacks followed. We were now being taken care of by the people. In the meantime, the train left Narkopi village.

Soon, it was dusk. I was tired of talking. The people looked exhausted too, especially the older people who had been protesting since the morning.

'*Sir, ab aap jaiye. Lagtaa hain SP aur DM saheb ab nahin aayenge.* You can leave now. It doesn't seem that the SP and the DM will come,' the people told me.

'Okay. Thank you for your warm hospitality,' I replied.

The villagers folded their hands. I marvelled at their simplicity. Their houses had been burnt, some of them had been beaten up but they had accepted their fate.

'At least let me have a look at the destruction caused by the Naxals. I will recommend some compensation to the government for your losses. Also, I want your statement to lodge an FIR and investigate this case.'

'*Sir, kya muawaza?* What compensation? We have lost everything. This is our fate,' said a villager, whose house had been burnt down.

I felt terrible. The Naxals had unleashed violence on their own brethren—people who were farmers, labourers, the very people they were supposed to emancipate.

'*Sir, humne pataa kar liya hain.* I have found out,' said Hari Shankar. 'The Naxals believe that Bindu Pahan and Kalu Oraon are police informers. That is why their houses were burnt down. They could not find those two. It was bad luck that two innocent villagers were mistakenly beaten up by the Naxals.'

I surveyed the burnt houses—whatever little was left of them. I vowed to bring the perpetrators to justice.

'*Sir, ab chalna chahiye.* We should leave. It's getting dark. This area is unsafe,' Hari Shankar said.

'We were extremely lucky that the mob did not get violent and attack us. *Maa Bhavani ki kripa hain.* Maa Bhavani has been kind,' said Inspector Prasad.

I nodded. There is no formula when it comes to dealing with a mob. You can only keep an open demeanour, be ready to listen and rely on your presence of mind. And a lot of luck.

* * *

We reached the police station around 8 p.m. The munshi came running tome as I got out of my Gypsy.

'*Bade Saheb aaye hue hain ek ghante se.* A senior official has been waiting for an hour. He is resting in the quarters of Bada Babu, the SHO,' he said.

I immediately went to Bada Babu's residence, assuming that the senior must be waiting for me to brief him. But I was in for a surprise.

He was lying on the bed, with an orderly massaging his legs.

'*Amit, aa gaye tum?* You've finally arrived. I am a little tired. You know the life of a policeman is very tough. That is why I'm enjoying this massage,' he said, explaining his spa ritual in the middle of Naxal territory.

I felt awkward being there while he got massaged, but tried my best to ignore it as I informed him of the sequence of events in detail.

Bada Saheb suddenly sprang to his feet. I thought he was planning to launch an operation. Instead, he coolly dialed a number on his cellphone.

'*Ji Sir, main Narkopi gaon jaakar aa gaya hoon.* I have just returned from Narkopi village. I have a young ASP probationer. I will put him on the job to lead the operation. He will get some good experience.'

'Yes, Sir, you are right. I need some rest after spending hours in the village. Goodnight. Jai Hind.' He disconnected the call.

I was shocked at the blatant lie I had just heard.

'Amit, I will send you some force from the headquarters tomorrow. You plan and lead the operation. I hope you get some results,' he said, before he got into his car and drove away.

'*Huzoor, aapka bhi deh dabaa de?* Should I give you a body massage too?' asked the masseur, his hands glistening with oil. I stared hard at him.

11

Dugdugi Baj Rahi Hain!

'Diwakar, let us start in half an hour. Ask all the men to check their weapons. And eat something,' I instructed Inspector Prasad.

I had just briefed the men on the operation against the Naxals that we were about to embark upon. The police headquarters, Ranchi, had instructed us to go to villages that were supposed to be Naxal hideouts. Most of the villages were tribal areas whose inhabitants were simple people. They could get violent over small issues, particularly under the influence of mahua, the local liquor. After consultation with my team, we decided to start our operation from Moru village, a safe haven for Naxals and hence dangerous.

I was tense but also excited. This was my first 'raid' against criminals. I kept going over the guidelines and the operation in my mind through the almost non-existent roads. No doubt the Naxals were taking full advantage of the poor infrastructure and poverty of certain areas. Moreover, the people living in those regions were disconnected from the outside world, as if they existed in a different India. Over the years, the government has continuously worked against the Naxal menace.

The recent successes against Naxalism can be largely attributed to sustained development by the government in the hitherto underdeveloped areas and, of course, continuous operations by our security forces.

When we reached the village, nothing seemed out of the ordinary. Everybody was going about their work. But the moment they noticed the police contingent, the expression on their faces changed. I could clearly make out that we were not welcome.

'*Sir, jaldi se saare ghar check kar lijiye. Yahaan se nikalna hoga.* Please check all the houses quickly. We will have to get out of here fast,' said Haamid Khan, an inspector who had come from Ranchi with the force.

'It's okay, Inspector Saheb. What is the problem?' I asked, surprised at the inspector's hurry. We had enough men and had cordoned off the village. We were well prepared for any eventuality. The policemen entered the huts and started checking for anything suspicious.

'*Sir, kuch bhi nahin mila.* We didn't find anything,' said the first few constables. One by one, the policemen started coming out of the huts and reporting the same thing.

I was disappointed. We had come quite far based on credible inputs provided by the special branch.

Suddenly a constable shouted, '*Sir, yahaan aaiye. Humko Naxal sahitya mila hain iss ghar se.* Please come here, I have found Naxal literature in this house.'

I got excited and quickly ran to the hut. There were a lot of pamphlets and books on Naxal ideology lying in a corner.

'This guy, the owner of the house, is definitely a Naxal sympathizer, if not a Naxal himself,' I told Inspector Prasad.

'Sir, this kind of literature can be found in a quite a few of these households. The villagers have no choice. They either join the Naxals or support them,' he replied.

I knew he was right. Nevertheless, I wanted to meet the house owner and ask him about the source of the literature. Maybe it would provide a lead, if not anything else.

A young boy standing in a corner looked scared.

'*Babu, tumre baba kahaan hain?* Where is your father?' asked Hari Shankar.

'*Khet mein gaye hain.* He has gone to the fields,' he replied.

I sent a section of the force with the boy to get the man.

After ten minutes, the policemen came back covered in dust and straw. They had a man clad in a lungi and a vest with them.

'Sir, this man is Kalu Pahan. He is a hardcore Naxal. Look, we found this desi *kata* [a locally made gun] on his person,' said the section commander.

'*Sir, badhaai ho!* Congratulations! You caught a Naxal on your very first raid. You are really lucky. The police usually do not find Naxals in the villages,' said Inspector Prasad.

This was the first arrest of my career, and it brought me a strange sense of satisfaction, nothing like anything I had felt before. I had never seen a man with a gun in his hands outside of the police force either.

Suddenly Hari Shankar came running, Tension was writ large on his face.

'*Sir, jaldi kariye. Yahaan se bhagna padega. Dugdugi baj rahi hain.* Quick, we will have to leave right now. The villagers are playing the drums,' he shouted to me.

I did not understand the fuss but was also bewildered by the sound of the drums.

'Let us make an arrest memo. And a seizure memo for this guy. Also get two independent witnesses to sign on these memos.' I directed Inspector Prasad to follow all the instructions of the CrPC. This was how we had been trained at the NPA.

'*Sir, chhodiye memo-shemo.* Forget the memos. There is a crowd of villagers coming to surround us. We are outnumbered. The dugdugi means that the villagers are about to attack. *Aap Gypsy mein baithiye.* Please get into the Gypsy,' Hari Shankar pleaded.

The sound of the drums was getting louder. As I got out of the hut, I could see 200–300 tribals armed with bows and arrows. They were just about 150 metres away. I had seen such scenes only in the *Tarzan* films. The sound of the cymbals and drums was cacophonic now. The tribals' chants were starting to worry me.

'You are right. But please get some witnesses for the memo. How will we forward this Pahan guy to judicial custody without proper papers?' I said.

'*Bithao ASP Saheb ko!* Get ASP Sir to sit in the car!' shouted Hari Shankar.

My bodyguard physically pushed me into the Gypsy. Kalu Pahan was also pushed into the Jeep of Inspector Prasad.

'*Sir, nikaliye yahaan se!* Get out of here! I will get your witnesses, don't worry,' shouted an exasperated Hari Shankar.

Hari Shankar caught hold of two villagers, noted down their names on a piece of paper and took their thumb impressions remarkably quickly.

'But you have to give a copy of the seizure memo to the witnesses,' I shouted from the Gypsy.

The tribals were getting closer.

Hari Shankar looked at me and said, 'Sir, these tribals are furious. We won't be able to tackle them in any way. Remember the Lalu Oraon case?' The face of Lalu Oraon flashed in my mind.

Just a few days ago, an intoxicated tribal had come to the Bero police station with a sack in his hand. 'My name is Lalu Oraon. I have come to surrender,' he had said.

'For what offence?' the munshi had asked.

Lalu Oraon put his hand in the sack and took out a bloody mass. It was the head of a woman.

'I have killed my wife as she was not letting me drink,' Lalu had said without batting an eyelid. We were all shocked at how remorseless the man seemed. An angry tribal is quite dangerous, and here we were facing a mob of them. We didn't want to face a mob of enraged tribalfolk when we were unprepared.

The tribals were infuriated for some reason and their eyes clearly showed they were in no mood for dialogue. We were far too few in number to be able to counter-attack.

'*Agar jaan bachi toh aake saare kanoon follow karenge.* If we live, we will come back and follow all the laws.'

Suddenly, a spear flew past my Gypsy.

'*Driver, bhagao!* Let's go!' I shouted.

I realized that day that discretion was the better part of valour.

12

Police Officers Ko Kya Kya Karna Padhta Hain

'Sir, I am an IPS probationer calling from the Bero police station. The NPA has directed all probationers to get a first-hand experience of a religious procession. It's Ram Navami tomorrow. I will be grateful if you could let me accompany you to oversee the arrangements,' I said to B.S. Raiprasad, a senior police officer, on the phone.

He paused for a moment and said, 'Okay, come to my house tomorrow at 10 p.m.'

The next night, I reached his sprawling bungalow and waited anxiously. He emerged after about ten minutes.

He was wearing Jodhpuri breeches, riding boots and sunglasses, even though it was night. His handlebar moustache added to his look. I tried hard to control my laughter.

'Chalo, let us go, young man,' said Raiprasad nonchalantly.

It was a new experience for me to travel in an Ambassador car with a red beacon on it. A number of policemen saluted as our car drove through Ranchi.

As we reached the venue where the Ramnavami procession was to culminate, the crowd got really excited to see such a senior police officer among them. Raiprasad Sir was decked with garlands by the people when he got down.

'*Arre, iske bhi kandhe pe IPS likha hain.* Even he has IPS written on his shoulders. Put some garlands on him too,' said someone.

I was embarrassed and tried to avoid being garlanded, but some people managed to put one or two on me as well.

I wished all the senior officers sitting on the stage. The DM, Sulkhan Singh, was also there. He smiled and asked me to sit beside him.

The atmosphere was electrifying. Soon, the noise around us reached a deafening crescendo as the procession reached the venue. It was led by a man painted as Hanuman. He carried a mace and jumped around. He was followed by two children dressed as Luv and Kush, the children of Ram and Sita.

Suddenly, Raiprasad Sir got up and jumped down from the almost 12–13-foot-high stage.

'Why has Sir jumped down? Is there a problem in the crowd?' I wondered, a little worried. Instinctively, I drew my Glock out of the holster.

'Relax, Amit. Everything is fine. *Bas tum tamasha dekho.* Just enjoy the show,' said Sulkhan Sir. He patted my shoulder and gestured to me to sit down.

Raiprasad Sir took the *gadaa*, the mace, from Hanuman and started dancing and jumping around. He even puffed up his cheeks to resemble Hanuman. The crowd went wild, and hundreds of people cheered him on. He kept dancing for about fifteen minutes. It was quite a spectacle. A policeman wearing riding boots and sunglasses, madly swinging a gadaa!

Raiprasad Sir came back to the stage, drenched in sweat, but visibly elated by the response of the crowd.

'*Dekha, Amit? Crowd control ke liye ek policewale ko kya kya karna padhta hain.* Look at what all a policeman has to do control the crowd,' he told me in a matter-of-fact manner.

I just nodded, not wanting to point out that it looked like he had thoroughly enjoyed himself in the process. Raiprasad Sir then proceeded to mingle with the people again. He sure knew how to play to the gallery.

After sometime, I turned to Sulkhan Sir and asked him sheepishly, '*Sir, kya sach mein police officers ko ye sab karna padhta hain law-and-order situation mein?* Do police officers really need to do all this to control a law-and-order situation?'

Sulkhan Sir smiled and said, '*Nahin, ye sab nahin karna padhta hain. Aur tumse hoga bhi nahin. Yeh kaam kewal Raiprasad hi kar sakta hain.* No, you don't need to do these things. And it's not your cup of tea anyway. Only Raiprasad can do such things.'

I sighed in relief. I had been wondering if I would be a successful police officer, for I did not have Raiprasad Sir's dancing and acting talents.

'What makes an officer successful, Sir?' I continued with my juvenile questions.

'Very simple. *Mehnat aur kismet.* Hard work and luck. Just do your work sincerely, the so-called "successes" will follow.'

'Amit, our services have a great proclivity to produce such weird characters,' he continued, offering me biscuits.

'You know, the civil service is one of the finest jobs in the country! Thousands of brilliant, hard-working, highly qualified candidates appear for the exam every year and only a few hundred are selected. Their lives change overnight,' he continued, sipping his tea. 'Imagine, an ordinary person, a young man or woman, suddenly given the responsibility of running a district that has lakhs of people. You become "sir" or "madam" for everyone. For some people, the power is too much. It goes to their head. They start behaving in an autocratic manner and develop strange whims over a period to time. Don't let this power override your humility. Always remain grounded.'

Sulkhan Sir looked at me and said with all earnestness, 'Just do your job, don't try to look for adulation.'

'Sir, I will definitely follow the best traditions of our services,' I replied.

I remembered the dilapidated condition of the Bero police station and made a request to him. 'Sir, I'm posted at the Bero police station. The building is in a shambles. The jawans and the officers are living in difficult conditions. Can you please help us? My officers told me that the DM has a lot of financial power.' I asked, hoping that I had not overstepped my bounds.

Sulkhan Sir smiled.

Of course. I will sanction a community hall for Bero. You can use it as a barracks for your constables. Remind me when I go to office tomorrow.'

'The community hall should be completed in two to three months. I will be glad to have your jawans shift into it,' said the DM. People talk about rivalries between services, particularly between the IAS and the IPS. In general, and in my particular experience, I have never witnessed it. Every service has its own clear area of work, though we often have to support each other. The services have to work in close cooperation for the efficient functioning of the government. Of course, some people's egos create problems, but that has nothing to do with a particular service.

I have had great relations with officers from across the services. All the DMs I have worked with, who were, of course, IAS officers, have been excellent.

I rushed back that night to Bero to break this great news to Tanu and all the policemen. I realized just how much Tanu's presence meant to me. I no longer wanted to stay in Ranchi, which I would earlier find any excuse to run off to every few weeks. I wanted to return to Bero as soon as possible. Home truly is where the heart is.

A few weeks later, Tanu and I did the puja for the foundation-laying ceremony for the community hall in Bero, just before my probation in Ranchi was about to end. The smiles on the faces of my trainer Hari Shankar and the police staff of Bero were the best testimonials to my successful training.

13

Mungeri Lal Ke Haseen Sapne!

'*Chun, apni posting aa gayi hain*. We have been posted as ASP Jamalpur, Munger,' said an excited Tanu.

'Munger?' I wondered. I had never heard of the place. All I had seen was the famous show *Mungeri Lal Ke Haseen Sapne*.

We packed whatever little stuff we had in Ranchi and sent it by truck to Munger. Tanu and I boarded the train at night, only to wake up to a tragic sight when we pulled into the Munger station in the morning. There were hundreds of people bathing, sleeping, eating and practically living on the railway tracks. Thousands of people had become homeless because of the devastating floods in the area a few days ago. The railway tracks and the platform were the few places high enough to give them sanctuary from the floodwaters. The administration was doing its best to provide food to the people, yet many went hungry.

But not all creatures in Munger were going hungry. When we reached the Munger circuit house, we were greeted by fat rats scurrying over the sofas and around the kitchen. Ironically they had been enjoying the 'sarkari' food and quarters.

* * *

The local officers came to meet me soon after. A few young netas or wannabe politicians also followed. They all wanted to welcome me to the district.

'*Huzoor, bada naam sune hain.* We have heard a lot about you. Please accept these cashews and almonds as gifts!' one of them, a bearded man, said. He was dressed in kurta pyjamas, the trademark 'uniform' of a neta.

'*Aaj hi toh join kiya hain maine, mere career ka pehla din hain.* I have joined today—this is the first day of my career— and you have heard my name?' I replied sternly. 'And don't get these dry fruits and other things for me. I don't need them.'

With experience, I've realized that a policemen's reputation is formed in the first four or five years of his career. Of course, I did not know this at that time, but my rejection of these gifts was a good foundation for the image people would have of me, and this went on to serve me well later.

I put on my uniform and stepped out of the circuit house with great trepidation. Every eye was on me, making note of every small step I took. I saw my blue Gypsy with a board that had 'ASP Jamalpur' painted on it. I felt very proud. And tense at the same time. I was no longer a probationer. I was a 'senior' officer responsible for law and order in my jurisdiction.

'*Ab kya karoon?* What am I supposed to do?' I thought.

Suddenly a voice crackled on the wireless set.

'*Ek murder ho gaya hain Jamalpur mein.* There's been a murder in Jamalpur. Please come soon,' said the constable from the district police control room.

I took a deep breath and got into the Gypsy.

'So this is how I begin my career,' I mused. But at least I knew where I had to go. By the time I reached, a mob had already got hold of the killer and beaten him black and blue.

'Sir, Parashuram was killed by his own *bhagna*, his own nephew, because of a property dispute,' said the SHO. I was appalled, but also a bit relieved that my first case had seemingly been solved without any complications. However, there was still an investigation to be carried out and proper procedures to be followed.

'Bada Babu, please take the blood samples from the murder site. Get the fingerprints,' I instructed, as hundreds of people looked at me. They weren't used to a young, boyish person in a police uniform directing the proceedings.

'*Huzoor, blood sample kaahe? Ye toh clear case hain. Aur fingerprint kaise lijiyega?* Why blood samples? This is a clear case. And how will you take fingerprints? We don't have any fingerprint toolkit,' said the SHO. He looked at me incredulously, as if I had committed a crime by asking him to follow the most basic steps of investigation.

In those days, Bihar Police had quite a resource crunch. But the policemen made up for it with their hard work. Now the situation has changed quite a bit, and the Bihar Police headquarters has a state-of-the-art forensic science laboratory, where due procedure is followed to investigate cases using new and advanced equipment.

But all that was still a few years away. I accepted that we hardly had any tools to collect scientific evidence, so I took the statements of the witnesses.

I gave a few more instructions and left for my office.

'*Huzoor, apna dera toh dekh lijiye.* Please see your house,' said my driver as we drove through the lanes of Jamalpur.

I felt quite excited. It would be our first house. I imagined decorating it, putting up new curtains and upholstery, and getting new furniture.

But I would have to hold on to my dreams for now. The bungalow was still occupied by my predecessor's family.

I thought that I would make a courtesy call to the lady of the house.

'*Saheb Patna gaye hain transfer rukwane. Zyada jaldi mat kariye ghar mein ghusne ki.* My husband has gone to Patna to get his transfer cancelled. Don't be in a hurry to enter the house,' said the DSP's wife before I could even wish her. This was the worst welcome one could get.

Her 'saheb' could not manage to get his transfer cancelled, but it did take us another two months to get the house.

Tanu and I were appalled when we entered the house. It was in a shambles, bereft of even the most basic amenities. There were no pelmets to hang the curtains on, no taps and even the pipes were missing in a few places.

'*Huzoor, purane saheb ka parivar sab nal, bulb aur pankhe Patna ke dera ke liye le gaye.* The DSP's family has taken all taps, bulbs and fans for their house in Patna,' said the home guard nonchalantly.

Tanu and I were shocked. We looked at each other and burst out laughing. At least they had left the walls behind!

I went to the residential office and saw that the pen stand did not have any pens or stationery. This time I did not even ask my staff. I knew even the pens must have gone to Patna with the DSP.

But I didn't let all of this bother me. I focused on work. I soon started pursuing the arrest of criminals with tremendous zeal. As Lady Luck smiled upon me, I arrested the two most dreaded criminals in Jamalpur soon.

* * *

'*Ye itne saare Parle-G biscuits kiske liye le jaye rahe ho?* Who are you taking so many packets of Parle-G biscuits for?' I asked Maqbool, one of my staff.

'*Huzoor, apne bachchon ke liye.* For my kids. I have twelve . . . no . . . thirteen children,' said Maqbool sheepishly.

Tanu started giving him a lecture as a 'considerate' memsaheb.

'Why don't you do proper family-planning? Why are you treating your wife as a child-producing factory?' said Tanu sternly.

'Tanu, let it go. It's a private matter,' I interjected.

'Chun, as responsible citizens, we must at least ask the people who work with us if they're aware of these things,' Tanu continued.

'*Ji, Memsaheb. Bas ye bachcha ho jaye, phir hum bhi nasbandi kara lenge.* After this child, I'll go for a vasectomy,' said Maqbool shyly.

'"*Ye bachcha?* This child?" You are having another child?' I shouted.

Maqbool nodded, looking down.

A few days later, I rummaged through my drawers and realized that my stock of 'protection' had run out.

I jumped into the Gypsy and asked my driver to take me to the chemist shop.

I got out of the Gypsy to buy some 'protection'. Much to my chagrin, I turned around to see my two tall and burly bodyguards standing behind me, giving me 'protection'. I didn't realize that the bodyguards would follow me. I could not ask for such a thing in front of my bodyguards. I sheepishly smiled at the shopkeeper and went to the next shop.

'*Shankar, Rajesh, tum dono wireless pe zara situation check karo.* The two of you check the situation on the wireless,' I ordered my bodyguards. They looked at each other and then at me. I kept my expression stern to show that I wanted them to follow orders, no matter how unnecessary they seemed.

I went to the next shop and was about to ask the shopkeeper for my stuff, when he smiled and welcomed me.

'*Arre, Amit Sir, aaiye. Hum bahut bade fan hain aapke.* Welcome. I'm a big fan of yours,' said the beaming shopkeeper.

'*Aap humein jaante hain?* You know me?' I asked.

'*Sir, aapko kaun nahin jaanta?* Who doesn't know you? *Poora Jamalpur mein aap phamous hain.* You are "phamous" in all of Jamalpur.'

I must have blushed a little. I walked out and got into the Gypsy.

'*Sir, samaan mila kya?* Did you get your stuff?' asked Shashi, the driver.

'*Ghar chalo.* Drive home,' I commanded.

An IPS officer certainly couldn't live a normal life!

14

Kadak ASP

'*Sir, aap ek young IPS hain. Aapse bahut umeed hain.* You are a young IPS. We have high hopes from you,' said the elderly townspeople sitting in front of me.

'Yes, of course. I'll definitely act on your information,' I said. I was now used to the letters marked 'Gupt Soochna' and 'tips' received on the phone. Some people, however, preferred to come see me directly.

My success rate of arresting criminals and solving crimes had been reasonably high, helped by the cooperation of the people and, of course, luck. Word spread fast in Munger that the new young ASP would actually act on the information given to him. Things got a bit tricky when I started getting information on matters outside my jurisdiction. The DIG was not happy when I raided places that were not within my jurisdiction for suspected criminals. He gave me a call and asked me why I was acting on these tips.

'But Sir, what do I do? Should I just sit on the information I get?' I protested.

'The DSPs don't like it when you conduct raids in their areas. They think you are trespassing in their jurisdiction,' said the DIG.

'Sir, I have to go to areas outside my subdivision. So many people send me information. There is so much crime taking place all around.'

'Listen, crime is taking place in a lot of places in Bihar. Will you start raiding in Lakhisarai, Khagaria and other districts just because you get information related to those districts? *Crime toh Russia aur Afghanistan mein bhi ho raha hain—wahaan bhi jaaoge?* Crime is taking place in Russia and Afghanistan—will you go there too?' he asked sternly.

I remained quiet. He was right.

'I know you are sincere. You are charged up and want to do as much as possible. You have taken it upon yourself to bring about change. A lot of young officers have this missionary zeal. But remember, you are no vigilante—no Batman or Spiderman. You are a police officer who is supposed to do his job within the scope of law. In future, always share the information with the DSP or the SP of the concerned district or area. Have faith in the police of other areas. They are also sincere and trustworthy. God bless you,' he said as he signed off.

A few days later, we got news that a local boy had died because of electrocution. A case had been registered against the superintendent engineer (SE) and the junior engineer (JE) of the state electricity board. I decided to visit the site to investigate and find out if the SE and the JE were at fault.

Anil, my ever-smiling reader, accompanied me. He was in an even better mood that day—I found it a little odd.

'Sir, we must thoroughly investigate the case. These engineers are so careless. *Kisi ki jaan ki inhe parwa nahin.* They don't care about anyone's life,' he said.

I listened to him but decided to check all the evidence before implicating the engineers.

After a thorough investigation, I concluded that the engineers were innocent. The boy had died as he had accidentally touched a live wire where some work had been going on. In spite of barricades, he had wandered into the area and unfortunately come in contact with the wire.

The engineers came to see me in my office.

'*Dhanyawad, Sir. Aapne bachaa liya.* Thank you, Sir, you saved us,' they said with folded hands.

I felt good that I had done justice. It's so important to not instantly believe and act on what is in front of you, even though it may seem like the most obvious choice. Good police work is a result of following procedure, carefully examining evidence, questioning witnesses and then coming to a conclusion.

* * *

After a fortnight, I was given a call by the DGP Bihar. 'Amit, we are posting you to Patna. We need a young officer there. Reach Patna in two days,' the DGP said.

'But Sir, I have been posted to Munger just three months ago. I am just settling in. Moreover, I am going to Jaipur in two days to drop off my pregnant wife at her parents' house,' I protested feebly.

'Lodha, it seems you don't understand orders. You're a policeman now, an IPS officer. Next time, don't argue with a senior officer. Patna is more important than Munger. Do I need to tell you that? It's not for you to decide how long or where you will be posted. So pack your bags and reach Patna,' he thundered.

'Right, Sir, but can I at least drop my wife to Jaipur?' I said earnestly.

'Boy, we've all had kids. Send her to Jaipur with someone. What role do you have to play in the delivery? It's the doctor's job. *Hum bhi apne bachchon ki delivery ke time nahin the.* Even I wasn't present for my kids' deliveries,' said the DGP, ending the conversation and making it clear there would be no further discussion.

I was sad. We had just shifted to our house, after waiting for it to be vacated for two months. Even the paint had not dried in some parts.

I found out that a few people known to me were travelling from Munger to Delhi soon. I arranged for Tanu to travel with them.

I went to the railway station to drop her. My driver, my bodyguards and the house staff also came with us.

'*Memsaheb, apna khayal rakhna.* Please take care of yourself. *Chandi Mata ki hamesha kripa rahe.* May Goddess Chandi always bless you,' said my driver Shashi.

'*Bahut jaldi aapka transfer ho gaya. Aap toh parivar ki tarah the.* You got transferred very soon. You had become like family,' said Rajesh, one of my bodyguards, who usually remained very quiet.

The entire staff had become emotional.

As police officers, we frequently get transferred to other postings. And most of us who go to cadres different from our home state usually don't have any friends or relatives in those places. It is our staff, our guards and our drivers who become our family. They take care of us like we are their own, help us raise our children and defend us with their lives.

'Chun, please reach in time to be there with me. I'm very nervous. I'll miss you,' said Tanu, her eyes welling up. I knew she was not only going to miss me, but also the staff—she had become emotionally attached to all of them. Later on, whenever we got transferred, Tanu was the most sentimental of all. The staff also cried for her.

'*Sir, aap acche hain par Memsaheb aur bhi acchi hain.* You are nice but Madam is nicer,' the staff used to tell me. I never understood what that meant. Was it a back-handed compliment?

Two or three days later I packed my bags, all set for Patna. My staff had organized a farewell dinner for me. Everybody wished me well for my Patna stint. I felt humbled that I had had such a short and yet satisfying tenure in Munger.

Anil came tottering up to me. He was clearly intoxicated. I was angry with this show of indiscipline but decided to overlook it. It was my farewell—my staff was getting emotional. So I let it be.

'*Sir, aapka bahut badhiya karyakaal raha.* You had an excellent tenure,' said Anil.

'Yes, I tried my best. Thank you,' I replied controlling my anger.

'Personally, this was my best time too, the most profitable,' Anil continued.

'Excuse me? Profitable?' I asked.

'*Sir, aapke time hi toh sabse zyada kamaaya hain.* I have earned the most in your tenure. I took a full 2 lakh rupees from those two engineers,' Anil said happily. The alcohol had acted as a truth serum for him and he had proceeded to blurt out all his misdeeds.

'*Aap itne honest aur strict the, toh humne bhi apna rate badhaa liya.* You were so honest and strict that I also increased my rate,' he slurred.

Unscrupulous people such as Anil take advantage of honest officers. Anil was privy to the fact that I had found the engineers innocent. After all, he was to type the order. So he had called the engineers and struck a deal with them.

'*ASP sahib bahut kadak hain.* The ASP is very strict. But I will manage to type a report in your favour. The rate will be high, though,' Anil had told the engineers.

Of course, the engineers did not know that I had already absolved them. Anil was making money for something that I had anyway done right.

I was devastated. I had done my job with the utmost devotion and yet my own staff had cheated me. Sensing my seething rage, my driver Shashi and the other policemen took Anil away. Of course, I ensured that strict action was taken against Anil.

That day on, I decided that I would announce my decisions about all my cases publicly once I had completed the investigation, so no one could take advantage of the situation like that again.

15

Charlie Mike Ki File

I was initially quite hesitant about joining the force in Patna as I had heard that there was a lot of pressure from all quarters. Everything was not perfect, yet Patna Police performed brilliantly within its limitations. There were quite a few policemen of all ranks who were extremely committed to their work.

On the very second day of my joining Patna Police, I got a letter marked 'Gupt Soochna'.

'*Saheb, aapka bodyguard Abhay sharaab mafia aur jua se juda hain.* Your bodyguard Abhay is involved with the liquor mafia and the gambling cartel. Please beware of him,' said the letter. This was worrying because it was a tip about the very man who was supposed to protect me, whom I was supposed to trust my life with.

I trusted my intuition and summoned Abhay.

'*Abhay, tumhari shikayat hain. Mujhe bahut dukh hua hain jaan kar.* There is a complaint against you. I am quite upset. It is true?' I said as I pushed the letter towards him.

Abhay read the letter and stood at attention.

'*Ji sir, ye sach hain.* This is true,' Abhay said.

I was speechless for a moment.

'*Par sir, humare ek puraane saheb iss mein shamil the, toh hum bhi apna cut lete the.* One of my old bosses was involved in these deals, so I also took a cut. *Par ab hum apni galti sudharenge.* I will mend my ways. I will help you put an end to these illicit activities,' he said confidently.

'*Toh chalo, gaadi mein baitho.* Then come, sit in the Gypsy,' I said immediately.

For the next few days, we raided all the gambling dens and storehouses of illicit liquor. Abhay knew all the secret nooks and corners in Patna that were helping these illegal activities flourish.

By the end of it, I was satisfied with the results. Abhay had indeed helped Patna Police ensure that all such illegal activities were stopped.

'*Sir, hum log toh mitti ki tarah hote hain—jaise aap aakaar denge waise bann jayenge.* We are like clay—we will take the shape that you give us,' said Abhay with a smart salute, as if still trying to justify his own greed.

I realized early on in my career that the subordinate police officers and the constabulary adapted their working styles, attitude and even value systems according to those of their bosses.

* * *

'Why are these files pending?' I asked the SHO of Sultanganj.

'*Sir, ye toh Charlie Mike ne manaa kar rakhi hain.* Charlie Mike has asked us not to touch these files,' replied Vinay Sharan, the SHO.

'Who's Charlie Mike?' I asked.

'Sir, Charlie Mike stands for CM,' replied Sharan. 'He has strictly told us not to arrest the people whose names appear in these files.'

I was taken aback. I was in a dilemma as these were routine cases, including one of dowry, where the accused was still sitting at home, and another of embezzling funds. Should I try to arrest the accused and incur the wrath of the CM or ignore these files and concentrate on other issues? I went home conflicted that night.

'Tanu, what should I do? I joined the service to uphold the principles that are so close to my heart, and yet I am unable to take action. I feel miserable,' I said after narrating the day's events to her on the phone.

'Chun, the CM has not asked you directly to not arrest the accused in those cases. I think you should go ahead and investigate. In case he calls, you can say that you were not aware of any such instructions,' she said calmly.

'Moreover, you are doing your duty. Have the courage to tell the CM,' she continued.

'Tanu, why don't you come back? I am feeling lonely without you! And I can get constant guidance from you. You are like my home minister.'

'Of course, Chun. I'm also keen to be with you, but you know I have to stay here till the baby comes,' she said. We chatted some more before ending the call.

I was happy with the solution my wife had given me and could finally relax.

The next day, I immediately went to a high-profile businessman's house whose name figured in one of the pending cases. The businessman was enjoying a game of cards with his friends. I was taken aback at his audacity. An arrest warrant had been issued against him and he was coolly living at home, unafraid!

'*Sir, Charlie Mike ne manaa kar rakha hain.* Charlie Mike has forbidden these arrests,' said Sharan, who had reached just after me. The tension was visible on his face.

'I haven't received any such phone call. *Jab aayega, tab dekhenge.* We'll see when the phone call comes,' I said sternly, and took away the flummoxed businessman. His friends kept looking at him, speechless.

I waited for the call to come from the CM's house. A few hours passed, then a few days. But I received no call.

I took out another file and raided the house of the accused. Again I received no call from the CM. I realized that this was all the SHO's doing. The SHO must have struck deals with the accused in all those files. To prevent any other officer taking action against the accused, the SHO used the name of the CM. The ploy must have worked until then. I reported the matter to the SSP Patna, who promptly suspended the SHO.

The next day, I went to the Sultanganj police station and looked at the bundle of files lying on the table.

'*Aur kaun si Charlie Mike ki file hain? Sab dikhao.* Show me all the Charlie Mike files,' I told the staff with a smile.

16

Patna Police Zindabad

I've been a sportsman my whole life. Playing a sport or doing some form of physical activity every day, whether swimming or playing squash, is ingrained in my system. When I was in Patna, I managed to find the only squash court in the city at the Indian Club. The club was in a shambles, with the squash court frequently used as a makeshift kitchen or a storehouse during wedding functions organized on the clay tennis courts. Obviously, encouraging sports was low on the list of priorities of the club management.

'Sir, welcome to Patna. You'll get a *salaami* soon, a salute from criminals,' said Pranav, one of the regular squash players at the club.

'Salami? What do you mean?' I asked.

'Arre, Sir, every IPS officer gets to hear the news of a big crime when he joins a new posting. It is a welcome from the criminals. I have heard this from my uncle, who was DIG Patna some years ago,' Pranav said.

'Anyway, Sir, there is so much crime here, all of us have either had a very bad experience ourselves or had someone close to us been harmed or affected because of a crime,' said Vikas, another squash player.

'Sir, I was shot in my ankle by an extortionist. It was the Almighty's blessing that saved me,' said Ravi, another player, lifting his trousers to show me the scar from the bullet.

'*Ye toh kuch nahin hain, sir*. This is nothing. My chacha was kidnapped and killed even after we paid the ransom,' interjected Pranav.

The horror stories continued for quite some time. Tanu, who had been listening quietly, suddenly said, 'Is that the reason all of you travel by scooters and modest cars even when you can afford much better things—so criminals don't think of you as a target?'

'Bingo, Madam. You are very smart. And that's why a lot of us have not even renovated our houses. *Kaun criminals ki nazron mein aaye?* Why flash our lifestyle and attract the attention of a criminal?' laughed Pranav.

I did not find anything funny in the conversation. Especially as a policeman, I found the crime situation in Patna appalling.

I was still thinking about this when I reached home. I was about to go for my shower when the landline rang.

'Sir, ASP Saheb . . . I'm Doctor Mishra's wife,' said a woman's voice on the other end. '*Doctor Saheb ko rangdaaro ne goli maar di hain!* Doctor Saheb has been shot!' She sounded hysterical.

'*Rangdaaro ne?* Why would painters shoot at a doctor? Was there any payment dispute?' I asked incredulously.

'Rangdaar is Hindi for extortionists, not painters! Please come soon,' sobbed Mrs Mishra.

I reached the clinic and was shocked to see blood splattered all over. The doctor had already been taken to the hospital and was in a critical condition. On the doctor's table I saw a handwritten poster with the letters written in bold, '*BIRJA KAHAAR NAHIN, KAHAR HOON MAIN.*' '*Kahar*' means disaster. So this was the salami or salute Pranav was talking about. How prophetic. I cursed silently.

'Mrs Mishra, my father is a doctor. I know how much social service a doctor does. I promise I'll arrest this Birja Kahaar.' I left the clinic praying for Dr Mishra.

As a rookie officer, I did not know exactly what to do. In policing, there is no book or set of rules that tells you how to deal with a particular situation. I quickly gathered myself and called all the officers of Patna to the Khajekala police station.

'Come what may, I want this Birja Kahaar. Put all your might into the search, use all your resources,' I said with unflinching resolve in my voice.

All the officers could make out my sincerity and seriousness. '*Sir, aapko hum Birja Kahaar khoj ke layenge.* We will find Birja Kahaar for you,' they said. They immediately formed teams and activated their 'sources'.

I learnt that day that if a senior police officer shows his intent, his subordinates respond wonderfully, particularly during a crisis.

* * *

Just after midnight I got a call from Lalbabu, an officer I was not particularly fond of. It was an opinion that had been formed from what I had heard of him.

'*Sir, main jaanta hoon aap mujhe pasand nahin karte hain.* I know you do not like me. But please listen to me. I have some concrete information about the man you are looking for,' he said.

'Birja Kahaar?' I asked indifferently, because I wasn't confident of the kind of officer he was.

'Yes, Sir. My source has informed me that he's just been shot by his own accomplice over a drunken brawl. He is being treated at a private nursing home,' said Lalbabu confidently.

'Which nursing home?' I asked, beginning to think there might be something in this lead after all.

'Sir, I don't know, but if we send teams everywhere, we will find him. *Police toh pataal se bhi criminals ko khoj leti hain.* The police can find a criminal even in the netherworld,' said Lalbabu.

I immediately called all my officers and told them about the information. The entire strength of Patna Police checked each and every ICU and emergency ward of every private hospital and nursing home in the city that night. I checked a number of clinics and hospitals myself.

'*Hay bhagwan, Birja Kahaar mil jaaye.* Oh god, I hope we get Birja Kahaar. I hope Lalbabu's information is correct,' I thought in desperation.

My prayers were answered soon. Around 4 a.m., a jubilant Lalbabu contacted me on the wireless.

'*Sir, mil gaya.* I have got him. My "spy" has given me the location of Birja Kahaar. Come quickly to Dr Sumeet's nursing home in Machchuatoli.'

I was delighted and asked my driver, Tirkey, to drive as fast as possible. I saw a beaming Lalbabu outside the nursing home. He saluted smartly.

'Sir, I got him!'

I patted him on the back and entered the nursing home. I thought about how I had had preconceived notions about Lalbabu just on hearsay. I had assumed that Lalbabu was corrupt and inefficient. Ironically, this is the image an average citizen also has of policemen. And they are hardly given the benefit of the doubt.

Never have I since let myself give in to preconceived notions about my subordinate officers. I give people time to prove their credentials. Every time I get posted somewhere new, I tell everyone that I'm giving them a month to perform their duties to the best of their abilities. And most of the policemen rise to my challenge and prove to be excellent officers.

To my utter shock, I saw an emaciated person with ruffled hair, who must have been about five-foot-two, lying on a cot. He was on a drip, with a bandage on his thigh. It was a flesh wound; otherwise he seemed to be fine. So this was Birja Kahaar—the dreaded Kahaar, the infamous extortionist of Patna. I wondered why nobody had managed to overcome him physically. I guess if fear pervades, the human mind thinks of even the puniest people as giants.

I motioned to Lalbabu to get Birja off the cot.

'Sir, what are you doing? He's my patient. He's under treatment,' the doctor protested.

'Dr Sumeet, this guy just shot your peer Dr Mishra,' I said, my eyebrows arched.

'Oh, I can't believe this guy is an extortionist! *Jo karna hain kariye.* Do what you have to,' said Dr Sumeet.

Lalbabu and two constables lifted Birja off the cot, ignoring his feeble protests. One of the constables snapped the drip out of Birja's arm. Birja tried to cling to the cot, much to the amusement of the constables.

'What about the treatment records, Doctor Saheb?' I asked Dr Sumeet.

'*Chinta mat kijiye.* Don't worry,' Dr Sumeet said, tearing off Birja Kahaar's medical sheet and other records. Luckily, those were not exactly the days of computers and CCTVs.

We loaded Birja into the back of the Gypsy. I wasn't sure what to do next, where to take Birja. '*Kya kare, Tirkey?* What should we do?' I asked Tirkey.

'Sir, let us go near the Ganga river. You will get some peace of mind and can think up a strategy,' he replied.

Tirkey, who was to retire in another three months, started the ignition and drove straight towards Mahatma Gandhi Setu, or Ganga Bridge, as it was more popularly called. Ganga Bridge is the third-longest in India, almost 6 km long. Bihar is separated into two parts by the mighty Ganga, and the bridge is the only connection between the north and the south of Bihar. The bridge was in a shambles because of wear and tear over the years. Thousands of vehicles plied on it every day. One side of the bridge was badly damaged and vehicles used only the other side. Whenever a vehicle would break down, it would create a terrible traffic jam. This was quite common and the police would have a harrowing time trying to get traffic moving again. Moreover, because of its inherent design, the bridge wobbled a lot, making quite a few commuters jittery.

But the bridge was perfect for us that night. We were in luck—there was no traffic. Tirkey slowed down and stopped on the middle of the bridge.

'*Lalbabu, iska kya karna hain?* What do we do with him?' I asked loudly, making sure Birja could hear me.

'*Karna kya hain, isko khatam karna hain.* We need to finish him,' said Lalbabu nonchalantly, playing along.

'*Kaise?* How?'

'Sir, how do you want it? Should we shoot him and show it as an encounter? *Ya Gangaji mein fenk de?* Or should we throw him into the Ganges?' asked Lalbabu, ignoring Birja's whimpers on hearing this.

'*Nahin, nahin, sir. Kya keh rahe ho?* No, no. What are you saying?' Birja pleaded with folded hands, tears trickling down his cheeks. '*Main aapke bartan aur kapde dhounga zindagi bhar.* I will wash your utensils and your clothes my whole life. Please spare me. I have young kids!'

Lalbabu gave him a whack and said, '*Abey,* you are the most dreaded extortionist in Patna—why are you so scared? And did you not think of the doctor's family when you shot him? You scoundrel!'

Abhay and Lalbabu put a cloth over Birja's face and dragged him out of the car. Abhay picked up Birja's legs and Lalbabu held his arms.

'*Fenk dete hain isko Gangaji mein.* Let us throw him into the Ganga. *Iske saare paap dhool jayenge.* All his sins will be washed away,' they said as they started swinging Birja's body as if to throw him over.

'Sir, please spare my life! Give me a chance!' cried Birja. 'I'll mend my ways and help you arrest all my gang members. Why only them, I will help you arrest other criminals too,' said Birja, hoping his offer would 'change our minds'. He had fallen for our scare tactics easily. Of course we could not have harmed him, but I was glad we were so successful in scaring him. We happily accepted his offer.

'Let us get started, then,' I said with a smile.

Birja started singing like a canary and led us to the hideouts of all the criminals he knew. We started that night itself, and over the next few days, raided a number of hideouts and arrested dozens of the most wanted criminals of Patna. It seemed like Birja did not want to go to jail alone. It's something I've seen again and again. Every time a notorious criminal is arrested, it leads to the arrest of their accomplices too. Once they know there is no way out for them, they want to bring others down too.

Incidentally, the SSP was on leave during this little Birja Kahaar episode, but he called me from Shimla early in the morning after Birja's arrest.

'Well done, Amit. Keep up the good work,' he said proudly.

Birja Kahaar was paraded on the streets of Patna. The man who had struck fear in the hearts of the people, particularly businessmen, was walking with his head bowed, avoiding their eyes.

When I finally reached home, I saw hundreds of people at my residence.

One of them was Mrs Mishra. '*Amitji, Doctor Saheb ab theek hain.* Doctor Saheb is all right now. Thank you for getting rid of the menace of Patna city,' she said, with tears in her eyes.

I had no words. I was exhausted both physically and mentally. I nodded and turned to enter my house.

Suddenly Mrs Mishra shouted, 'Patna Police zindabad!'

Everyone else joined in.

17

Aapke Pati Nirdosh Hain

I was travelling with the SSP Patna to supervise the arrangements for the panchayat elections. A man of few words, the SSP was a thorough professional, who stood by his men during any crisis.

'*Sir, Saheb aapko yaad kar rahe hain*. Saheb has asked for you,' the wireless crackled.

'Saheb' was one of the most powerful persons in Patna. But the SSP hardly flinched on hearing the message.

'*Keh do Danapur mein hain. Raaste mein hain. Thodi der mein aa rahe hain*. Tell him I'm in Danapur, on the way to Patna. I'll reach in some time,' said the SSP over the wireless.

Just five minutes later, the same message was repeated on the wireless.

'*Aa rahe hain*. I'm coming,' said the SSP, a trifle irritated. We continued towards Patna.

But again after a few moments, the now familiar voice sounded on the wireless.

'*Sir, Saheb yaad kar rahe hain*. Sir, saheb is asking for you.'

This time the SSP lost his temper.

'*Unko keh do koi helicopter nahin hain jo udke aa jayenge. Time lagega*. Tell him I don't have a helicopter to fly to him in. Tell him I'll take time,' replied the SSP over the wireless.

There was silence on the wireless. The 'saheb' realized that the SSP was made of different mettle. There were no more wireless messages.

I already had great respect for the SSP, but that day I realized that he could get angry if rubbed the wrong way.

We reached the SSP's office to discuss a few cases.

'Amit, are you sure you have taken the right decision in the Suman Kashyap case?' the SSP asked.

Yes, Sir, it is a clear case of attempt to murder,' I said confidently.

'I'd still say that you investigate the case again,' said the SSP. 'The accused Sanjay Sahu's wife had come to see me. She claims her husband has been falsely implicated.'

'Okay, Sir, give me some time,' I saluted and left the office.

* * *

Suman Kashyap had come to meet me about a month ago. He had had a property dispute with Sanjay Sahu, a leading businessman of Patna.

'Sir, why don't you help me sort out the property matter? It's worth crores. Sanjay is creating so much trouble for me,' Kashyap had said.

'Sumanji, the police cannot settle property disputes. You will have to go to court or the SDO's office,' I replied.

'But Sir, it will take ages for a decision to be made. Why don't you send him to jail? I can then start construction on the land.'

'Sumanji, please don't ask for something that is not right. This is not a police matter. I hope I have made myself clear.'

A few days later, I found out that Kashyap had met with a serious accident. I visited him in hospital. He was badly injured.

'Sir, Sanjay Sahu drove a truck straight into my car. I was almost crushed to death. Sanjay tried to kill me just to get the disputed land. I have lodged an FIR against him. *Bhagwan humko bachaa liya*. God has saved me,' said Kashyap, lying on the hospital bed.

Seeing his condition, I immediately ordered the arrest of Sahu. I was convinced that he had attempted to kill Kashyap.

Now the SSP's order to investigate the case made me rethink my decision. I realized I had just relied on the statement given by Kashyap instead of talking to witnesses or even properly examining the accident site.

This time I went to Agamkua Chowk, the place where the accident had taken place. All the witnesses agreed that a truck had rammed into Kashyap's car, but that the truck had vanished after the accident. No one had noted down the details of the number plate.

On seeing the spot, it was clear that the accident had not been deliberate or an attempt to kill Kashyap. It was simply not possible, considering the busy traffic on the chowk. The best way to kill a person in a car is to collide head-on with it. In this case, the divider on the road simply did not permit that. Kashyap's car was damaged only from the side, clearly indicating that it had not been a head-on collision.

I went to the hospital and talked to the nursing staff.

'Did you attend to the patient Suman Kashyap on his arrival at the hospital a few days ago?' I asked the head nurse.

'Yes, Sir, I took him to the emergency room,' she replied.

'Did he tell you what had happened? Was he in his senses?'

'Sir, he was conscious. He told me that a truck had crashed into his car. It was probably because Sumanji was a little careless when driving that day. He tried to cross a busy intersection without looking out for traffic.'

'He did not take anyone's name? That somebody tried to kill him?'

'No, Sir, he did not mention anyone. He said that the truck was driving too fast for him to see anything.'

'Thank you,' I said.

I immediately realized that I had made a blunder. If Kashyap had actually seen Sahu in the truck, he would have naturally told the nurse and doctor about it.

Kashyap had lodged the FIR after twenty-four hours of being admitted to the hospital. Sure he had met with a dangerous accident, but he had used the situation to his advantage. It was a golden opportunity for Kashyap to put Sahu behind bars for a crime he had not committed.

I took the statements of the doctors, the nursing staff and other witnesses.

I immediately directed the investigating officer to submit a report in court the next day.

Early in the morning, I went to meet Sahu's wife. She looked to be in great distress. I felt miserable for being the cause of her agony.

Her eyes were swollen due to constant crying. Her daughter, who was just a child, stood next to her, trying to make knots with her mama's pallu.

'*Aapke pati nirdosh hain.* Your husband is innocent. Please apply for his bail immediately. I'm hopeful he'll be out soon,' I said softly.

'Thank you so much, Sir,' she said, her eyes welling up. I did not know what to say. I was guilty of not investigating a simple case properly. On my way out, I promised myself that I would never again let an innocent man go to jail.

18

Hum Hain Aapke Saath

'Tanu, you need to take care of yourself. You are six months pregnant,' I said while driving to Dr Malti Geeta Mishra's house. Dr Mishra was one of the most famous gynaecologists in Patna.

'*Dekh ke, Sir, thokar hain!* Watch out, there's a speed breaker!' shouted Tirkey, my fantastic driver from the back of the Gypsy.

Before I could realize the import of Tirkey's warning, I bumped into a speed breaker, our Gypsy jumping high in the air. It landed with a thud.

'*Chun, yahi pe delivery karaoge kya?* Will you make me deliver here on the road?' said Tanu, laughing.

'I'm really sorry. I hope you're all right. There are so many of these bloody *thokar*s everywhere,' I said.

Once at the hospital, the check-up went up well. The doctor made me touch Tanu's abdomen.

'You can feel your child kicking inside,' said Dr Mishra.

I was going to be a father soon. I was excited but also a little worried. I did not know a thing about raising children.

'Don't worry. *Jaise ASP bann gaye aur police ka kaam seekh liya, waise hi papa ka kaam bhi seekh loge.* Just the way you became an ASP and learnt police work, you'll also learn to be a father,' said the jovial doctor with a big smile.

On our way back, we talked and laughed about the various names of boys and girls we had thought of for our baby.

We entered the busy area of the Patna city market. I slowed the Gypsy down as the road was chock-a-block with people.

'*Chun, uss autowaale ko loot rahe hain.* See, an auto driver is getting robbed,' shouted Tanu. I thought she was joking. The market was teeming with people. How could someone be robbed in front of so many people?

But she was right. I saw an auto driver being thrashed by four people, two of them carrying desi *katta*s, country-made pistols. Without thinking, I applied the brakes and jumped out of the Gypsy. I started running towards the auto.

The four robbers looked at me in shock. They were bewildered to see me coming after them. They left the auto driver and ran into the lanes.

'*Abhay, Saheb ke peechhe jao.* Go after Sir,' Tanu commanded Abhay, my bodyguard.

But Abhay stayed next to Tanu, holding his carbine tightly. He was in a dilemma—should he come after me to help or stand guard by Tanu, his madam?

Tanu understood his predicament.

'*Abhay, tum Sir ke peechhe bhago.* You run after Sir. Tirkey is here with me,' Tanu said.

Abhay nodded and bolted after me into the lanes. Meanwhile, Tirkey took out a cane from the Gypsy and stood next to Tanu. '*Hum hain aapke saath hain.* I am with you, Madam,' he said. Tanu felt proud that she was being guarded by Tirkey. The dedication he had shown to his job for so many years was still strong.

I lost track of three of the four criminals. Luckily, the fourth was slower, probably because he was carrying a bag on his shoulders. He was just a few feet ahead of me. I jumped on him and pinned him to the ground with my elbow.

The robber managed to wriggle out of my grip and took out something from his bag. It was a country-made bomb. He hurled it at me. During our training, we were told to lie down when a bomb or grenade was hurled at us—this was the best way to avoid the shrapnel and splinters flying out after the grenade or bomb bursts.

I ducked and immediately lay down flat on the ground. The bomb exploded, sending shrapnel flying all around. Fortunately, none of them hit me. Nevertheless, I was blinded for a few moments by the blast.

I heard two gunshots. Abhay had fired at my assailant. But, unfortunately, he had managed to escape.

I got up, patted down my clothes and went back to the Gypsy. Tanu and Tirkey were waiting anxiously for us.

'Chun, are you okay?' said Tanu, hugging me. I was too dazed to respond.

We reached our house to see a number of policemen gathered outside. The news of the 'attack' had travelled fast.

'*Sir, kaise hain?* How are you?'

'Is Madam all right?'

All the policemen, the officers and the constables were concerned about our safety.

'Yeah, we are all right, thank you,' said Tanu graciously. I was understandably upset. A robbery had taken place in my jurisdiction right in front of my eyes and one of the criminals had escaped from my grip.

'I need those four criminals,' I said. Sub-inspectors Sunil and Mustafa, two of the bravest officers of Patna Police, stepped forward.

'Sir, we'll get them,' said both in unison. I knew they would deliver on their promise. They had a fantastic network of 'spies', or sources.

* * *

After two days, all four criminals were in front of me.

'*Sorry, Sir, humko pataa nahin tha aap police mein hain.* We did not know you were in the police,' said the guy who had thrown the bomb at me.

'*Matlab tum policewaalon par hamla nahin karte—unka dhyan rakhte ho.* You don't attack policemen—you take care of them!' said SI Sunil. I could not help but smile.

The criminals were sent to judicial custody. I was proud that my men had arrested them so soon. Some cases require immediate action because of the far-reaching consequences they can have in a district or an area, or the impact they have on people. An attack on a police officer, after a botched-up robbery, is obviously a serious incident that can cause a lot of panic among the public. The police put such cases on high priority, and, naturally, results also tend to be achieved more rapidly. The only problem is that by the time the police solve one crime, another incident has already taken place. A policeman can never feel that his work is over for the day.

I often think about the way I ran after the criminals that day. Then I was young and brash, but today, after two decades of service, I don't think I can run after four armed criminals. Maybe I have become sensible. Or old.

19

Jai Bajrang Bali!

I had sent Tanu back to Jaipur to her parents as her delivery date was nearing. I planned to join her immediately after Saraswati Puja.

'Sir, I have applied for seven days' paternity leave. The date the doctor gave us is approaching,' I requested the SSP.

'There is no concept of paternity leave in our field. Moreover, Saraswati Puja is round the corner,' said the SSP, laconic as always.

'But you can go immediately after the puja is over,' he added. 'Communal harmony is the priority of the government. You are in charge of a very sensitive area. There have been regular instances of riots over trivial matters. Please be alert in your area.'

'Yes, Sir, I'll do my best,' I said, worried about whether I would be able to go to Jaipur in time. It just added to the stress of being away from Tanu at such a time.

Patna had had a major conflagration between two communities just before I had joined. Certain areas were potential tinderboxes. I had been told to chalk out the list of sensitive areas and deploy extra forces there. I also knew from other police officers' experiences that a communal situation had to be controlled right at the beginning, otherwise a riot could spread quickly to other areas. If not handled properly, the situation could often escalate to a major crisis, leading to grave damage to life and property.

I had briefed my men thoroughly and activated my sources to keep an eye on mischief mongers. I had also organized a number of peace committee meetings. The members were respected citizens of that particular locality and had a hold on the local people. They could, hence, influence their opinions. It was always good to have these members on our side to diffuse potential problems. I ensured that all the processions got the requisite licences too.

Soon, the Saraswati Puja celebrations began. They were to continue for a few days. I was camping in the most sensitive part of the city, from where the processions of revellers were passing.

'*Bada Babu, teen din nikal gaye hain.* Three days have passed. I am confident that the celebrations will happen peacefully,' I said to the SHO of Alamganj, Manoj Pal. Pal was an old, experienced policeman.

'*Sir, police mein ek kahawat hain—jab tak sab kuch theek se na ho jaaye, kuch bhi ho sakta hain.* There is a saying in the police—until everything is over, it's not over. Anything can happen,' he said.

'I hope we see the end of it soon,' I said.

'Sir, thirteen processions have passed. Only the last two *akhada*s are left. *Sabse badmaash hain ye akhade.* They are the most notorious,' said Pal.

'Chalo, let us see that these processions also pass peacefully,' I said, picking up my wireless set.

A large crowd had gathered to witness the last two akhadas. The crowd was in a frenzy when the processions entered the chowk area. The akhada members were young boys, almost all of them intoxicated. They danced crudely to loud Bhojpuri and Hindi music.

'*Bada Babu, ye kya ho raha hain?* What is happening? I did not expect rowdies dancing during a religious procession,' I complained to Pal.

'*Sir, abhi shaant rahiye.* Stay calm. If somebody hears you, it will create a major problem,' replied Pal, signalling me to keep quiet.

'*Aajkal aisi hi prabhu ki bhakti hoti hain.* Nowadays this is how gods are worshipped,' added Pal grimly.

I understood. 'Just let it be over. I need go to home and rest,' I thought. It had been three consecutive nights that I had been out on the road, ensuring that the processions passed peacefully.

Suddenly I saw one of the akhada members dancing and brandishing a desi katta. Clearly drunk, he was about to fire the gun.

Our first thought was to immediately rush towards him, but we held back as we thought it was probably just a stunt; it would create a ruckus as the akhada members might get agitated in their inebriated state. So we just walked casually and mingled with the crowd. In the ensuing melee, we caught hold of the man firmly, took away his pistol and escorted him away. We then promptly sent him to the police station.

The procession took almost three hours to cross the chowk before the idols were immersed in the Ganga. It was early morning. In just some more time, the last procession would be out too, I told myself.

'*Sir, jaldi aaiye.* Come quickly. *Danga hone wala hain!* Riots are about to start!' shouted Abhay.

'Wh-what happened?' I asked nervously.

'Sir, somebody defaced the statue of Bajrang Bali near the chowk. The crowd thinks that someone from the other community has done it deliberately,' said Abhay.

'This is bad. Shit! I thought everything would end peacefully,' I said, rushing towards the chowk, which was quite close by.

I saw a lot of people shouting and raising slogans.

I knew I had to control the people before they turned into a bloodthirsty mob.

'*Shaant ho jaiye.* Please calm down,' I requested the people.

'*Nahin, humari murti todi hain.* Our idol has been damaged. We want revenge,' they shouted.

'We will get the idol repaired, please remain calm,' I tried to reason with the people.

'No, we know who from the other community has deliberately defaced Bajrang Bali. Arrest those people immediately or Patna will burn.' Now the crowd was getting unruly.

I saw that most of the people were just following the leader of the procession. Whenever he raised a slogan, the people shouted with him. Otherwise they didn't seem particularly bothered or angered.

I realized that I had to take immediate action or things would spin out of control.

Without wasting a moment, I entered the crowd and grabbed the leader. In full public view, I dragged him away from the group.

'I know that you people outnumber the police, but I will not spare anyone who creates trouble. And this, your leader . . . I will ensure he stays behind bars for a long time,' I shouted at the top of my voice.

I had taken a calculated risk. Luckily for me, the protesters got scared. They didn't want to be taken away by the police like their leader. Most importantly, they had lost the person who was adding fuel to fire. The agitation lost steam and the people dissipated. They also seemed to be tired.

'Phew, that was close,' I said. Just earlier in the evening we had taken away the gun-toting youth quietly, but now I had detained the leader publicly. Two different strategies with the same result. But in each situation, things could have well gone awry.

I briefed the SSP over the phone about the tense situation that we had managed to avert.

'Well done. Take some rest,' he said.

I went home, had a hot shower and a very heavy breakfast.

I then hit the sack and slept through the day.

The problem with a policeman's job is the odd working hours that we have. That night, I was wide awake. I tried to rest but kept tossing in bed.

Suddenly, the landline rang.

'*Sir, hum Malsalami se Bada Babu bol rahe hain. Ek aur Bajrang Bali ki murti tod di gayi hain.* I'm the SHO of Malsalami. One more idol of Bajrang Bali has been defaced,' said the tense voice of Ram Avatar.

'Oh no, this is bad,' I muttered.

'Sir, the good news is that we have caught the perpetrator. He's the same guy who had defaced the Bajrang Bali idol in the chowk as well. *Dimaag se disturbed lagtaa hain.* It seems he has some mental issues,' continued the SHO.

'That's one good news—at least we have the offender. Otherwise he would have gone on an idol-defacing spree,' I said.

'Now, Ram Avatar, is there a crowd near the Bajrang Bali temple? Any tension right now?'

No, Sir. It's 2.30 a.m. There is no one there,' he replied. 'But the pujari is upset with the vandalism.'

'Then wait, I am coming over.'

I reached the temple. It was quite cold at night. I was freezing and my teeth were chattering.

'Gosh, how does Patna become so cold at night?' I asked Ajay.

'*Sir, Ganga nadi ke kaaran.* The Ganges makes it cold outside. We are quite close to the banks of the Ganges right now,' he replied.

We reached the temple at 3 a.m. and saw a posse of policemen and the pujari huddled outside the temple.

'Panditji, is everything all right?' I asked.

'*Nahin, sir. Bajrang Bali ka murti kharab kar diye, ab toh bawaal machega.* The statue of my god has been vandalized, now there will be problems. We will protest and take revenge,' the pandit replied.

'*Panditji, koi hungama nahin hoga, shaant rahiye.* No agitation will take place, keep calm. You quickly replace the idol. And no one should know about,' I said as sternly as possible.

'*Sir, abhi toh mere paas koi murti nahin hain.* I don't have any other idol now,' said the pandit.

'Doesn't matter. You go with the SHO and get another idol from anywhere. That's your problem. Till then, do not open the temple. Make an excuse,' I ordered.

The pandit sensed my seriousness. 'Okay, I know the person who made the idol. I'll go to him,' he said.

The SHO of Malsalami immediately escorted the pandit in his vehicle. I put a few constables outside the temple to guard it.

'Ensure that the temple is not opened until I order it to be,' I told the constables.

I checked the watch. It was 3.45 a.m. We still had almost two and a half hours before the temple was due to open.

Soon, I got the call I was waiting for.

'*Sir, mil gayi doosri murti.* We have found a replica,' said the delighted SHO, Ram Avatar. Luckily, the idolmaker had one more statue of Bajrang Bali with him.

'Great, get back quickly and replace it,' I said cheerfully.

By 6 a.m., the new Bajrang Bali idol was in place. We opened the temple to the public. Soon, devotees started thronging the temple.

'*Panditji, aarti shuru kariye.* Please start the aarti,' I told the pandit.

'Jai Bajrang Bali!' the constables shouted.

It was the best aarti I had ever seen. After all, the gods had answered my prayers.

* * *

I somehow managed to get tickets for the Patna–Delhi Rajdhani. Before I boarded the bus from Delhi to Jaipur, I called my brother-in-law to talk to Tanu.

'Congratulations, Amit. You have become a father,' Kapil said.

'Really?' I asked. I could not fathom that I had become a father, for I thought I was too young for such a responsibility.

'But the date of delivery was supposed to be two days from now!' I protested.

'Arre, these are natural things—they can happen any time,' Kapil replied.

I reached Jaipur in the evening and immediately went to the hospital to see Tanu and our son.

'*Late kar diya aapne.* You got late. I wanted you by my side during the delivery,' Tanu said smiling under the pain of her stiches from the C-section she had just gone through.

'*Police toh har jagah late hi pahunchti hain.* The police always reach late everywhere!' I replied, embracing Tanu and my son.

20

Truck Ka Number Kya Hain?

'It's such a huge house. Eight rooms—and we're just two-and-a-half people,' said Tanu, looking wide-eyed at the huge bungalow of the ASP Patna. She was back in Patna with one more member of our family. Avi, our month-old son, was snuggling in his mother's lap.

'Why, have you forgotten all these rats? There are quite a handful to give us company,' I said, putting my feet up on the chair. One particularly fat rodent had come really close to us. He was probably eyeing a piece of toast lying on the table. Suddenly, the rat jumped onto the dining table. I was caught by surprised and lost my balance.

Tanu started laughing and our son gurgled along.

'*ASP Saheb, chooha bhi aapse nahin darta, par aap zaroor usse darte ho.* Even a rat is not scared of you, but you are sure scared of it.'

'*Toh kya jail mein bandh kar doon?* Should I put it in prison?' I said in an irritated tone.

'*Filhal to choohedani mein hi bandh kar do.* For now, a mousetrap will do,' replied Tanu.

Our banter continued for some time. On nights such as these, I was really thankful for everything I had. A lovely family and a great job that I really enjoyed.

A little later, the phone rang. I looked at the clock. It was 10.40 p.m. I knew it could not be good news at this hour. The later it is, the worse news it is for a policeman.

'*Sir, Fatuha ke paas ek accident ho gaya hain.* There has been an accident near Fatuha. People have blocked the road. They might create a ruckus. Please come soon, Sir,' said the SHO of Fatuha.

I looked at Tanu and Avi, sighed and got up to change into my uniform. I went out and asked the guard to get everyone ready. Within five minutes, we were on our way to Fatuha.

'*Sir, jaldi pahunchiye, public oogra ho gayi hain.* Please reach fast, the public has become violent.' This time the SHO sounded nervous on the wireless.

'*SHO Alamganj, SHQ Sultanganj, aap bhi turant force lekar pahunchiye.* Reach Fatuha immediately with the force,' I shouted on the wireless. For a moment, I felt bad about calling these policemen. They must have just reached home or their barracks to take rest. Maybe they were spending time with their families or making some time for themselves.

But such is the nature of the job of a policeman that we are expected to forget our personal lives and answer the call of duty whenever required.

'We all know what we have signed up for,' I mused and quickly got over these thoughts.

'*Sir, gaadi yahi rok lete hain. Kaafi bheed lag rahi hain.* Let us stop the Gypsy here. There seems to be a big crowd ahead,' said the driver.

In a few moments, the SHO Fatuha came running to me, his uniform drenched in sweat.

'Sir, I tried my best to persuade the crowd to disperse. But they are not willing to budge.'

'What are their demands?' I asked.

'Sir, they want a compensation of Rs 25,000, accommodation at the Indira Gandhi Awas Yojana housing plan and a job for one of the relatives of the deceased, a young boy.'

The first two promises were usually fulfilled, but getting a job for the relative of the deceased was tricky. There was no provision to provide a government job in such cases.

I pitied the poor family that had lost a future breadwinner, but there was nothing I could do.

'Sir, yahaan se hatiye. Log truck mein aag lagaa rahe hain. Please move from here. People are setting trucks on fire,' shouted Rajbir, the SHO Alamganj. The mob was in no mood to listen to us. A number of drunk hooligans also started smashing the windshields and windowpanes of trucks. Some of them tried to vandalize closed shops.

Traffic on the national highway connecting Patna and Ranchi came to a standstill.

'Where is the SHO Sultanganj? We will fall short of men. The crowd seems to have gone berserk,' I said, the tension in my voice palpable.

Luckily, within minutes, the SHO Sultanganj reached the spot.

'Sorry, Sir, my Jeep had a flat tyre. So I had to get hold of a private vehicle,' he said.

Suddenly, I saw a few flashlights and video cameras. 'The press,' I muttered.

Every police officer hopes that the media will not reach a site, whether it is a murder or an accident. But it is unavoidable in most cases. After all, the press also has to do its job.

While I was issuing instructions and trying to control the mob frenzy, a reporter came to me and asked, 'Sir, kya aap mujhe uss jalte huye truck ka number bataa sakte hain? Can you tell me the number of that burning truck?' I was too busy to get angry. It was a ridiculous question and deserved an equally stupid answer.

'*Aap khud hi paas jaakar dekh lo.* You go and find out yourself,' I retorted.

The flames burnt higher. The intrepid reporter ran back as fast as possible.

'We will have to resort to a lathi charge. Ask all the jawans to put on their helmets and body protectors,' I said.

The SHOs looked at me incredulously.

'*Sir, kahaan body protector aur helmet?* Where will we get body protectors and helmets? They are in short supply. Whatever we have is lying in the police lines,' they said.

I knew he was right. Resource crunch has always been a problem with the police. But there was no time to waste. If we did not control the mob right now, things could go from bad to worse.

During our training, we had a riot-control drill, where we were taught to use force only as a last resort, after we had exhausted all our options—from warning the mob to using tear gas. In fact, we were supposed to announce, '*Aapka mazma najayaz karar diya jaata hain.* Your gathering is declared illegal.'

It was a different matter that, in reality, there was hardly any situation where we could happily use those lovely Urdu words! Today was no different.

'*Dhyan se chot karna—kamar ke neeche.* Be careful when hitting—hurt only below the waist. Lathi charge!' I shouted at the top of my voice, using all my lung power. The already charged-up force just needed to hear this command. In five to ten minutes, the situation changed completely. The mob disappeared when they saw so many police officers wielding lathis.

We cleared the area soon. Only a few wailing relatives were sitting in the middle of the road around the young boy's body.

I felt terrible for them.

'*Baba, mujhe bahut dukh hain. Main sarkar ki taraf se waada karta hoon ki aapki poori sahayata hogi.* I'm sad for your loss. I promise that I'll do my best to get you all the government aid that is due to you,' I said.

The poor people did not utter a word, just folded their hands. The hooligans had nothing to do with the poor family and yet they had created a major ruckus. Such situations bring out the anger in people, whether it is frustration about their situation, anger at lack of employment opportunities or just rowdiness under the influence of alcohol.

Though most of the people had run away into the lanes and bylanes of Fatuha, my jawans had managed to round up six to seven of the troublemongers.

'*Le jao inko. Bandh karo hawalat mein.* Take them away and put them in lock-up,' I said.

All of a sudden, a few pyjama-kurta-clad people got out of an SUV. I immediately understood they were small-time politicians looking to take advantage of the situation.

'*ASP Saheb, pranaam. Kripya inn logo ko chhod dijiye. Ye humare aadmi hain.* Please let these people go. They are our men,' said a bearded man in an authoritative tone.

'*Kis baat ke liye chhod de?* Why should they be released? They have created so much trouble,' I said firmly.

'*Toh phir aapko oopar se kehlana padega. Hum log Santo Bhaiyya ke khas hain.* Then we'll have to ask some higher-ups to call you. We're Santo Bhaiyya's special team,' said another guy in the group.

Santo Bhaiyya was the relative of a senior minister. He was supposed to have strong clout in the city.

This time I got really angry.

'*Kisi bhaiyya se phone kara lijiye. Main wahi karunga jo sahi hain.* Get any bhaiyya to call me. I'll do what is right,' I snapped at them.

One of the guys took out his cellphone and started dialling a number.

'*Haan, lagaao phone.* Make the call. Let me speak to your bhaiyya personally,' I shouted. The person got scared and put the phone back in his pocket. He was most probably feigning the call and testing waters with me.

'*Achha sir, pranaam. Aapko jo sahi lage kariye. Hum jaate hain.* Do whatever you feel is right. We are leaving,' the leader said.

The group of local politicians beat a hasty retreat and left the accident site. I turned around and saw all my men standing there, with faint smiles on their faces.

In my years of experience, I have realized that true politicians largely understand what is right and wrong. They never pressure for illegal things. It is often the unscrupulous elements who try to take advantage of a situation.

If an officer is honest and fair, politicians also appreciate him. Of course, there can be times when an officer does not fit into the scheme of things of the establishment, and he might be sidelined for a brief period. Nevertheless, all governments need 'good' officers to run the administration, so the right officers are invariably put at the right post.

I came back home tired, and saw Tanu and Avi sleeping peacefully. Without thinking twice, I got into bed and held Tanu tightly.

21

Papaji

'*Sir, ye aapke liye hain.* This is for you. Happy Diwali,' said the amiable sardar, meeting me in my residential office on the day of the festival.

'What for? Why have you got this cellphone for me?' I asked sternly.

'Sir, please don't mind. You don't have a cellphone, so the Patna chamber of traders thought it would be a good idea to gift you one so that the public can be in touch with you directly,' said Paras Kanaujia, speaking up in support of the sardarji.

In 2000, a cellphone was a luxury. Only the SSP Patna and very few senior officers had official cellphones. It was not until about 2007 that we were issued official cellphones by the government. Having one was a double-edged sword. Though we could communicate with our staff and officers easily, some officers complained that they received hundreds of calls, some unwanted and/or irrelevant. I, for one, think that one should always receive all calls. It just takes a few minutes, and a patient hearing can act like a balm to an aggrieved individual. Of course, it can lead to the detection of a major crime and arrest of criminals too. And it is definitely better to be accessible to the public in real life than just having a personal Facebook page extolling one's virtues, with thousands of virtual followers.

The Patna businessmen probably had the right intentions, but I didn't feel comfortable accepting the phone.

'Dekho, any IPS officer's reputation is built not only upon his professional competence but his integrity too. Your entire career is dependent on the reputation that you have established,' I remembered K.C. Pritam, my DIG, telling me that.

'I appreciate your concern but I'm sorry, I cannot accept this cellphone. You all know that I pick up the landline myself at home and office. Moreover we have an excellent police wireless network, which is quite effective in passing on information to me,' I told them.

'Okay, Sir, as you wish,' said both the businessmen, taking back the cellphone.

The moment they left, someone else showed up. People didn't seem to realize that it was a holiday for me as well and came to greet me. '*Namaskar, SP Saheb. Aapko Diwali ki badhaai.* Best wishes for Diwali,' said Dinkar Jha, a small-time politician who loved to hobnob with the who's who of the district. I avoided meeting such people, but it was tough to do so on Diwali.

'*Lijiye.* Have some,' I said, pointing to the sweets on my table.

'*Arre, ye to bahut badhiya hain.* This is very good,' said Jha, putting two pieces in his mouth.

'*Haan, Jaipur se aayi hain.* These have come from Jaipur, from my parents and relatives,' I replied, a little irritated.

'*Oho, tab to aur leni padegi.* Then I'll have to take some more,' he said, biting into another piece. And then he picked up the remaining sweets and put them in his pockets. I was livid, somehow managing to control my anger.

'Why did Tanu have to send out these sweets for the guests?' I muttered to myself.

'*Accha, Sir, ek tho parivee hain.* I have a request. *Woh jo Anoopgadh ka thana prabhari hain, usse badal dijiye.* Please change the SHO of Anoopgarh. *Suna hain galat logo se uske mili bhagat hain.* I have heard he is in connivance with some bad people.'

I knew that the SHO of Anoopgarh was a fine officer. Jha's unsolicited advice infuriated me beyond control now. I was already annoyed at his 'pocketing' of my favourite sweets.

'How dare you! Get out! Out, right now!' I shouted at him angrily.

Jha beat a hasty retreat.

Once outside, he told the cronies who had come with him, '*Badhiya raha. Amit bhaiyya ne badaa khayal rakha.* The meeting went very well. Brother Amit took good care of me. Bhabhi personally met me and gave me these sweets,' said Jha, taking out the sweets from his pockets.

'*Lo khao.* Help yourselves,' he said, handing them the sweets.

'*Aur haan, aage se kuch kaam ho Amit bhaiyya se, mujhe bataana—ho jayega.* From next time if you have any work with Brother Amit, let me know—it will be done,' said Jha, triumphantly.

'*Accha, abhi tumke bataate hain.* I will tell you your place,' said Abhay, my bodyguard. Unfortunately for Jha, Abhay had overheard the entire conversation. He dragged Jha to my chamber.

'*Arre, ye phir aa gaya.* He has come again!' I said irritatedly.

'*Hum laaye hain.* I have got him,' said Abhay, and narrated the conversation he had heard taking place outside.

'*Aapne mooh toh meetha kar hi liye hain, ab kuch namkeen bhi khao.* You have already had sweets, now have something salty too,' I said.

Abhay glared at Jha and moved towards him threateningly. Jha yelped and left in a hurry. After that, no one else came to eat sweets for the rest of the day.

* * *

My telephone rang.

'Sir, this is Pramod, SHO Khajekalan. One of the prominent businessmen of Patna, Mani Prabhat Chaurasia, has been missing since yesterday afternoon.'

'Have you done the preliminary investigation?' I asked.

'Sir, I'm at his house. Since Chaurasia is widely respected, the public is getting uneasy as he is still untraceable. A lot of people have conspiracy theories,' he said.

'I'm on my way,' I said, signalling to Abhay to get the vehicle out and alert the force.

Abhay was dressed in a kurta-pyjama, with a *teeka* on his forehead. This was the first time I had seen him wearing anything other than his uniform. Being my bodyguards, both Abhay and his brother Ajay were like my shadow. Whenever I went out, even for a private event, they were always in uniform, carrying carbines and pistols.

Abhay, used to being summoned to duty any time, walked swiftly towards the barracks to change into his uniform.

'*Tanu, bas thodi der mein aata hoon.* I'll come back soon,' I said.

'It's all right. *Poori raat baaki hain Diwali ke liye.* The entire night is there for Diwali,' she said. Being a policeman's daughter certainly made her understand the demands of my job.

* * *

All of Patna was decked up in lights and diyas. The *patakha*s, or crackers, were creating quite a din. My Gypsy waded through the lanes of the beautifully decorated markets; my mind was unable to take in all the festivity around.

SHO Pramod was waiting outside Chaurasia's house. I looked at the crowd that had gathered. A number of people had come, some out of curiosity and some to help us with the investigation.

'Sir, Chaurasiaji lived alone in this house. Though his sons have a well-established business in Ahmedabad, Chaurasiaji refused to live with them. He preferred to stay in his ancestral house,' said Pramod.

'Then who took care of him and his house? He must have had some staff or servant, at least,' I asked.

'*Sir, hum rahte hain Chaurasiaji ki saath. Humara naam Gautam hain. Woh humare pitah samaan hain.* I live with Chaurasiaji. My name is Gautam. Chaurasiaji is like a father to me. In fact, I call him Papaji,' said a young, good-looking lad.

'Hmm, were you with him yesterday? Where did he go? Did you get any ransom call?' I asked.

'*Sir, hum toh Fatuha gaye the dost se milne.* I had gone to Fatuha to meet my friend. I have no idea,' Gautam replied.

The way he said it made me think something was off. It was a gut feeling, I didn't trust the boy. Just like a doctor can understand what the ailment is by looking at a patient, a policeman also develops an intuitive power that gives them an idea of a person's character.

'*Kisi ne Chaurasiaji ko jaate hue dekha?* Did anyone see Chaurasiaji leave the house?' I asked to the people around.

A man stepped out of the crowd.

'*Sir, hum dekhe hain. Akele nikle the scooter par.* I have seen him. He went out alone on his scooter. *Hum unke naukar hain.* I'm his servant, Ram Prakash.'

'Any other detail you remember?' I asked, hoping for some clue.

'*Sir, woh nikkar-banyan mein nikal gaye.* Sir, he was wearing a vest and shorts when he left,' replied the servant.

What was the rush, I wondered.

'*Sir, ek phone aaya tha. Uske turant baad nikal gaye.* There was a phone call. He left immediately after,' the servant added.

I nodded and took Pramod aside.

'Have your got a tower location for Chaurasia's cellphone?' I asked Pramod.

'No, sir. Chaurasiaji did not have a cellphone,' Pramod replied.

'Then get details of the landline. There is a high probability that somebody well known to Chaurasia had called him. Either it was an emergency call or he must have gone somewhere close by. Otherwise why would anyone leave in just shorts and a vest?'

'*Sir, sahi keh rahe hain aap.* You are right,' Pramod replied.

'I don't think it's a case of kidnapping. His relatives, his sons, someone should have received a call for ransom if it was,' I said. 'Was he fighting with anyone? Any property dispute?'

'Sir, until now, from whatever I could find out, he was a loner. He did not have animosity with anyone,' Pramod said.

'And what about Gautam, this foster son?'

Pramod shrugged.

'I need you to find out about his family and background. Does he have any bad habits, such as gambling? What kind of company does he keep?' I continued.

'Sir, let us ask some more people close to Chaurasiaji. We'll meet some of his relatives too. Hopefully we'll get some important information,' Pramod replied.

The loud noise of crackers made it difficult for us to converse. I had almost forgotten it was Diwali and that Tanu was waiting for me.

'Send a message through PIR to check all hospitals, in case Chaurasia has met with an accident. Share the details of the scooter with the police stations and see if any of them have found it. Let me know if you get any other information,' I said, getting into my Gypsy.

Tanu was waiting for me, with Avi asleep on the cot. Neither of us knew exactly how to do the puja, so we stumbled through it and did our best to sing the few bhajans and aartis we knew. I started singing *Om Jai Jagadish*, but it came out shriller than I had expected.

'*Chun, mat gao itna besura.* Don't sing so badly. Even the gods will get angry!' said Tanu, laughing deliriously.

'I'm sorry, sweetheart, I couldn't celebrate Diwali with you properly,' I said as I bent down to caress Avi's hair.

'Chun, a man is missing. It's more important to find him. We'll celebrate when you crack the case,' she said lovingly.

* * *

'*Sir, aapse Patna city ke Agarwalji milne aaye hain. Lagtaa hain Chaurasia case ke baare mein batiyane aaye hain.* Agarwalji has come to meet you. Seems like he wants to speak to you about the Chaurasia case,' Abhay said. I had just woken up and was getting ready for work.

I met Agarwal in my residential office.

'ASP Saheb, I have a strong suspicion that Gautam might have done something to Chaurasiaji,' he said.

'Why do you think so?'

'Amitji, Gautam has been brought up like a son by Chaursiaji. *Par lobh sab ko ho jataa hain.* But everyone gets greedy.'

'Gautam knows that Chaurasiaji will bequeath all his property to his sons. *Khoon toh khoon hi hota hain.* After all, those are blood relations. Though Gautam took great care of Chaurasiaji, I'm sure the latter would have named his sons as his inheritors,' Agarwal continued.

I listened intently.

'Sure, Agarwalji. I will definitely investigate this aspect,' I said, as I ushered him out.

* * *

I called Pramod to my office.

'Pramod, did you investigate Gautam? Do you suspect him?' I asked him.

'*Sir, Gautam kaafi tez hain.* He's quite sharp. He likes to live a good life. I have also heard that he has lost a lot of money in gambling. I don't have a good feeling about him,' Pramod replied.

'And did you find out the details of the number from which Chaurasia received his last call on the landline?'

'Sir, we found out the details from BSNL. The call came from a PCO in Agamkua.'

'Then?'

'The PCO owner does not remember the caller. It's quite a busy PCO, with hundreds of people using it every day.'

'It was definitely someone close to Chaurasia who called him. That's why he rushed out in his vest and shorts,' I said, channeling my inner Hercule Poirot.

'*Gautam ke baare mein aur pataa lagaao.* Find out more about Gautam. Also find out if he had gone to Fatuha that day.'

'Right, sir. I'll talk to the SHO Fatuha, Vinod. He is my batchmate,' said Pramod.

Pramod came to see me in the evening.

'*Sir, Fatuha toh gaya tha Gautam.* Gautam did go to Fatuha. I asked Vinod to find out about Gautam's location that day. Vinod sent the chowkidar to Fatuha to find out, and he confirmed that Gautam had gone to his friend's house. He has a solid alibi.'

'So we have reached a dead end. Let us hope we get a clue soon.'

* * *

I kept pacing the large verandah of my house. The guard could make out that I was not in good spirits. I was desperately looking for some information, some breakthrough in the Chaurasia case.

The landline rang.

'*Sir se baat karaiye.* Have me talk to Sir. I'm the SHO Fatuha speaking,' said the voice on the other end.

'*Hum ASP bol rahe hain.* This is the ASP speaking,' I said.

'Sir, I have just come back from Fatuha. *Ye Gautam kaafi gadbad lag raha hain.* Gautam seems like a dubious chap. He does not have a good reputation. There is a murmur in Fatuha village that he might have killed Chaurasia. I got this information just now. I am sorry I did not go personally to Fatuha earlier as I was busy with another case.'

'But you are the one who confirmed that Gautam was in Fatuha,' I said in a slightly brusque tone, barely hiding my frustration.

'*Sir, woh toh theek hain.* That's right. He did go to Fatua. But he might have gone back to Patna or he might have called an accomplice to carry out the kidnapping,' said Vinod.

'*Sir, thoda karai se pooch-tachh kariye.* Interrogate him intensely. Maybe he'll tell us something,' added Vinod, before signing off.

I immediately called up Pramod.

'Pramod, does Gautam have a cellphone?'

'Yes, Sir. It's a status symbol to keep a cellphone and Gautam is a flashy character—he likes to flaunt expensive things.'

'Great. Get me the call log of Gautam's number.'

In those days, it used to take some time to get call details of a cell number. The Reliance Communications office was under the jurisdiction of Patrakar Nagar police station. Policemen from all districts of Bihar called the Patrakar Nagar police station to ask for the call details of their respective cases. The SHO of Patrakar Nagar was a harried person.

It took two day of continuously calling the Patrakar Nagar police station to get the call records.

The tower location showed Gautam at Fatuha the night before Chaurasia went missing. The next day, Gautam's location was at Agamkua. Chaurasia had got a call from a PCO in Agamkua. It could not be a coincidence.

I had no doubt that Gautam was involved.

'*Pramod, Gautam ko utha ke lao.* Bring Gautam in immediately,' I ordered.

* * *

'Pranaam, sir,' said Gautam, looking fresh, his hair carefully styled.

'*Kahaan pe rakha hain Chaurasiaji ko?* Where have you kept Chaurasiaji?' I snarled at him.

I had learnt instinctively that a criminal would never admit to a crime if you asked them if they were involved. But if you confronted them directly and kept asking them pointed questions, there was a good chance of them cracking.

'*Sir, kya keh rahe hain? Hum unhe kyun marenge? Main toh unhe pitah samaan maanta tha.* What are you saying? Why would I kill him? I considered him my father,' said Gautam, stammering, the glow gone from his face.

'*Arre, log paise ke liye apne sage baap ko maar dete hain.* People kill their own father for money. So what is the big deal in killing a father figure?' said Pramod.

'Wait, I never mentioned that you killed him! I just asked you where you have kept Chaurasiaji,' I shouted at Gautam, interrupting Pramod.

Before I could continue, Abhay began to shove and intimidate Gautam. The latter began to whimper. I told Abhay to hold off before gesturing to him to shove Gautam again.

'*Hum sab bataate hain—maariye mat.* I'll tell you everything—don't hit me,' Gautam said.

'Speak.'

'Sir, over the past few months, I had lost a lot of money in gambling. I was under severe stress from the local gambling dons to repay them. Earlier, I used to ask Papaji for money on some pretext, but this time the amount was quite big.'

'Don't you dare call him Papaji,' I said.

'*Toh aur kya kahe?* What else should I call him? I have been calling him Papaji my entire life,' Gautam replied.

Pramod and I looked at each other and shook our heads.

'I was in a debt of Rs 20 lakh. The only way to repay it was to sell off some of Papaji's property. I requested Papaji to sell off his motor garage and give me the money. I thought it was my right. After all, I grew up with him. His own sons left him a long time ago. I was the one who took care of Chaurasiaji every day, I was the one who tended to him when he fell ill. I was the only one who kept him company. I thought that for all my devotion, he would definitely help me. When I asked him to sell off the garage, he refused point-blank. He said all his property would be bequeathed to his sons,' Gautam said.

I could clearly see the hatred in his eyes now.

'I was crestfallen. I felt cheated. I had given my entire life to Papaji, but for what? Only to be ultimately treated as an orphan,' Gautam spat out.

'I met a few of my friends and told them about my situation,' he continued. 'Then one of my closest friends, Raju

Azad, suggested that I kidnap Chaurasiaji and force him to sign the garage property papers in my name. I would have mortgaged the garage and repaid my debt to the dons.'

'So my friends and I hatched a simple plan,' Gautam paused for a few moments. 'My friend Suleiman called Papaji from a PCO near his motor garage in Agamkua. He told Papaji that my fingers had been crushed under a car being repaired in the garage. On hearing this, Papaji immediately started for the garage. I had expected this. After all, he loved me so much,' said Gautam, looking at us.

'Don't you dare talk about love, you selfish person!' shouted Pramod.

'Then? Go on,' I prodded.

'The moment he reached the garage, we caught him and asked him to sign the property in my name. We thought it would be easy to intimidate him, but the old man was a tough nut. He abused me and threatened to expose us.'

Gautam took a deep breath, and then uttered very softly, 'We are all inexperienced people, we got scared. We grabbed him around the neck and held on tightly. Before we even realized we were throttling him, he was dead. Baldev, another friend, took Chaurasiaji's scooter to dump it somewhere. Azad Bhaiyya then took the body and threw it in the Ganga.'

I shuddered at what they had done just for money. I could not control my rage any more and let it all out on Gautam. He lay on the floor, his face expressionless.

'Pramod, the case is solved. But we need to arrest all the people involved in this murder. Form teams and get going. Once we get Chaurasia's body and the scooter, we will have the evidence we need against these rascals,' I said.

'Yes, Sir,' Pramod saluted and left the room.

Within five hours, we had arrested Suleiman and Baldev, but there was no trace of Raju Azad, the mastermind.

I called Agarwalji, the elderly businessman from Patna. 'Agarwalji, you were right. We have solved the case. Gautam is behind Chaurasiaji's disappearance.'

'*Ishwar ki kripa hain.* God has shown mercy. Now we will get Chaurasiaji home soon,' he said happily.

I could not break the bad news of Chaurasiaji's murder to him right away.

'Do you know of Raju Azad?' I asked.

'Of course. He is the nephew of Councillor Ganesh Azad. Should I ask for his whereabouts?'

'Please connect me to Ganesh Azad.'

'Sure, sir. *Kal usse leke hazir hote hain.* I'll come to you with him tomorrow.'

'*Kal nahin—abhi, Agarwalji.* Not tomorrow, right now, Agarwalji,' I said.

'Okay, Sir, though it's quite an odd time. It's 6 in the morning.'

'Yes, I know. But please do it right now.'

Time was of the essence. If Raju Azad came to know that his accomplices had been arrested, he would vanish.

After fifteen minutes, I got a call from Ganesh Azad.

'Sir, pranaam. This is Ganesh Azad. *Agarwalji ne kahaa aap yaad kar rahe the.* Agarwalji told me that you asked me to call you,' he said.

'Ganeshji, I know you are a respected councillor and that you are in line for a ticket for MLA from Patna. But your chances will go down if I reveal a secret.'

'*Sir, hum kuch samjhe nahin.* I don't understand,' said a worried Azad.

I told him about the Chaurasia case and Raju Azad's role in it.

'If you don't get him to me in the next few hours, I'll come to raid your house. With the media in tow,' I threatened.

'*Sir, thoda time dijiye.* Give me some time.'

'*Zyada time nahin hain aapke paas.* You don't have much time.'

Azad knew that Chaurasia was popular in Patna. If the police came to his house in connection to the Chaurasia case, Azad would lose a lot of goodwill in the trader community. The businessmen formed a majority of voters in Patna.

Soon, he was in my office. And with him was his nephew, Raju Azad.

I stared coldly at Raju, making my anger and disgust apparent.

'*Sir, bahut badi galti ho gayi.* I have made a big mistake,' said Raju immediately, realizing that the police had discovered the truth.

'Where did you dump the body?'

'Sir, *chaliye*, I'll show you where,' Raju said.

Abhay and Ajay hauled Raju into the Gypsy. Councillor Azad stood outside my office, speechless. He could not believe his nephew had murdered Chaurasia.

'PIR, send at least six teams to the Ganga ghat at Alamganj,' I ordered over the wireless.

Within an hour we were swarming the ghats. We searched everywhere but did not find the body. We were slowly losing hope.

'Sir, the body must have been washed away by the river,' said Razi Ahmed, one of the police officers.

'You are right. But the body has to come to the surface somewhere,' I said. It was getting dark and it was dangerous for the police team and the divers to stay in the deep waters of the Ganga beyond a point. Disappointed, we decided to return.

'On my way back, I got a message on the wireless.

'Sir, we have found the scooter. Baldev has led us to it.'

I sighed with relief. 'At least we have the scooter,' said Pramod.

'But we still need to find Chaurasiaji's body,' I muttered.

I reached home. As I was slowly climbing the stairs to my house, Abhay came running.

'*Sir, Bada Babu Alamganj baat karna chahte hain.* SHO Alamganj wants to talk to you,' he said, giving his cellphone to me.

I was surprised. I didn't know Abhay had a cellphone.

I took his phone and said, '*Haan, boliye.* Yes, tell me.'

'Sir, we have the body. It was found about 5 kilometres from the ghats. Some fishermen noticed it floating in the water.'

'Okay, take it for post mortem. Also take pictures of the body,' I said. I took a long pause. We had reached closure in the case but I was numb. I hated these cases, where we ended up solving a murder case rather than working with the hope that we would safely bring home a victim of kidnapping or a missing person.

I looked at Abhay and said, '*Lagtaa hain ab ek cellphone lena hi padega. Kaafi kaam ka hain.* I think I'll have to get a cellphone. It is quite useful.'

22

D Ho Gayi

'Amit, congratulations! You have been posted as SP Nalanda. It's a prestigious charge. You are lucky to get it as your first posting as a superintendent of police,' said Pandit Sir, who had been one of my trainers. 'I'm happy that I'm handing over the charge of Nalanda to my probationer.'

I was delighted to receive the news of my posting as SP. Because of certain circumstances and my inter se seniority, I was the first in my batch to become an SP. I was quite excited to be serving as the chief of the district police. The responsibilities are challenging yet extremely fulfilling, and this is one post any IPS officer looks forward to holding.

Tanu and I had a small celebration at home. We also made phone calls to our parents and a few friends.

The very next day, I left for Nalanda, which was about two hours from Patna. On reaching Nalanda, I was welcomed by Pandit Sir.

'*Baitho, ab ye tumhari kursi hain. Bahut zimmedari ka kaam hain SP ka.* Sit, this is your chair now. The SP has a lot of responsibilities,' said Pandit Sir affectionately.

* * *

It was a completely different feeling being an SP. For the first time I was sitting on the opposite side of the table, listening to the brief introductions of all my officers. I realized that problems were aplenty and resources limited. After a slew of long meetings, I went home in the evening. I felt proud to see my name plate outside the house: 'Amit Lodha, IPS, Superintendent of Police, Nalanda.' I surveyed the house and instructed Onkar Pandey, the cook-cum-orderly of the house, to have the walls painted.

I didn't have the energy to do anything else, so I hit the sack. I was woken up early the next day with the ringing of the phone.

'*Haan, bolo.* Yes, tell me,' I said gruffly.

'*Sir, Bada Babu Rahui baat karna chahte hain.* The SHO Rahui wants to speak to you,' said the telephone orderly. It felt so different but also good to have a telephone orderly now. Even the ramshackle Ambassador I had driven home the previous evening had felt more authoritative than my Gypsy.

While I was happily pondering these differences between an SP and an ASP, the telephone orderly transferred the call.

'*Sir, D ho gayi hain.* There has been a D,' said the SHO.

'D? What is D?' I asked.

'*Sir, dacoity ho gayi.* A dacoity has taken place. *Sab barbaad ho gaya hain.* Everything is finished. And, Sir, two of the residents of the house have been beaten to death.' The SHO started crying.

'Why the hell are you crying?' I said, a little angry.

'*Sir, hum abhi join kiya tha.* I have joined recently. I am a newly recruited SI. Now this crime has taken place. I have failed you,' said the SHO.

'What is your name?'

'Sir, Nikhil SI, '94 batch.'

'Nikhil, please control your emotions. Crimes will take place. Our job is to prevent a crime to the best of our abilities. If we can't prevent a crime, as in this case, it is important for us to investigate the case properly and arrest the criminals. That is why you and I have been posted here. *Ab rona bandh karo.* Now stop crying,' I said like an elder brother to him.

During my training, I had realized that the SP always had to look in control of their emotions and appear cool even in the most difficult times. It was the SP's job to boost the morale of the police force.

I felt bad about what had happened, but it wouldn't help to let everyone else know and be affected by my mood. It was horrible that whenever I joined a new place, I would receive news of a serious crime.

'Yes, Sir. Jai Hind. Thank you, Sir,' Nikhil replied. Feeling a little more confident, I sat in the Gypsy, which I used for travelling longer distances with my guards, and started towards Rahui.

'*Sir, ye to accha shagun hain—aate hi crime ho gaya. Ab aage nahin hoga.* This is a good omen—a crime has taken place the moment you have landed. In future nothing will happen,' said the driver Mangeshwar, a chatterbox.

I wanted to rebuke him for his stupid theory but realized he meant well. I wanted to remind him that something bad had already happened to the people who had been looted and killed.

* * *

Nikhil was at the scene of the crime.

'The house owner told us that about six to seven robbers had entered the house and looted some ornaments and cash. Then they thrashed the family members,' he said.

'Do you have a fingerprint kit? Have you called the forensics team?' I asked as I looked around the house for clues. Nikhil looked at me blankly.

After a minute of silence, Inspector Vijay Yadav said, '*Sir, ye sab facilities yahaan kahaan hogi? Ye sirf rajdhani Patna mein milegi.* These facilities are not available here. These are available only in the capital, Patna.'

'*Of course, phir kutta toh hoga hi nahin?* Then we don't have a sniffer dog either?' I asked.

'*Sir, koi baat nahin, par hum apradhiyon ko pakad lenge.* It does not matter, we will find the criminals,' said Vijay confidently.

I took the statements of all the family members.

'*Sir, hum keh rahe hain. Humare parivar ko Munna Pehalwan aur uske logon ne maara hain.* I am telling you, our family members have been killed by Munna Pehalwan and his goons,' said Haroon, the patriarch of the family. Interestingly, the other family members did not mention Munna Pehalwan. Rather, they said they could not identify any of the robbers.

'*Anjaane chehre the.* They were unknown faces,' said the lady of the house.

'Sir, Munna is from another community. Haroon and Munna have a long-standing property feud. It is possible that Munna was involved in this crime,' said Vijay.

Nikhil, being a greenhorn, remained quiet.

'But Vijay, the family members' statements are contradictory. Let us go by the evidence. From whatever I can see, it seems to be the job of habitual criminals. Doesn't seem like a planned crime to me,' I said.

* * *

I returned home and was shocked to find my bedroom painted a garish green, with pink curtains.

'*Ye sab kisne kiya?* Who has done this?' I asked, annoyed.

'*Huzoor, thekedar aaye the. Bole Saheb jawaan hain, unhe aise rang acche lagenge.* The contractor had come. He said that SP Saheb is young, he will like such colours,' replied my orderly Onkar.

'Onkar, you could have at least asked me. Call the contractor again. I'll tell him my choice,' I thundered.

I could not stand the colour and the smell of paint in my room. I went out for a stroll in the garden.

Suddenly, I saw my telephone orderly Tariq running towards me with the cordless phone.

'*Sir, Sir, Patna se Bade Saheb ka phone hain.* Big boss is calling from Patna.'

Feeling a little nervous, I took the phone.

'*Aapke yahaan do XYZ caste ke logon ka murder hua hain?* Have two people of XYZ caste been killed in your area?' said the unmistakably familiar voice on the other side.

'Yes, sir. Two people have been murdered. I don't know their caste but I am monitoring the investigation myself,' I replied.

'*Aap jile ke SP hain.* You are the SP of the district. You should know the caste and community of the people. *Nahin toh phera mein pad jayenge,*' he said and disconnected the call.

'*Phera mein pad jayenge?* What does it mean?' I asked Tariq.

'You will land in trouble,' he replied.

* * *

The next day, the Bada Saheb himself came to meet Haroon's family. The visit was sudden but not unexpected. Haroon was from a community that was quite influential.

'*Hum elaan karte hain ki police jaldi hi Munna Pehalwan ko giraftar karegi.* I announce that the police will arrest Munna Pehalwan soon,' he declared to the large crowd that had gathered.

'But Sir, the investigation is on. The dacoity seems to be the work of a professional gang,' I complained to the IG, who had accompanied the boss.

'Lodha, the boss has made a decision. Now don't argue, just follow the instructions. I have been in service long enough to know how things work. Your idealism will die soon,' said the IG, R.K. Krishna.

'But Sir, you are known for your no-nonsense reputation. You could take a stand on behalf of the police,' I said

Krishna Sir smiled and said, 'You know, when I was a young SP like you one of my SHOs told me, "Sir, *aap log bamboo ki tarah hote ho.* You officers are like the bamboo plant. The more you grow in rank, the more you bend.'

We fell silent after that.

'*SP Saheb, jaldi hi giraftari honi chahiye.* The arrests should be made soon,' ordered the big boss as he sat in his car.

The motorcade left, leaving behind a trail of dust.

* * *

Nikhil, though a newly recruited policeman, was diligent and took the investigation seriously.

'*Sir, maine Haroon waale case ke apradhi pakad liye hain.* I have arrested the criminals of the Haroon case,' he said triumphantly on the phone when he called me two days later.

I reached the Rahui police station immediately. The criminals had confessed to the crime. They even led us to the recovery of the looted ornaments and the weapons used in the murder. Moreover, the criminals had a number of old cases against them. We called Haroon to the police station.

'*Kya ye tumhara samaan hain?* Is this your stuff? The jewellery?' Nikhil asked.

'Sir, these are my looted ornaments. *Bahut bahut dhanyawad.* Thank you so much,' he said happily.

'*Par tum toh keh rahe the ki Munna Pehalwan dakaiti kiya hain.* But you were saying that Munna Pehalwan was behind the dacoity,' I said angrily.

'*Sir, woh to hum aise hi keh diye.* I said it just like that. I suspected him as he is my enemy,' Haroon replied.

I came back to my office and immediately issued a report declaring Munna Pehalwan innocent, as the real culprits had been arrested.

* * *

'Amit, have you changed the report? Have you removed the names of the original accused in the Rahui dacoity–murder case?' said the angry voice of the ADG Patna.

'Yes, Sir, but after proper investigation,' I replied.

'I don't know about that but you had better pack your bags. I think you'll be posted to Arwal. And yes, the DIG has been asked to suspend Nikhil Kumar with immediate effect too,' said the ADG.

'But Sir . . . ' I protested, only to hear the phone getting disconnected.

I was crestfallen. I had done the right thing, and yet I was being transferred within just a few days of my posting to Nalanda. Arwal was one of the least developed places in Bihar and rumoured to be a very difficult posting!

'*Aap Papa se baat kar ke dekho.* Talk to Papa,' suggested Tanu, after hearing my conversation with the ADG.

'Beta, I think you should talk to the Big Boss. Maybe he will appreciate the truth. At least you would have tried,' said my father-in-law, using his years of experience as a police officer.

I dialled the Big Boss's number. '*Main SP Nalanda bol raha hoon.* This is the SP Nalanda. I want to speak to Sir,' I told the PA of the Big Boss.

'*Achha Sir, dekhte hain Saheb ka mood.* Okay Sir, let me check on Saheb's mood,' the PA replied.

A few moments passed. They felt like infinity.

'*Haan, boliye.* Yes, tell me,' said the familiar voice.

'*Sir, mujhe pataa chalaa hain ki mera transfer hone wala hain.* I have come to know that I'm being transferred. *Maine wahi kiya jo sahi tha.* I have done what was right. I will be disappointed if I am punished for doing the right thing,' I said in a single breath.

'*Aisi baat hain?* Is this true? Let me find out,' he said and hung up.

After an hour or so, I got a call from Patna. '*SP Saheb, Bada Saheb baat karenge.* The Big Boss wants to speak to you,' said the PA.

'SP Saheb, you were right. *Badhiya se kaam kariye.* Now work at ease,' said the Big Boss.

'Thank you, sir!' I said, elated.

'Sir, one more thing,' I hurried to add, 'SI Nikhil has been put under suspension for no fault of his.'

'*Achha, toh aisa karte hain, usko release kara dete hain.* We will get him released from suspension. But don't post him to Rahui again. *Kuch humari bhi baat rahe. Let my word also hold true.* Post him to any other important police station,' he said.

'*Aur haan, aage se aisi baatein phone pe nahin karna.* In future, do not discuss these matters on the phone,' the Big Boss said firmly.

I was delighted. I had such a different image of politicians, particularly the Big Boss, but I need not have feared. And I was glad I had stood my ground. As an officer, I had to stand by the truth and could not take a step in the wrong direction.

I called Krishna Sir and told him of my conversation with the Big Boss.

'I hope you do not become a bamboo tree like us. Well done, boy. Proud of you,' he said.

I'm glad I had the courage to make that one phone call. I remained SP of Nalanda for three years.

* * *

'*Sir, aapko aur ADG Sir ko Bada Saheb ne bulaya hain.* Big Boss has called you and ADG Sir,' said the MLA of Nalanda.

'Okay, I'll be there.' I said and soon started for Patna.

The ADG and I reached the sprawling bungalow of the Big Boss.

After some time, the PA ushered us towards the outhouse. The MLA was waiting for us there. Big Boss usually had his afternoon siesta there.

'*Sir, aapko andar bula rahe hain.* Big Boss is calling you inside.'

The ADG started taking off his shoes.

'Sir, what are you doing?' I asked, my eyes wide in surprise.

'Arre, we are going inside his bedroom. Why make it dirty?' the ADG replied.

I did not even think of taking off my shoes. Inside, the Big Boss was lying on a bed, getting a massage from a servant. It was quite a funny sight.

I pulled one of the plastic chairs and sat on it. I gestured the ADG to sit too, but he ignored me.

The Big Boss discussed a few things and dismissed us. After a few days, the Nalanda MLA met me with a big smile.

'*Saheb keh rahe the SP bahut innocent hain.* Big Boss was saying that the SP is very innocent.'

'Why?' I asked.

'Ha, ha. He said the ADG did not sit but the SP pulled up a chair and sat.'

'*Toh kya nahin baithna tha?* Was I not supposed to sit?'

'*Nahin, nahin, aisa nahin hain.* No, no, it's not like that. Actually, nobody sits in front of him. But, interestingly, he neither stops people from sitting, nor asks them to sit. *Aapka aatmasamman aapke haath mein hain.* Your self-respect is in your hands,' said the MLA.

That day, it was another lesson learnt. You need to respect yourself for others to give you respect.

23

The Kidnapping of a Rikshawallah

As soon I as had settled in, I started visiting all the police stations under my jurisdiction. On one of my inspections, I saw quite a few boxes lying in the SHO's chamber.

'*Bada Babu, ye itne saare cartons kyun rakhe hain?* Why have you kept so many cartons?' I asked.

I was rather curious because I had seen similar boxes in a few other police stations too.

'*Arre Sir, ye toh purana saheb ke gaano ke cassettes hain.* These are the cassettes of the earlier DSP. He used to sing a lot of songs, so he got his own cassettes released,' replied Malti, the SHO.

'But what are these cassettes doing here?'

'*Sir, DSP Saheb bole hain inko bikwane ke liye.* DSP Sir has asked us to get them sold.'

'And how will you sell them? Have you opened a shop in the thana?' I asked angrily.

'*Arre, Sir, it's not difficult to get them sold. Jo bhi thana mein case karaane aata hain, hum usko ye cassette ke bare mein bataate hain.* Whoever comes to the police station to lodge an FIR, we tell them about the cassettes. Then it's up to them whether they buy them or not,' said Malti smugly.

'I can't believe it, Malti. This is unacceptable. What is even on these tapes? Put on one of them. *Ek cassette chalao. Sune, kaise gaane hain.* Let's hear what kind of songs they are.'

Malti took a cassette from one of the cartons. The cover had a dancer in a lewd pose.

'*Jao tape recorder lao.* Go get the tape recorder,' Malti ordered a constable. Ten minutes later, I heard the worst music ever. The DSP had sung some really ear-splitting, cacophonous Bhojpuri songs in his exceedingly shrill voice.

'*Bas karo, bandh karo!* Enough, stop it!' I ordered, irritated and unable to take any more.

The constable immediately stopped the cassette from playing. We were all quiet for a few moments. We needed to recover from the shock caused to our eardrums.

'Malti, you will not display any more of these cassettes here. This is a police station, not a shop! Do you understand?' I said sternly.

'But yes, you can make all the criminals you arrest hear these songs. There can't be worse torture.' I added.

All the policemen burst out laughing.

I sat in the car, eager to get home and play with my son Avi. I had been continuously travelling across the district since I had joined Nalanda. I could hardly spend any time with Tanu and Avi. But I was not complaining. My work was challenging but also exciting.

My cellphone started ringing, breaking my train of thought.

'*Sir, kidnapping ho gaya hain.* There has been a kidnapping,' said the SHO Deep Nagar.

'Give me the details,' I said, quickly controlling my feelings. Of course, news of any crime made me nervous and upset, but I had to focus on the details and not panic. After all,

I was paid to listen to bad news and act to convert it to good news.

'Sir, a rikshawallah named Abdul Sattar has been kidnapped,' said the SHO.

'A rikshawallah? Are you serious?' I asked.

'Yes, Sir. Abdul had recently sold off his ancestral land for Rs 3 lakh. Some of his neighbours must have been eyeing the bounty,' the SHO replied.

'Damn it! Make a list of all the suspects. I'll reach the police station in an hour.'

We spent almost the entire day looking for possible clues to the kidnapping and sent off various teams after the suspects.

I returned home, exhausted, only to see the SP Nawada waiting in my residential office.

'Jai Hind, Sir. How come you are here?' I asked Ganguly Sir.

'Amit, a kidnapping has taken place in my area,' he said. 'Dr Hiralal Sah, a reputed doctor of Hazaribagh, had recently returned from London. He was travelling from Patna to Ranchi. He was kidnapped on the way in my district. I have come to seek your assistance in conducting joint raids in your area.'

'Thank god this kidnapping did not take place in my area, and Sir has not attributed it to my district,' I sighed.

Just a few days ago, a PWD engineer had been kidnapped from Patna, quite a few kilometres from Nalanda.

'Amit, why haven't you registered an FIR?' the ADG had asked me.

'But Sir, the kidnapping has clearly taken place in Patna,' I had said.

'Don't argue. Patna is already seeing a wave of crime. We can't let a high-profile kidnapping further tarnish the image of Patna Police. Moreover, the kidnapping has taken place at the border of Nalanda and Patna; it might have actually happened in Nalanda itself. It will have to be registered as a case in Nalanda.'

'But Sir—'

'Nothing doing. You will understand as you grow older in service,' said the ADG.

My protests were of no avail. I knew that the ADG was not very supportive of me.

Nalanda Police had to a register an FIR for the kidnapping of the engineer. In spite of our best efforts, we had no leads of his whereabouts.

Then, at 11 p.m., I had got a call from the son of the engineer.

'Sir, the kidnappers have just called us. They have asked for a ransom of Rs 20 lakh,' said Jameel, the son.

'Let us fix a rendezvous for the delivery of the money. We can trap the criminals there,' I had said excitedly.

'*Sir, aap se haath jodte hain, aisa kuch mat karna.* I beg of you, please don't do any such thing.'

'Jameel, have faith in the police. We have been working hard, you know that.'

'I know, Sir, but I am concerned about Baba's safety. Please understand. *Baba ne itna paisa kamaya hain, kis kaam aayega?* Baba has made so much money, what is its use?'

Before I could argue further, he had hung up. Those days, we did not have sophisticated techniques such as call observation, dump data analysis, etc. I could not move forward in this case as I had no support from the victim's family.

After two days, I read the headlines splashed in the newspapers, 'Engineer released under police pressure.' I crumpled the newspaper and threw it in the dustbin.

I had failed as a policeman.

'Good, the matter is over,' the ADG said, sounding relieved.

* * *

I had promised myself that I would not let anyone pay ransom under my watch. I tried to channel my frustration and redoubled my efforts in the rickshawallah's case. At the same time, I had to think of Dr Hiralal Sah too.

'Sir, do you have any suspects? Any known gangs?' I asked Ganguly Sir.

'Yes, of course. We have so many professional gangs working in this belt,' he replied.

'Professional?' I couldn't help but smile as I wondered that some people must call kidnapping their profession.

Ganguly Sir and I had a long discussion. We dispatched teams to different areas of Nalanda to conduct raids on all possible hideouts of the area's kidnapping gangs.

Ganguly Sir left for Nawada and I retired to my bedroom.

Avi was crying non-stop. Tanu tried to keep him quiet using various tricks but I lost my patience. '*Tanu, sulao isko, yaar.* Please put him to sleep.'

'Chun, he is not a baby doll that I can switch off. I am trying my best. Why don't you go to another room?' replied Tanu.

I went to another room and tried my best to sleep.

I kept turning restlessly as I pondered the kidnappings.

After a few hours I had almost fallen asleep, only to woken up by the buzzing of my cellphone.

'*SP Saheb bol rahe hain?* Is this SP Saheb?' said a voice in a hushed tone.

'*Haan, hum SP bol rahe hain.* Yes, this is the SP,' I said.

'*Sir, ek aadmi ko humare ghar ke paas wale tubewell pe rakha hua hain.* A man has been kept at the tube well near my house. I have a suspicion that he has been kidnapped.'

'Are you sure?' I asked.

'*Ekdam* 100 per cent,' replied the man.

Alert, I noted down the address quickly.

'Ajit, get the guard ready. We have to leave right now,' I told my bodyguard. I was almost certain I had information on the whereabouts of the rikshawallah. I immediately called DSP Shankar Thakur to accompany me. On my way, I kept hoping we would safely bring him back.

After a bumpy ride, we reached the village named by the informer.

We got down about 500 metres before the supposed tube well where the man was being held. It was pitch-dark as there was no electricity in the village. As my police team, led by DSP Sadar Shankar and I, advanced towards the spot, we saw silhouettes moving.

Thakur immediately switched on his torch. There were three people just about a few feet from us.

'*Haath upar karo, nahin to goli chalaa denge.* Hands up, or we will shoot,' challenged the DSP.

The men tried to scamper but were trapped by our teams from all sides. Seeing that the police clearly meant business, they did not put up any resistance.

We rushed towards them and caught them.

'*Arre, Sir, ye to Chhotka Santosh hain.* This is Chhotka Santosh. He's a dreaded kidnapper of Patna,' said the SHO Vena.

'Yes, Sir. This is a big win,' said Thakur.

Though I was satisfied we had done a good job, I was still perplexed about something. Why had such a notorious criminal kidnapped a poor rikshawallah?

'Where is Abdul, the rikshawallah?' I asked.

'Abdul? Abdul who? We don't know any Abdul,' replied one the accomplices of Chhotka Santosh.

'Don't talk nonsense. Tell us where you have kept the kidnapped person,' said Ajit in a threatening tone.

'*Hum toh doctor ka kidnap kiye the.* We had kidnapped a doctor,' said Chhotka Santosh. '*Woh toh tubewell ke paas rakha hain.* We have him kept near the tubewell.'

We made him lead us to the tubewell. After just a few minutes, we heard the voice of a man groaning.

We rushed towards the spot where the sound was coming from.

'It can't be Abdul, the rikshawallah,' I said, looking at the 'suited booted' man lying on the ground. His expression changed from extreme fear to relief when he saw the men in uniform rushing towards him.

We untied the man and removed the gag from his mouth.

'Sir, you are the angels of God. Thank you for saving me.' The man hugged me and started crying.

'Oh my god, this is Dr Hiralal Sah, who was kidnapped from Nawada,' said Thakur.

I was surprised.

We took Dr Sah to my house. It was early morning. Tanu was pacing on the verandah with Avi in her arms.

'Tanu, this is Dr Hiralal Sah. Please arrange for some tea for him,' I said.

Tanu was surprised.

'*Aap raat ko kab nikale?* When did you go out in the night? At least you should have told me,' she complained.

'*Tum dono neend mein the.* Both of you were in deep sleep. I did not want to disturb you,' I said with a smile.

I called Ganguly Sir. 'Ganguly Sir, this is Amit. We have got Dr Hiralal Sah. Yes, he's with me.' He was clearly very happy with the news.

'Excellent, Amit. I am proud of you. And thank you,' said Ganguly Sir graciously.

* * *

I was happy with our lucky break, but we were yet to recover the rikshawallah. After the sustained efforts of my team, we also got Abdul back that night. He had been kidnapped by his neighbour, Sartaj.

'Sartaj, why the hell did you kidnap a poor rikshawallah?' I questioned.

'Sir, hum bhi toh gareeb dukandaar hain. I am also a poor shopkeeper. I needed this money to start work as a government contractor,' he replied. I wondered if kidnapping had become an 'industry' or an alternative source of employment in Bihar.

The next day, the newspapers were splashed with the headlines such as, 'Famous doctor recovered by Nalanda Police.'

Dr Sah's kidnapping got a big headline while poor Abdul was hardly mentioned. To us both cases had been equally important, but the news sadly only wanted to report about the man who came from a certain class and background.

I realized that my habit of answering phone calls personally had again paid rich dividends.

I also realized that the harder we work, the luckier we get.

24

Sambhav

'*Sir, yahaan Bhagwan Buddha aur Mahavir kuch na kar sake—hum aur aap kaise karenge?* Even Lord Buddha and Mahavir could not do anything here—what can you and I do?' shouted a young man, clearly disgruntled with the state of affairs around him.

I had gone to interact with the college students of Nalanda just to listen to their problems and improve the functioning of the police. Instead, I saw disenchantment and apathy among the students. They were not only angry but seemed to have very little hope for the future too. The establishment had failed them and the police were no role models either. The only silver lining they seemed to find was that I was young and that they could interact with me easily.

I wanted to channelize their energy to augment the work of the police.

'*Tumhari yuva shakti se badi taaqat kuch nahin hain.* There is no force greater than the power of the youth,' I said.

'*Sir, ye toh har neta, vidhayak bhi bolte hain. Isse kya hoga?* Every politician and MLA says the same thing. What difference will it make?' retorted one of the students.

'*Hoga, zaroor kuch accha hoga.* Something good will definitely happen. *Sab sambhav hain.* Everything is possible,' I replied with conviction.

'As SP of Nalanda, I'm announcing a police–public partnership today. I'll call it Sambhav, meaning "possible",' I said.

'I want volunteers from among you to come forward and help the police. You know the police is quite understaffed and we have a shortage of resources. It is very difficult for the police to perform even their basic duties properly. But it will be a big boost to us if you join hands with us,' I told the packed auditorium.

There was a deafening silence for some moments. I thought that my idea had been outright rejected by the students. But suddenly the auditorium erupted.

'Sir, I am ready!' said one student.

'SP Sir, SP Sir, I also want to support Nalanda Police,' said another.

I felt wonderful to see almost all the youngsters embracing my idea. And it was heartening to see quite a few girls also participating with equal zeal.

'Okay, now, it's a great beginning. My office will issue special identity cards to you. From tomorrow, you will be known as the Sambhav volunteers. I will make a charter of duties for you in consultation with my team of police officers,' I said enthusiastically.

I came back to my office quite excited and immediately called a meeting with my senior police officers.

'I am starting a police–public partnership called Sambhav,' I said, relating my interaction with the college students.

Most of the policemen somehow did not seem very enthusiastic about this idea. After a moment of hesitation, DSP Sadar said, 'Sir, these college students are troublemongers. They often create trouble during festivals such as Holi and Saraswati Puja. How can they assist the police?'

'DSP Saheb, that is exactly the point. Let us give some responsibility to these "errant" youngsters. I am sure it will channelize their energy positively,' I said.

'But, Sir, what work will we give them? We can't ask them to investigate a case or arrest a murderer,' said the town inspector, Vijay Gopal.

'There are quite a few things the youth can help us with. For starters, depute them at all the sensitive points during this Durga Puja. They can help us control the movement of the public through the crowded areas. The youngsters can also ask the revellers to move their processions faster,' I explained.

'This will be like giving our powers to the students,' protested the DSP Hilsa.

I was disappointed at the attitude of my colleagues.

'What powers are you talking about, DSP Saheb? Let us stop bickering about these small things. Let us experiment during this Durga Puja. I am hopeful of a successful result,' I said, dismissing my officers.

I was nervous on the day of Durga Puja. What if the young, inexperienced students could not carry out the basic tasks assigned to them? I was also apprehensive that my own policemen would not welcome the efforts of the volunteers.

Much to my surprise, I saw the college students positioned at all critical points, wearing big smiles and lovely T-shirts with 'Sambhav' printed on them. I got out of my Gypsy and asked one of the volunteers, 'I am sure you are enjoying your job. By the way, who gave you these smart "Sambhav" T-shirts?'

'Sir, Inspector Uncle got these T-shirts for us,' replied the students cheerfully.

I looked around and saw the town inspector directing the traffic. Along with him were three Sambhav volunteers, shouting at the public to move forward. Suddenly an old passer-by lost his balance and fell off his cycle. The volunteers immediately rushed to the man, took him to the 'Sambhav' kiosk and offered him water.

'*Sir, bahut accha lag raha hain bachchon ke saath kaam karke.* It feels very good working with these kids. *Inn mein abhi bhi kitni masoomiyat hain.* They still have so much innocence in them,' Gopal said.

I gave him a big smile.

Soon, 'Sambhav' became quite popular. Nalanda Police enlisted a number of students to act as volunteers. The youngsters started helping the police not only during festivals but also for traffic management and relief to accident victims. Both girls and boys came forward and joined our mission. The atmosphere of the district slowly started changing. The 'scary' policemen soon became 'police uncles' for the youngsters. The parents also felt reassured that their children were using their time and energy positively. The police started organizing various sporting and literary events for the youth. As a young man myself, I started enjoying this fruitful partnership with the youth.

One evening, when I was sitting in my garden looking at the beautiful flowers, the DSP Sadar came to meet me.

'Sir, I just wanted to tell you—*sab sambhav hain.* Everything is possible.'

Both of us smiled.

25

Matric Exam

'Why should the police be concerned with the conduct of the matric examination?' I asked my reader.

The police headquarters had issued an order asking all SPs to deploy police at all the centres for the matric exams.

'Sir, the matric certificate is extremely important as it is mandatory for all government jobs. People are so desperate for the certificate that a lot of cheating takes place in these exams. Even parents help their children cheat. Sometimes widespread cheating may even lead to law-and-order problems,' replied my reader.

'*Chalo, phir nikalo order.* Then issue the order for police deployment at the schools earmarked as centres for the exam. *Police ko har cheez mein involve hona padhta hain.* The police has to be involved in every issue,' I said.

On the day of the exam, the DM insisted that both of us take a round of the centres to see that everything was going well.

'SP Saheb, I want Nalanda to be an example for all districts of Bihar. I want to ensure that no cheating takes place here,' the DM said.

Our motorcade went to different schools.

'Let us check the Balika Vidyalaya, the girls' school,' said the DM.

'Did you check the girls? They can hide slips and chits in their socks and sleeves,' the DM asked the invigilators there. The police were vigilant. Even the invigilators and the teachers were doing their job seriously. The DM was pleased.

We went to a few more schools and were planning to go to a few more, but we suddenly saw a huge crowd outside an exam centre. They held bricks in their hands and were ready to throw them at us.

'*Prashashan haye haye!* Down with the administration!' shouted the public, raising their arms in protest.

'*Ye kya ho raha hain? Ye bawaal kyun?* What is happening? Why this commotion?' asked the DM.

'Sir, the parents have spread a rumour that the girls were checked indecently by the male invigilators. That is why the people are getting so angry,' said the DM's driver.

'But this is not true. *Aisa to kuch nahin hua hain.* Nothing like that has happened,' said the DM. His face had turned pale.

The volley of stones had increased in intensity.

It was difficult facing the crowd. The people were raising slogans against the administration. We did not have enough force, so I called all my officers to the girls' school.

'DM Saheb, the crowd is getting violent and I think their anger is directed at you. *Aap yahaan ruko.* You wait here. Since it is not exactly a police problem, let me try to talk to the mob. Hopefully, I will be able to reason with them.'

I got out of the car and walked towards the crowd. My bodyguards Shukla, Ajit and Ritesh accompanied me.

I had been in Nalanda for one-and-a-half years now and thought I could connect well with the public. The moment I raised my hands to dissuade the people, I was welcomed with a volley of brickbats. My bodyguards immediately formed a protective cordon around me, standing as human shields between the mob and me.

Even before I could react, my fit and agile bodyguards picked me up and put me in the Gypsy. Though shaken, I was grateful and proud of my excellent team, which had saved me.

As I sat in the Gypsy, I saw a brick coming straight at me. I ducked and covered my face. The windscreen cracked, the glass pieces hitting me. Chhotu, my driver, drove the Gypsy in reverse in high speed for a good 300-400 metres.

I was dazed for a few moments and a little unnerved by the turn of events. I gathered myself and shouted over the wireless, 'Inspector Rajender, quickly get reinforcements and reach Balika Vidyalaya.' All police vehicles near the area immediately moved towards the school on hearing my command.

Once the reinforcements had reached, we returned to the epicentre of the ruckus.

'*Aap shaant ho jaiye.* Please calm down. All the rumours of indecent checking of the female students are false,' I announced on the megaphone.

It hardly made any difference to the mob. Rather, it got even more violent. I was exasperated to see young students and even their parents vandalize school property. Unable to bear this senseless mayhem any more, I ordered my men to resort to the use of light force.

The police caught hold of a few troublemongers who were closest to us and gave them a thrashing. Since the crowd was leaderless, it did not know what to do. Some of the students ran and hid in the classrooms.

My men and I followed them with lathis in our hands, ready to use light force against anyone who was causing trouble. Inside, I saw the students huddled in a corner, fear writ large on their faces. All my anger vanished on seeing their young faces.

'Why the hell are you doing this?' I said.

'Sorry, Sir. *Galti ho gayi. Maaf kar dijiye.* We made a mistake. Please forgive us,' replied the students fearfully. Many of them started crying.

'Shame on you. You are going to be the future of the nation and this is what you are doing,' I said, admonishing them.

'Do you know that if your names are mentioned in an FIR, your careers are finished? Then what will you do with the matric certificate?' Inspector Rajender reprimanded. The students were absolutely quiet; some parents also folded their hands and apologized. Except for a few vandals, we decided to let go of the remaining students and parents. We made a queue of the students and asked them to leave for their homes.

I was taken aback as I had not anticipated such a public outburst against the police.

'*Sir, iss baar bahut tight checking ho rahi hain. Cheating namumkin hain.* This time, the checking is very strict. Cheating is impossible,' said Rajender.

'This anger is not exactly about the rumour. It is basically the frustration of the students, parents and relatives at not being able to cheat in the exams,' he continued.

'But why this mindless violence?' I asked.

'Sir, the people wait for the matric certificate. They want it by hook or by crook. You know the education system is in a shambles in the state. Sometimes there are no school buildings; if there are schools, there are no teachers. So the children hardly have any formal schooling. They hardly know what to write in the exam. So what do they do? They cheat, as a matter of right. Plus, it has become a culture. Like other ills of the society, cheating, too, has become acceptable.'

I remained quiet. I wondered how so many students from Bihar still made it into the IITs, the IAS, the IPS. They were the few who worked hard and chose to make their own destiny.

'Most of the people try for government jobs. That is why they even have fake birth certificates reducing their real age by at least two or three years,' Rajender said.

I managed a smile. I thought about a few of my colleagues who certainly looked older than me and yet were 'officially' younger. In fact, a few of them even had children when they had joined the services.

26

Mauka Sabko Milta Hain

As a young SP, I wanted my district to be crime-free and, of course, make an impression on everyone. I made a list of the most dreaded criminals and started hounding their hideouts almost every other night.

Though my raids had a salutary effect on the criminals, I was soon exhausted. One of my very able officers, SI Ravi Jyoti, accompanied me for almost all the operations.

Seeing my state, he asked me after a raid one day, '*Sir, ek baat boloon?* May I say something?'

'*Haan bolo, Ravi.* Yes, tell me,' I said, trying not to doze off.

'Sir, generals don't fight wars,' he said.

'Huh? What do you mean?' I asked.

'Sir, the SP of a district is like a general. He is the chief of the district police. His job is planning, delegating and ensuring execution.'

'Sir, as an SP you are supposed to make us work. You are not supposed to do our work,' he continued.

'Go on,' I said.

'Sir, it is not desirable and, of course, not possible for you to raid every criminal's house. You will burn yourself out.'

'Then should I sit at home? What kind of leadership would that be?'

'Of course sir, you should lead a few important operations. But you must also know how to delegate. You must have faith in your subordinates. Let me assure you we will not let you down.'

'And, finally, if we land in some kind of trouble, we want our boss to be safe so he can bail us out. In policing, a lot of controversial things happen. It's for the district SP to see that his policemen stay out of trouble. *Agar SP saheb khud hi musibat mein padh jayenge, unhe kaun bachayega?* If the SP himself lands in trouble, who will save him?' Ravi said.

I thought about Ravi's words and realized he had a point. And soon enough, something else did need my attention.

* * *

'Nalanda becomes a hotbed of kidnapping; crime at an all-time high,' screamed the headlines of *Dainik Khabar*, a local newspaper.

I was annoyed seeing the headline, as crime was well under control in Nalanda. All the other newspapers gave factual news, but *Dainik Khabar* was always critical of the police. In fact, it exaggerated the crimes happening in Nalanda to the point that it was even publishing false 'court cases' as actual proceedings.

Unable to tolerate this misrepresentation of facts any longer, I called the bureau chief of the newspaper and asked, 'Akhilendraji, why are you publishing such negative news about Nalanda Police? What is your problem?'

'*Arre, Sir, aap humara dhyaan hi nahin rakhte.* You don't take care of us,' replied Akhilendra.

'*Dhyaan?*'

'*Sir, kuch maans, machhi, madira bhijwaiye kabhi.* Send some meat, fish and drinks sometimes. You should take care of us. And, of course, easy access to you will help me get some fringe benefits.'

'Akhilendraji, nothing of that sort will happen. Let us maintain a professional relationship,' I replied tersely.

'*Sir, phir toh khabar chhapti rahegi.* Then such news will keep getting printed.'

'Then so be it,' I said angrily.

As it turned out soon after, Nalanda was in the news as developments in some really high-profile national cases had taken place there. One of them was the firing at the American Centre in Kolkata. The terrorist act was carried out under the direction of Farhan Ansari, whose passport was made in Nalanda. On investigation, it was discovered that Ansari had given a fake address of a village in Nalanda, though he had never lived there. The ASI of the concerned police station gave a certificate to Ansari without any verification, for a bribe of just Rs 500. And the office head clerk had forwarded it to the passport office in Patna for another Rs 1000. I arrested the ASI and the head clerk and provided some valuable clues to Kolkata Police, leading to the arrest of Farhan Ansari.

Since it was big news, journalists descended on my office to get 'bytes' and all the news channels and newspapers wanted 'exclusives'. I entertained all the mediapersons except Akhilendra.

Akhilendra lost out on a lot of first-hand news and could not cover such an important national event linked to Nalanda.

He did not take this rebuff well. His attacks became more vitriolic and sometimes even personal.

I wasn't immune to the attacks and spoke to my wife about it. 'Tanu, yaar, this newspaper is printing such nonsense about Nalanda Police every day. Most of the news is fake,' I complained.

'Relax. Why do you react at all? The best solution is to stop reading *Dainik Khabar*. That way, you will not even know what is being printed against you,' she replied.

'But what about the public? The people are being fed so much negative news about us.'

'No one can fool the people all the time. Just keep doing your work sincerely. Ultimately, the people will know what the truth is.'

She then called Tariq, my telephone orderly.

'*Kal se ye akhbar*, Dainik Khabar, *bandh kar do*. From tomorrow, stop the subscription of *Dainik Khabar.*'

'Ji, Madam,' replied Tariq with a smart salute.

* * *

It was a huge relief to not read all the vitriol in *Dainik Khabar* every day. But soon, I had to contend with another adversary. A newly appointed *jila adhyaksh*, or district officer, had a grudge against the police and wanted to keep us under his thumb. He encouraged Akhilendra to go all out against Nalanda Police.

'*Sir, ab toh ye kuch zyada ho raha hain*. Now things are getting a little too much,' said Inspector Tiwari, one of my most competent and loyal officers.

'It seems the jila adhyaksh is giving a lot of advertisements to *Dainik Khabar*. This funding has further emboldened Akhilendra to print negative news about us,' he continued.

'Let us be patient. *Mauka sabko milta hain*. Everyone gets a chance to get even,' said Mithilesh, the SHO Lahiri.

I forced a smile. Things were getting difficult for Nalanda Police. It wasn't easy to just stand by while a newspaper spewed venom against us every day—that, too, with the help of the jila adhyaksh.

We didn't have to wait long before an opportunity came knocking on our door.

* * *

Mithilesh stood outside my office with a man.

'Sir, this is Chandan, a civil contractor. He has been getting threats from Akhilendra, the bureau chief of *Dainik Khabar*,' he said.

'Ji huzoor. Akhilendra has been blackmailing me that he will write against my construction work in his newspaper and use his relations with the jila adhyaksh to blacklist me,' Chandan said. 'He has been extorting money from me for the past two months. I can no longer comply with his demands. *Ab ati ho gayi hain*. It's gone too far now.'

'Sir, we have lodged an FIR under Section 384 of the IPC for extortion. We can arrest him whenever you order us to,' said Mithilesh.

'Raid his house tonight and arrest him. He might create problems, as he is well connected. Keep me posted on any development. I will be awake,' I said, before dismissing the police officers.

I went home and switched on the TV to watch the US Open. My favourite player, Andre Agassi, was playing. I loved his game and couldn't but envy his long, flowing hair.

The match was quite exciting and went well into the fifth set. I checked the clock.

It was 3 a.m., the perfect time for the police to raid Akhilendra's house. This is the time a man is in his deepest sleep, this is the time for non-REM sleep. The heart rate and breathing rate are at their lowest in this part of the sleep cycle. But for us policemen, it's normal to stay awake at such unearthly hours.

As I was watching the match, my cellphone buzzed. It was the DIG Patna.

'Jai Hind, Sir,' I said, and instinctively sat up in attention in my bedroom. It was all a result of the discipline and training that had been ingrained in me over the years. Such is the Pavlovian reaction of a policeman!

'Amit, have you sent a police team to a journalist's house? The jila adhyaksh of your district just called me,' said the DIG. He sounded a little irritated, possibly because his sleep had been disturbed.

'Why did the jila adhyaksh not call you directly? What was the need to wake me up?' he asked.

'Sir, the jila adhyaksh and I do not get along. He has a problem with the police. That is why he called you instead of me,' I said.

'And Sir,' I explained further, 'Akhilendra is a rogue of a journalist. He has been booked in an extortion case. The police is right in arresting him.'

'Okay, I trust you. You are free to take your decisions,' said the DIG. I was glad to hear that. Sir never interfered in my work.

After five minutes, my phone rang again. The match was at an enthralling tie-breaker, but it seemed like I wouldn't be able to enjoy it that night.

It was Inspector Tiwari.

'*Sir, Jila Adhyaksh Saheb khud hi aa gaye hain.* The jila adhyaksh is here. He is standing outside Akhilendra's house. He is asking us to not arrest Akhilendra,' Tiwari said.

I was angry.

'Tell the jila adhyaksh to not interfere in police work. I have faith in you that you will handle the situation well,' I said.

'*Sir, hum chattan ki tarah khade rahenge aapke aadesh par.* I will stand like a rock at your command,' replied Tiwari. I felt proud that I had men like him on the force.

Sadly, it didn't end there. I got a call from Tiwari again about half an hour later.

'Sir, the jila adhyaksh was insisting that we at least arrest Akhilendra in the morning. So I got a chowki, a small bed from the thana, for him to lie on until dawn. Of course, he was quite embarrassed and left,' said Tiwari.

Agassi had lost the match. It so happened that Agassi's hairpiece did not stay in place and he got distracted trying to keep it in place, which affected his shots. I was shocked when I realized the long hair I admired was a toupee. Agassi had fooled all of us for years!

I switched off the TV and tried to get some sleep.

Meanwhile, Tiwari and Mithilesh took Akhilendra into police custody early in the morning. But instead of taking him straight to the police station, they decided to make him walk through the lanes and roads of Nalanda. This did not sit well with the other reporters in Nalanda. They assembled outside the town's police station and started raising slogans against the police.

Inspector Tiwari tried to reason with the media.

'*Dekhiye, Akhilendra par extortion ka case darj hua hain.* An extortion case has been lodged against Akhilendra. The police has just followed the law,' he said, trying to placate the journalists gathered there.

'*Police murdabad!* Down with the police!' the crowd shouted. They got more aggressive and started hurling stones at the police. Soon, they ransacked nearby shops too.

Tiwari called me immediately when it started to get out of hand, waking me up from my sleep.

'*Sir, mediawaalon ne bawaal machaa diya hain.* The media people are creating a ruckus,' said Tiwari, explaining the situation to me.

'Tiwari, when somebody takes the law into their hands, the police has to take action. Go ahead, do your job,' I said.

'Just videograph the rioting. It will help us get evidence. You know the media will create a major issue when we take action against them,' I added, before disconnecting the call.

That day, Nalanda Police came down heavily on the troublemakers. FIRs were lodged against all the reporters who had taken law into their hands.

The next day, every newspaper wrote against us. The press representatives also went to meet the Big Boss to complain against police 'atrocities' and the 'murder of democracy' by the attack on the fifth estate.

'*Sir, SP ko suspend kariye.* Suspend the SP,' the press demanded.

'*SP ne bilkul theek kiya.* The SP did the right thing. I won't suspend him.' The Big Boss took a stand.

'*Par Sir, transfer hi kar dijiye.* At least transfer him,' said a media personnel.

'*Ab aap humko sikhayenge ki sarkar kaise chalani hain?* Now you will teach me how to run the government? No action will be taken against the SP. Period. Of course, the jila adhyaksh will be shown his place,' the Big Boss thundered.

The matter was closed. Akhilendra was released on bail after a month, as a much-chastened man. And the circulation of *Dainik Khabar* dropped to an all-time low.

27

Police Yadav

'*Sir, Avi Babu ab bade ho rahe hain. Aap bhi ek gai rakh lijiye doodh ke liye.* Your son Avi is growing up now. You should also keep a cow so he can have fresh milk every day,' said Onkar Pandey, my cook.

'*Gai?* A cow? In my house?' I asked.

'*Haan, Sir. DM Saheb toh poori gaushala rakhe hain.* The DM has kept quite a few cows in his house' he replied.

'Chun, I think he is right. Even if we don't keep a cow, at least get fresh milk from the DM's house. That milk will be pure, unadulterated,' said Tanu.

It was quite common in Bihar for officers to keep cows in their sprawling bungalows. Having grown up in urban areas, I found the idea of keeping a cow in my house quite strange. But it would certainly be nice to have fresh milk every day.

So we started getting milk from the DM's house. But things didn't work out as we had planned.

'*Chun, iss doodh mein to khoob paani hain.* There is a lot of water in this milk,' said Tanu, and showed me the bowl.

* * *

'*Arre, Amit, doodh kyun rok diya?* Why did you stop taking milk from us?' asked the jovial DM. He was a friendly neighbour and often came to say hello.

'*Sir, aise hi.* Just like that,' I said sheepishly.

'There must have been a reason,' the DM said.

Tanu could not control herself. She had never been diplomatic anyway.

'Sir, there was a lot of water mixed in the milk. We wanted pure milk for Avi,' she said.

'Accha, I will check. I am surprised,' said the DM, looking embarrassed.

He called me later in the evening.

'Amit, you were right. My staff was pilfering milk. To make up for the theft, he was adding water to the milk. I'm really sorry for the poor quality of milk supplied to you,' he said.

'Tanu, can you believe it? The DM's own staff was cheating him,' I said when I had disconnected the call.

'Why are you surprised? Even I have caught Onkar, our own cook, stealing from the kitchen,' she replied.

'Really? What was he taking? I hope nothing valuable.'

'*Buddhu,* what will be valuable in the kitchen? Anyway, we don't have anything expensive in our house. He was taking the usual stuff—ghee and onions,' she said, laughing.

'*Police ke ghar mein chori, woh bhi SP ke yahaan!* Theft in the house of the police, that, too, at the SP's house!' I was shocked and angry.

'*Zyada tension mat lo.* Don't get worried. I fired him.'

'You should have taken strict action.'

'*Kya jail bhej dete ghee churane ke liye?* Would you have sent him to jail for stealing ghee? Concentrate on more important work,' Tanu said, ending our conversation.

* * *

The next morning I got a call from Mathur Sir, IG, Patna zone.

'Amit, a famous neurophysician, Dr Ramesh Sethi, has been kidnapped from Patna. I want you to go to Mokama immediately,' he said.

'But sir, I'm the SP of Nalanda. Mokama falls in Patna district. What will I do there?' I protested.

'It doesn't matter. You make a list of all the possible kidnappers in Mokama and raid their hideouts. This might lead to the recovery of the kidnapped doctor. The government and the public will also have faith that the police is doing their work seriously.'

'Sir, looking for the doctor in the vast area of Mokama will be like looking for a needle in a haystack. And how do we even know if the doctor has been taken to Mokama?' I argued.

'Amit, even I don't know if the doctor is in Mokama. But this is an order—don't argue anymore.'

I started for Mokama, which was quite far from Nalanda. I knew it could be a futile exercise, yet I had to follow orders. On my way, I called my father-in-law, who was serving as the ADG Intelligence in Jaipur.

I told him about my conversation with the IG Patna.

'Beta, we had a similar kidnapping just a few days ago. We cracked the case pretty easily by just using the IMEI numbers,' he said, explaining to me in detail how the IMEI numbers of cellphones could be used to track a person.

'It's that simple?' I asked.

'Yes, of course. Use technology to your advantage,' my father-in-law replied.

I called Mrs Sethi, the wife of the doctor, and introduced myself.

'*SP Saheb, kuch kariye.* Please do something.' Mrs Sethi started sobbing.

'Mrs Sethi, let me assure you that the police is doing everything to get your husband back safely,' I said.

'Could you please give me the cell number of Dr Sethi? And what was the model of the cellphone?'

'SP Saheb, the number is 931x2@622 but it is switched off.'

'Doesn't matter. The model?'

'It is a Samsung cellphone, one with a colour screen.'

'Okay, I'll get back to you soon.'

The model of the cellphone used by Dr Sethi was quite an expensive one. Back in those days, a colour-screen cellphone was a novelty, and I knew only a handful of people who had those. I knew for sure that the kidnappers would not throw away such a fancy phone.

I immediately gave the details to Arvind Chatterjee, the affable GM of Reliance Communications.

'Can you please run the IMEI and find out if any other SIM card has been put in this cellphone set?' I requested.

He replied in ten minutes.

'Yes, Sir. A new SIM card was inserted in the phone a few hours ago.'

As expected, one of the kidnappers had put his own SIM card into the doctor's handset.

'Great. Can you send me the call details of the new SIM card? I will ask someone from Patrakar Nagar thana to get the details from the Patna office of Reliance Communications. Should I send my police team after two days?' I asked.

That was the time such work usually took.

'Arre, Sir, why would we take two days to give you the details? I will send it right away to your email address,' said Chatterjee.

'Really? Then why does it take two days for Patna Police to get a printout?' I asked.

'Because they have never called us earlier in case of an emergency. They always follow the typical bureaucratic procedure. First a requisition by Patna Police to the Reliance Patna office; then the Patna office asks the Kolkata Reliance office and they then send the details to Patna. I can send the call details directly to you,' Chatterjee explained.

I was baffled. There had been so much unwanted correspondence on so many cases until now.

As an SP I had a computer in my office, another luxury in those days. I was quite excited to get the call details of the kidnapper on my email in ten minutes.

I zeroed in on some frequently contacted numbers over the past few days and called Chatterjee again for the names and addresses attached with those numbers.

Forty-five minutes later, I had the details of five of those numbers. One name clearly stood out—Rajo Yadav.

Rajo Yadav was a known history-sheeter in Patna. I had heard about his foray into the world of crime when I was the ASP Patna. I immediately called Abhay, my former bodyguard, who had worked with me in Patna.

'*Abhay, Rajo Yadav ka koi gupt thikana hain?* Do you know of any secret hideout of Rajo Yadav? *Apna network use karo.* Use your network,' I said.

'*Ji sir, abhi thoda din pehle hi humara spy humko bataaya hain.* Just a few days ago my spy—my source—told me about his location. But he is not active nowadays. He is out on bail. He is not wanted by the police in any matter,' Abhay replied.

'Doesn't matter, Abhay. Find out where he is right now. But do it quietly.'

I got a call from Abhay in two hours.

'*Sir, mil gaya hain uska thikana. Bakhtiarpur ke paas gaon me hain.* I have found his location. It is in a village near Bakhtiarpur,' said Abhay.

Bakhtiarpur was halfway between Nalanda and Patna. Since the kidnapping case pertained to Patna Police, I immediately called the SSP Patna.

'Sir, I have found a clue in the neurosurgeon's kidnapping case. If we question Rajo Yadav, we might get some leads about the kidnapper,' I said, giving Yadav's details to him.

'Okay, meet me at Bakhtiarpur at 1.30 a.m. I'll come with my team,' said the SSP.

I was excited by the development. I was confident we would find out more about the kidnapper if we questioned Yadav. It was no coincidence that his number had been contacted so frequently by the new number in the doctor's handset.

We met SSP Sir's team at the designated time and, led by Abhay, set off for the hideout of Yadav. It was a big, dilapidated house. According to Abhay, the owner had left Bihar for greener pastures.

We could only hear the sound of crickets in the dark. There was absolute silence in and around the house. Our men surrounded the house and took their positions.

'Sir, should we keep our weapons ready?' I asked, taking out my Glock from the holster.

'Don't do it. Let us first check the house. If we go inside with loaded guns, there is a chance of accidental firing. Anyway, we just need to find Yadav,' said the SSP.

It made sense, but I was confused. What if there were criminals inside? I gestured to my personal bodyguards, Ajit and Shukla, to cock their weapons as silently as possible and stay alert.

Abhay broke open the door and we followed him inside. He switched on his torch and called out Yadav's name. Much to our surprise, we saw a group of people sleeping on the floor, with weapons lying next to them. They got up, startled by the commotion, and immediately tried to grab their desi kattas.

'*Thahro, nahin toh goli maar denge.* Stop or we will shoot,' shouted Ajit and Shukla, pointing their guns at the goons.

'*Sir, ye raha Rajo Yadav.* This is Rajo Yadav,' said Abhay, pointing the torch at one of the men. We took away the weapons from the criminals and tied them up.

'*Kaun ho tum log?* Who are you people? What are you doing here?' asked the SSP.

The goons kept quiet.

Abhay shoved Yadav.

'*Bataata hain ya do chaar aur lagaoon?* Will you speak or should I thrash you some more?' Abhay said, trying to sound intimidating.

Yadav pointed at a burly man.

'*Sir, bataata hoon.* I'll tell you. This is Police Yadav. And they are his gang members. They have brought a person to hide here. *Koi doctor saheb hain.* It's a doctor,' said Yadav, trembling now.

'Where is the doctor?' I asked.

'He is in the storeroom.'

We barged into the storeroom to find a potbellied man lying on the cold, damp floor. We removed the gag from his mouth and untied him.

We could not believe our luck. I had come to question Yadav about the kidnapping, and here we had not only rescued the doctor but also arrested one of the most dreaded criminals of Patna, Police Yadav.

The laconic SSP did not show much reaction. He dialled the number of the IG.

'Sir, we have the doctor,' he said.

'From where? Mokama?' asked the IG.

'No, Sir, Bakhtiarpur. Amit used cellphone technology to find the kidnappers,' said the SSP, explaining the details of the operation.

'We need to move out of our standard, old-fashioned policing at times, Sir,' said the SSP.

'You are right. I was wrong in ordering Amit to camp in Mokama. Put him on the line,' said the IG, graciously accepting his error in judgement.

'Congratulations, Amit. Well done,' he told me.

'Thank you, Sir,' I replied, elated at the faith reposed in me by my seniors.

We went to the Bakhtiarpur police station with the criminals and the doctor to see the formalities carried out. I looked at Police Yadav and could not resist asking him, '*Tumhara naam Police Yadav kyun hain?* Why is your name Police Yadav?'

'*Humara babuji bachpan se hi humein police banana chahte the.* My father always wanted me to be a policeman. This was his dream right from the day I was born,' he replied, avoiding direct eye contact with all the policemen.

All of us laughed at the irony. This was not the first time I came across a criminal with an interesting name. I crossed paths with Vakil Sharma, Mantri Prasad and Hero Singh too. But my favourite name has been 'Bholtage Yadav', named as such because his birth coincided with the time of steady voltage supply in his village after many years.

28

Parle-G

Even till a few months before I joined as the SP of Nalanda, the newspaper headlines were usually like, 'Apradhi mast, police past.' They had now changed to 'Apradhi mast, police chust'. Unfortunately, we had still not been able to stop kidnappings altogether. Kidnapping used to function as an organized industry in Bihar in those days.

Due to my knowledge of how to use cellphones to track people and a good network of 'sources', I was able to tackle most kidnapping cases with relative ease. It was the other problems that were more troubling.

When I had joined the IPS, I had the grandiose dream of becoming a top cop who would change the 'system' and solve all of my district's issues. I soon realized how this was next to impossible. Police officers face a plethora of problems every day. We have to account for all sorts of things that may anger people. If a girl elopes with her lover, we need to take into account that it could lead to a communal riot. If an examination is held and the police try to prevent cheating, we are mobbed. The worst are the land disputes. They can range from a dispute over a drain between two houses to a fight between two brothers over an expensive plot. These are problems that are usually never solved, because one party always ends up dissatisfied. The police are always beset with all kinds of problems and yet are expected to deliver results instantly. In those days, our resources were limited too. My munshi used to say, '*Saheb, iss desh ko yahaan ke taittees crore bhagwan hi chala rahe hain.* This country is being run by its thirty-three crore gods. Otherwise how can we progress so much in spite of so many humongous problems?'

I knew I could not solve every problem myself, so I began to delegate and prioritize my work.

Elections, whether Lok Sabha or panchayat, were always priority. Sabha elections were announced in 2003. It was a huge responsibility to make sure the elections were conducted in a free, fair and peaceful manner. I started making a list of sensitive booths that would require extra force a month earlier. The district police also started a drive against antisocial elements and troublemongers. Just a few days later, three observers of the Election Commission of India came to Nalanda to oversee our preparation for the elections.

The Nalanda district was allotted about 1200 men for the elections. These policemen had come from the Bihar Military Police, or the BMP, and the Home Guard. They were made to stay in dilapidated police lines and police stations. But the bigger problem was to send them to the various polling booths for duty. Nalanda Police needed a lot of buses, trucks and tractors to transport them. Unfortunately, at the same time, my relations with an officer of the administration had soured.

Despite repeated reminders, the vehicles were not provided to us. Until two days before the elections, I was worried, yet hopeful that things would fall into place. I had done extensive groundwork. Everything was under control in the district but the force was still in the police lines.

Late after midnight, I got a call from the police lines. It was the munshi.

'*Sir, aap jaldi aa jao, Major Saheb bahut tension mein hain.* Please come quickly, Major Saheb is in great tension,' he said worriedly.

'Why, what happened?' I asked.

'Sir, he cannot manage the huge manpower in the police lines. Things have gone haywire,' said the munshi.

I put on my uniform to go to the police lines.

'Where are you going at this hour?' asked Tanu.

'To the police lines. I should be back soon. You go back to sleep.'

She started filling up a water bottle for me. She also took out two Parle-G biscuit packets.

'*Inn biscuits ki kya zaroorat hain? Abhi aa toh raha hoon.* What is the need for these biscuits? I am coming back soon,' I said.

'*Arre, aap policewalon ka kuch pataa hota hain?* Can one ever tell with you policemen? Just keep the biscuits!'

I smiled and left home.

* * *

The scene at the police lines was scary. There was chaos among the hundreds of policemen. The generator wasn't working, some people were sleeping, others were looking for food—and there was no organization.

The munshi of the police lines came running towards me.

'*Sir, bahut bawaal chal raha hain.* There is a major crisis now,' he said, visibly tense.

'That I can see. *Samjhao.* Explain,' I said, trying to put on a confident face.

'Sir, Major Saheb had issued commands for all the parties for election duty. We had formed teams of the Home Guard and the BMP jawans,' he said.

'The parties kept waiting for the buses to take them to the polling booths. After some time, they lost patience and started moving, looking for food, going to the toilet . . . And now we are unable to locate the members of each team. Right now, we do not know if we'll be able to send the jawans in time for election duty,' he explained further.

'Where is Major Saheb?' I asked.

'Sir, he collapsed under stress. His BP is high. We have sent him to the district hospital,' the munshi replied.

The situation was grim. We only had a few hours before election duty. The elections could not be conducted without deployment of force. If I failed to send the men, the Election Commission of India would take strict action against me.

'*Sir, ghabraiye mat.* Don't worry. We'll send these guys,' said Mangeshwar, my driver, confidently.

'*Kya kare, Mangeshwar?* What should we do?' I asked him.

'*Hum log hain na.* We are with you, Sir,' said Devendra Yadav, the chief of the Bihar Policemen's Association. He was notorious for creating trouble for another SP of Nalanda, but here he was, supporting me in one of the biggest crises of my career.

They managed to get me a megaphone to address the crowd of jawans. I took it and shouted into it. The sound was shrill.

'*Sir, thoda dheere se.* Go a little easy on the volume,' Devendra said.

I realized my foolishness and spoke normally into the megaphone.

'Jawano, please assemble in front of me. Make your parties, find your mates. We have to reach the polling booths on time.'

There was momentary silence. Would they ignore a direct order from the SP? They all started moving, but there was no order and it only led to more chaos. I looked at Devendra.

'*Ye kya ho raha hain?* What is happening? Why so much indiscipline?' I said, exasperated.

'Sir, there are no vehicles. Unless the parties board the buses and leave, they will keep doing this. And right now, we do not have any mode of transport for these men,' Devendra replied.

'*Sir, hum inn logo ko apni gaadiyon mein le jaate hain.* Let us take these men in our vehicles,' said Mangeshwar excitedly.

'Which vehicles? We hardly have any vehicles, except for a few Jeeps. How will we send so many people?' I said.

'*Sir, hain toh sahi.* We do have vehicles. I will take them in the prisoners' van. The other drivers can take the parties in our trucks, even our ambulance,' said Mangeshwar.

'Are you sure? It is a huge number,' I asked, seeing a little ray of hope.

'Of course, Sir. We have almost twelve hours before the elections start. Let us not waste any more time,' said Mangeshwar confidently.

In ten minutes, I had fifteen drivers lined up in front of me.

'Please ensure that all the parties reach the polling booths. I am giving you the list of polling booths—we will start with the farthest booths first. The closer ones can be taken care of later,' I said.

The engines of the ambulance, police trucks and Jeeps roared to life.

Mangeshwar was in the prisoners' van, blaring its horn. I took the megaphone again.

'*Aap sab jaldi se gaadiyon mein baithe.* Please sit in the vehicles immediately. Move, move fast!'

The jawans were surprised to see their transport. '*Chalo, chalo!* Let's go!' Dheeraj shouted as he started pushing the constables towards the vehicles. Ajit and Shukla also joined him and started directing the men.

A group of constables reluctantly got into the prisoners' van. Mangeshwar did not wait for a moment. He quickly drove the van out the gates of the police lines. Soon, the other jawans started boarding the remaining vehicles. I saw the vehicles leaving the premises and heaved a sigh of relief. At least we had started.

'Now what? We wait for the vehicles to come back?' I asked my bodyguards.

'Sir, there is no other way. Mangeshwar bhai and some other policemen will have to do multiple trips,' said Constable Ritesh.

In a few moments, I saw my officers from the nearest police stations getting out of their Jeeps.

'*Arre, aap log yahaan kaise?* How come you people are here?' I asked, surprised by their unexpected arrival.

'Sir, we came to know about the crisis. How could we leave you to deal with all of it alone in this time?' said Mithlesh, SHO of the Lahiri police station.

'Sir, let us dispatch the remaining parties. They can be sent in our Jeeps,' said Vijay Sharma, another officer.

Pretty soon, another lot of constables left the police lines.

After an hour or so, I saw a vehicle coming in through the gate. It was Mangeshwar in the prisoners' van.

'*Sir, pahucha diye hain.* I have dropped those jawans off at a police station close to the polling booth. Ask the other parties to get into the van,' he said.

'At least rest for five minutes,' I said.

'*Sir, ek baar sab pahuch jaaye, phir rest hi rest hain.* Once all the parties reach the destination, there will only be rest for us,' he said with a smile.

I smiled back, marvelling at the commitment of policemen such as Mangeshwar, Devendra and everyone else who was there to help.

For the next few hours, vehicles kept moving to and from the police lines.

* * *

'Yes, we will do it,' I said to the men around me, my eyes gleaming with newfound hope.

I had been constantly moving around, ensuring that the men were being dispatched.

'*Sir, thoda susta lijiye.* Take some rest,' Vijay said.

'*Abhi toh theek hain.* I'm all right. When I get tired, I'll lie down for some time,' I said, looking at the police jawans all around me. Many of them had gone off to sleep on the ground itself. A few of them had woken up and gone to answer nature's call.

'Munshiji, how many people have reached the relevant polling booths?' I asked.

'Sir, about 480 constables have been dispatched. That means we still have about 800 left,' he replied.

'That's quite a number. Call all the Jeeps from the nearby police stations. Ask all the SHOs to seize the trucks and buses plying on the highways,' I ordered.

'Sir, I'll call the police Jeeps right away. But there are no buses or trucks on the highways. They have already been put to election duty,' replied the munshi.

'Election duty? I have been here since last night but I am yet to see any vehicles,' I said angrily.

I knew that the vehicles had deliberately not been sent. Over the past few days, I had sensed that the election observers were not particularly fond of me. They had probably been fed false stories that did not paint me in a good light.

I checked the time. I called one of the election observers and told him about the critical situation at the police lines.

He listened patiently and said, 'Amit, I have been made to understand that the vehicles have already been sent to the police lines but there is absolute mayhem there. You are not able to control your men and send them for duty. There are still some hours left before the elections. Let me be very clear with you—if the force does not reach on time, there will be serious consequences. In the meantime, I will tell the district authorities to ensure that you get the vehicles for transportation,' he said, repeating what I had already heard many times.

I was now determined to ensure that all my men reached their duty on time. Mangeshwar and the other drivers kept transporting the constables and home guards to their destinations. After a few hours, I saw a number of buses and trucks coming to the police lines. They had finally been sent by the administration!

Dawn was breaking and I was getting more hopeful. I took the megaphone to make announcements. My voice had become hoarse by now. I was barely audible, and yet the jawans understood my command. The police lines staff kept pushing the jawans into the buses and dispatching them. I lost track of time. When I checked my watch, it was 6.40 a.m. The election would commence at 7 a.m.

I saw a handful of jawans still waiting for vehicles. 'Why are you people here?' I asked them.

'Sir, waiting for the bus,' they replied in unison.

'Sir, they have to go to the town and Lahiri police stations. We had sent all the forces to the farthest place first, as you had instructed,' said the munshi.

'*Aap logo ko toh yahi jaana hain.* You people have to go nearby. Why don't you walk down to the booths? There are just a few minutes left. Hurry up,' I said.

The jawans picked up their rifles and bags, saluted and left.

At 7 a.m., my cellphone rang. It was the DSP Hilsa, Anwar Hussain.

'Sir, the election observers have started visiting the booths. They are satisfied with the security arrangements,' he said.

'Great!' I replied.

I had been lucky. I had guessed that the observers might start their rounds from the farthest and most challenging areas of Nalanda district. Hilsa was one of those areas. By the time the observers returned from Hilsa to the town, my men would have reached all the polling booths there too.

The wireless in my Gypsy crackled.

'Good morning, Sir. All peaceful in Nalanda.'

I saw the Parle-G packets lying on the seat of the Gypsy. I took out a few biscuits and offered them to Devendra and the other policemen. The two packets were not sufficient for all of us, so we broke the biscuits and shared them.

Parle-G had never tasted sweeter.

* * *

The election was conducted peacefully. But the police had to be on its toes throughout. Only the counting of the votes remained. I had to remain alert. I remembered the panchayat elections that had taken place a few years ago. I was deputed in the notorious Badh area of Patna. The entire day's proceedings had gone off peacefully. Just when I was about to get into my Gypsy, I saw a few villagers waving frantically at me.

They were shouting, '*Booth loota gaya, booth loota gaya!* The polling booth has been looted!'

I was amazed to see a few rifle-toting goons running with ballot boxes on their heads and shoulders.

'*Sir, chaliye, peechha karte hain!* Let us chase them,' said Abhay.

'Yeah, yeah,' I said, shaken. This was first time I had seen anything like this.

My constables and I ran after them. The booth looters had a head start and it was difficult to catch up with them. Moreover, they had climbed a small hillock. They started firing at us.

A few bullets whizzed past us. Along with the jawans, I took cover behind some rocks. I was dazed. I had imagined gun fights with Naxalites or mafia dons, but never with booth looters! People had really become audacious.

'Abhay, start fire,' I commanded, as I aimed my Glock at the criminals. I pressed the trigger. I expected a recoil but just felt a very soft thud. The bullet had misfired.

I fired again and got the same result. I was embarrassed and worried. My gun was as useless as a toy pistol! Another bullet flew past me.

Abhay and the other constables fired at the looters intermittently. As professionals, they were not supposed to waste ammunition. The firing continued for some time and then everything fell silent.

'*Lagtaa hain bhaag gaye.* It looks like they ran away,' said one of the constables.

We climbed the hillock and saw ballot papers scattered everywhere. This was before EVMs were used to count votes. Most of the ballots were soaked in blue colour. We moved further and saw a well.

'*Sir, oo raha ballot box.* There is the ballot box,' said a constable, pointing inside the well.

I peeped inside to see the ballot box lying at the bottom of the well. There were hundreds of ballot papers, all blue, floating in the water.

'*Ye neela kaise ho gaya?* How did they turn blue?' I asked.

'*Sir, syahi daal diya hain.* They have put ink in the ballot box.'

'And why have they done that?'

Abhay smiled.

'Sir, this happens in all elections. The losing party will always try to disturb the elections.'

I had failed in the conduct of elections because I had thought it was over. But nothing is ever over until it is really over. I was determined to learn from this lesson.

For the Lok Sabha elections, I deployed adequate force for the counting centre and was confident that this last part of the gigantic exercise would also go well. My relation with that one officer of the administration had gone from bad to worse. I had felt cheated when the district police had not been provided vehicles on time. But there was more to come. The officer of the administration issued orders for strict access control to the counting centre.

The orders specifically allowed only the vehicles of the administrative officers to enter the premises of the counting centre. Thus, it had prohibited the vehicles of police officers from going inside the campus. The police officers were supposed to get down from their Jeeps and walk to the counting centre.

I felt bad but was relieved, in a way. 'If I am not wanted, why should I go?' I thought.

So I stayed at home and played with Avi. He used to love wearing my police peak cap and stuff a toy pistol in his pyjamas.

'I am baby SP,' he would say and prance around the house, playing 'chor police' with my staff. That day I was the chor! I was hiding behind the curtains when my cellphone started ringing. What a stupid 'chor' I was! I had not even put my phone on silent before hiding. Avi heard the cellphone and wrapped himself around my legs. '*Pakad liya.* I have caught you,' he said happily. I patted his head before taking out the phone from my pocket. It was the DIG Patna.

'Jai Hind, Sir,' I said.

'Amit, how is the counting going?' he asked.

'Sir, it's going peacefully but I have not gone there.'

'Why?'

I told him about the administrative order and explained the reason for my not going to the counting centre.

'Tell me, who is manning the gates of the counting centre?' the DIG asked.

'The policemen of Nalanda district.'

'And who is the chief of those policemen?'

'Sir, I am.'

'Then who is going to stop you? Go to the counting centre and exert your authority as the SP of the district,' he said.

'Yes, Sir. Jai Hind!'

Sir was right. I got into my uniform in a jiffy. In fifteen minutes I reached the counting centre. As my Gypsy approached the gates, the policemen on duty there smartly saluted me and removed the barriers. I saluted back with a big smile. My motorcade roared inside the premises. I got down triumphantly and moved towards the centre. My bodyguards and the town inspector followed me.

'Sir, the observers are sitting in that room,' said the sub-inspector on duty.

I entered the room and greeted the three observers.

'How are you, Amit?' they asked warmly. Their attitude towards me had changed after they saw the efforts Nalanda Police had made to successfully conduct the elections. There was only one chair vacant in the room. Naturally, I sat on it. A few moments later, the officer of the administration came to the room, only to see me sitting on his chair.

He fumed and barged out of the room.

I could not control a smile.

'How could you let the SP come inside the campus in his car? I'll take strict action against you. I will suspend you,' the officer shouted at his subordinate.

'*Par, huzoor, hum kya karte?* What could I have done? *Saari police toh SP Saheb ki hain—unko kaun rokta?* The police is under the command of the SP—who would have stopped him?' the junior officer pleaded.

'You are suspended!' shouted the senior officer angrily.

'But you can't suspend me, Sir. It's not in your power,' the junior said, a little firmly this time.

29

Jile Ka Maalik

'Amit, the president is coming to your district next month,' said the IG Patna.

'Sir, president? Which president?' I asked.

'Don't be naïve. Which president? It is not the president of some club I would call you for. It's the president of India,' said the IG laughing, trying to hide his irritation at my foolish query.

'Oh, Sir . . . of course,' I said, realizing my mistake.

'He is going to inaugurate a defence facility in Rajgir. Start preparing for his visit. We will give you adequate resources and manpower.'

I called my team of officers and gave them instructions to start preparing for the visit. This was the first high-profile visit of a dignitary that I would be managing. I was excited that A.P.J. Abdul Kalam would be coming to my district. It would indeed be an honour meeting such an illustrious man.

I did a recce of the place a number of times, imagining all possible crises. I wondered if a sniper could take aim from the beautiful Rajgir hills or if a protesting citizen could plan to self-immolate in front of the president. I had to prepare for all scenarios.

The police headquarters sent me sufficient manpower to deploy at all strategic locations. Quite a few teams looking after the president's security came from Delhi to discuss all the eventualities. The team leader gave us a number of directions. We also had a rehearsal at the venue a few days before the inauguration.

'We need highly trained constables to be in the outer security cordon of the president. I hope those constables are proficient in the martial arts, such as jujitsu or krav maga,' said the team leader. My sergeant major squirmed at the mere suggestion.

'*Sir, kahaan aapko yahaan kung-fu, karate waale sipahi milenge?* Where will we get such kung-fu-karate-type constables?' said the sergeant major, raising his arms.

'Then who are the men that you have deployed?' asked the security team leader.

The sergeant major pointed to a few men talking under the shade of trees. The sight of a number of out-of-shape, portly constables casually scratching their bellies unnerved the team leader.

'Really?' he asked, looking at me.

'Boss, sometimes appearances can be deceptive. I don't know about their martial arts skills, but I do know that they won't hesitate to put their lives on the line for the safety of the president,' I said with full conviction.

The discussion ended there.

* * *

The president's visit was just two days away when the DSP Rajgir called me.

'Sir, I need to take my daughter to Delhi. She's got an interview call from an MNC,' he said.

'Jha, it's a difficult time. The president is coming,' I replied

'I know, Sir. But this opportunity won't come again. It is the question of my daughter's career,' the DSP pleaded.

'Okay, you can go,' I said. I understood his situation. Though DSP Sadar Shambhu was already on leave, I had two more DSPs who could take care of the visit on that day. That very night, DSP Abbas called me.

'Sir, my father-in-law is critical. He's had a stroke. My wife is crying non-stop. I have to go at once. Please permit me to go to Patna.'

'Okay, Abbas. You can leave as soon as possible,' I said. I had to allow him to go. His family needed him.

'Sir, inshallah, Abba should be fine. I'll try to come before the president's visit.'

The next day, while I was supervising another rehearsal of the deployment, I got a call from IG Sir.

'Amit, I have heard you have given leave to all your DSPs,' he said, sounding annoyed.

'Sir, that's true. But the situation was such that I could not refuse,' I said, trying to reason.

'There's nothing more important that the president's visit. Your large-heartedness can land you in trouble. You will be responsible for any problem,' said the IG, reprimanding me.

I knew Sir had a point. I only had the DSP Hilsa left to assist me. Nevertheless, I was confident that everything would go well.

By the evening, I got another order issued by the IG Patna. The IG had deputed one SP and three DSPs to assist me. Sir was concerned about the visit, but I realized he also cared for me. In the police, senior officers usually act as a shield for their juniors. They are like big brothers—they act tough but they are really kind and protective.

* * *

On the day of the inauguration, the DM and I waited at the helipad for the president to arrive. Out of the blue, we saw the president's helicopter flanked by two air-force helicopters. We ran to take cover behind our cars as the rotors of the choppers created a mini sandstorm while landing on the specially made helipad.

As the dust settled, a sprightly A.P.J. Kalam stepped off the helicopter. He shook hands with all of us with an infectious smile. He looked at me and said, 'Arre, you are quite young. *SP toh jile ka maalik hota hain!* The SP is the boss of a district. You are lucky to hold charge of a district so early in your career.'

'No, Sir, I am just a civil servant,' I replied. The president smiled again.

The president's brilliant but humble demeanour gave me the chance to see for myself why he was one of the most respected people in the country. As we escorted him to the site of the inauguration, I made sure all the security arrangements were in place.

One of the Cabinet ministers accompanying the president told me affably, '*SP Saheb, sab intezaam theek hain.* All arrangements are okay. Relax.' He seemed to be in a good mood.

'Thank you, Sir. But I have to be alert,' I replied.

'SP Saheb, I have heard you are an engineer. Why have you joined the police?' he asked.

'*Sir, aap bhi toh engineer hain, par aap bhi toh politics mein hain.* You are an engineer too, but you have joined politics,' I said immediately.

He smiled at my response.

The event was soon over and everything went to plan. The president boarded the helicopter and took off shortly afterwards.

Anwar, the DSP Hilsa, came to me and asked, 'Sir, you know what the best part of a VIP's visit is?'

I shrugged.

'When the VIP's chopper flies away!' he said.

Both of us broke into laughter.

30

Sourav Ganguly's Shirt

It had been a long time that I had watched a cricket match at ease, but I was really hoping to watch the final of the NatWest Trophy between England and India without any interruptions. England had scored 325 in 50 overs, which was a huge total for those days. India was in a precarious position, having lost the top order without it causing much damage. But the partnership of Yuvraj Singh and Mohammad Kaif brought some hope to me and millions of other Indians.

Apart from the fluctuating fortunes of the Indian team, I was worried about the fluctuating power supply. My TV would switch off every five minutes and even the stabilizer would be of no help. Nevertheless, I was enjoying the match. Avi was sleeping peacefully while Tanu was reading a novel by his side.

My phone rang. It was almost 2 a.m. It was the last thing I wanted.

'Sir, the chowkidar of Vena called just now. *Vena thana mein nau logo ka murder ho gaya hain*. Nine people have been murdered in the Vena police station area. The deceased belong to the same family,' said the telephone orderly, Tariq.

'Are you serious? Put me on to the SHO Vena,' I ordered Tariq, barely believing what I had just heard.

Two minutes later I was talking to SI Raghubir, the SHO Vena.

'What happened? Where have the murders taken place?' I fired off a barrage of questions.

'*Sir, humko nahin maloom. Hum abhi Patna mein hain.* I do not know. I am in Patna right now,' replied Raghubir meekly.

'You are in Patna? What the hell are you doing there? With whose permission did you leave the district?' I said angrily.

'*Sir, ek marriage attend karne aa gaye the.* I had come to attend a marriage. Sorry, Sir, I did not take your permission to leave Nalanda,' Raghubir said. I was furious, but this was not the time to lose my cool.

'Raghubir, you fly to Nalanda in a helicopter, I don't care. Get back as soon as possible,' I thundered.

I dialled the number of the DSP Sadar.

'Rashid, nine people have been murdered in Vena. I'm leaving. You also get there as soon as possible. Get the force from the neighbouring police stations as well. Things might get ugly.'

Rashid was a young but mature officer.

'Sir, nine people? This is shocking. I'm on my way,' he said.

It was quite a cool night for July. Maybe the rain earlier had brought down the temperature. I called the DIG while constantly listening to the wireless feed in my Gypsy. I had calmed down and was focused on getting there as soon as possible. My little experience had taught me when to keep my emotions in control and how to take charge of such situations.

'Really? Nalanda has had no history of massacres. It never had any caste wars, any Naxal attacks. What do you think?' said the DIG, sounding shocked.

'Sir, I think it could be a case of personal animosity. I will apprise you once I reach the scene of crime.'

The road was really bad. My back started hurting because of the bumps, but this was not the time to drive slowly. I just prayed that my ankylosing spondylitis wouldn't flare up again.

I was expecting a large, unruly crowd at the village, but there was just an eerie silence, as if nothing had happened. An old ASI was standing near the bodies. A few clueless constables were huddled in a corner. The incident must have been shocking for them too.

'*Sir, ye Kanhaiya Mali hain.* He is Kanhaiya Mali. *Ye mritak ke parivar se hain.* He is from the family of the deceased,' said the ASI, pointing to an old man sitting on his haunches.

'*Kya hua?* What happened?' I asked gently, expecting a furious reaction from the man.

'*Pataa nahin.* I don't know,' he said.

'Really?'

There was a long pause; still no reaction from the man.

Finally, the man took a deep breath and said, 'Sukhu and his brothers sent some criminals to our house. They were armed with swords and axes. They killed my family. Sukhu has a long-standing property dispute with us.'

'Are you sure? Can you identify all the assistants?'

'*Nahin, Sir. Hum kisi ko nahin pehchante.* I don't know anyone.' Kanhaiya said adamantly.

I asked a few other relatives about the incident. All of them feigned ignorance of the perpetrators of the crime.

By that time, DSP Rashid had also reached the spot. He took me to a corner.

'Sir, if he is sticking by his story, what can you do? I'll go and carry out a raid on the house of this Sukhu fellow,' Rashid said.

'Rashid, I have a gut feeling that he's not sure. Nevertheless, find Sukhu.'

Rashid took a few men with him and left the village. In the meantime, quite a few other police officers and their teams reached the spot. Luckily, the village was isolated and had a tiny population, so the outrage against the murders was not likely to get out of control. The villagers, outnumbered by the police, were too dazed to react anyway. Only the family of the victims was sitting quietly beside the bodies. Their tears had probably dried by the time we had reached the village. Seeing that the situation was under control, I got into the Gypsy and tried to alleviate some of the stress of the past few hours. I had realized that music helped me think more clearly and would listen to some 1970s' Bollywood music at a low volume in such scenarios. I switched on the cassette player in my Gypsy.

'Chhotu, who has put in this Bhojpuri cassette? Where are my Kishore Kumar songs?'

'*Sir, woh aaj shaam ko servicing ke liye le gaye the gaadi ko, to hum apna Bhojpuri gaana lagaa diya.* I had gone to get the car serviced in the evening, so I was listening to some Bhojpuri songs. I am sorry I forgot your cassettes in the barracks,' he replied sheepishly.

I grumbled at the way my night was unfolding. I had missed the cricket match to look at dead bodies. And now this.

Suddenly, I saw a Tata Safari coming towards us at full speed. It almost rammed into my Gypsy, halting just a few feet away. The door of the Safari opened and out jumped Raghubir, the SHO of Vena. He was dressed in a flashy velvet suit and reeking of perfume. He had come straight from the marriage function in Patna.

'Sir, I'm sorry. *Mujhe maaf kar dijiye.* Please forgive me,' he pleaded, flashing his paan-stained teeth.

I wanted to laugh but controlled myself.

'That I'll see later. These bodies should be removed as soon as possible. There should be no law-and-order problem in the morning, or you've had it,' I commanded.

I knew that the situation seemed normal right now, but it could change dramatically in the morning. The local politicians, people from the nearby villages, the family members and any Tom, Dick and Harry could create a ruckus. Their demands could vary from calling the chief minister to getting compensation for the family of the deceased.

'Now get going,' I commanded Raghubir.

Fortunately, there were a few things going in favour of the police.

Raghubir, the alleged murderers and the deceased were all from the same caste. Moreover, Raghubir had been an effective officer and had a good rapport with the locals.

I got back into the Gypsy and waited for Rashid and Raghubir to apprise me of any developments.

Twenty-five minutes later, I saw Rashid's Jeep.

'Sir, we have got all the five accused from their houses. This is Sukhu, and these are his brothers,' he said, pushing the men towards me.

I was surprised. How could someone kill nine people in cold blood and then go back home and sleep?

'Why have you killed Kanhaiya's family?' I asked sternly.

'*Na, huzoor, hum kuch nahin kare hain.* We have done nothing. *Humari purani dushmani hain isliye phasa raha hain.* We have old enmity with Kanhaiya, which is why we are being framed,' said Sukhu. He looked quite nervous.

I questioned him further and listened to his account without showing any emotion. I called the DIG and told him about the turn of events. He was a little gruff at being woken up again by me at 4 a.m.

'Amit, I would suggest you forward Sukhu and his brothers. When the complainant is adamant, why do you want to create problems? I hope the law-and-order situation stays under control,' he said firmly.

I did not argue with him. He was right. It was a serious situation that required immediate action by the police.

There was a sudden commotion. A tractor had arrived with a group of people. I saw Raghubir asking his constables and a few other people to take the bodies away.

'*Jaldi se shuru ho. Dhyan se uthao.* Get started. Lift carefully,' Raghubir commanded.

I was taken aback at the efficiency with which Raghubir was doing his job.

'*Sir, Kanhaiya se baat ho gayi hain.* I have spoken to Kanhaiya. I got him talking using my past relations with him. He is satisfied with the police action,' said Raghubir triumphantly.

'And who are these people who are lifting the bodies with the policemen?' I asked.

'Sir, these are our special helpers. We just give them some money. And, of course, some drinks for today's task.'

I stared hard at Raghubir.

'Sir, who would lift blood-soaked bodies with mangled limbs? You need to get a little intoxicated to soothe your nerves,' said Rashid, trying to calm me down.

'Okay, send the bodies for post mortem,' I replied.

After ten minutes, the spot was cleared.

'Raghubir, no more problems?'

'No, Sir, I assure you.'

'You ensure that. Anyway, I'll deal with you later. You have been extremely irresponsible,' I said as I got into the Gypsy.

I spoke to Rashid again.

'Rashid, I am not convinced by Sukhu's arrest. Do you think he is responsible?' I did not want an innocent man to go to jail.

'Sir, I am also thinking about it. *Par ye Sukhu bhi doodh ka dhulaa nahin hain.* Sukhu is not all innocent. I have put my "spy" on the job. He has given me a lead. I am going towards that area,' said Rashid, and left.

'Why don't we do something? It rained for a few hours before the murders took place. Let us walk back and look for footprints near the murder site,' I said to Inspector Kunal, one of the officers present.

The place already had a number of footprints, including ours. Unfortunately, there was no system of putting ropes around a scene of crime and cordoning off the area. I realized I had also adapted to policing according to the local procedures in place, relying more on common sense and our network of 'spies'. We moved further from the site, pointing our torches to the ground, looking for clues.

Suddenly, one of my guards, Shukla, shouted, '*Sir, yahaan par kaafi jooton ke nishaan hain.* There are lot of shoe prints here.'

'Chalo, let us follow this trail,' I said, and started moving in the direction of the prints. After around half an hour, the trail ended in a small settlement of just ten to fifteen houses. I directed my men to surround the settlement. One by one, we started checking the houses. The people in the houses were already awake as it would soon be dawn. Though surprised by the police presence, they did not protest at us checking their houses.

'*Sir, ye makaan maalik darwaza nahin khol raha hain.* The owner of this house is not opening the door,' Kunal said. We circled the house and broke open the door. In the corner of a room was a man with a country-made rifle and a dog.

The frail-looking man immediately dropped his rifle on seeing so many policemen.

Kunal grabbed the man.

'*Batate hain, Sir. Hum Kailash Prajapat ke aadmi hain. Hum hi Vena gaon mein narsanhar kiye hain.* I will tell you everything. I am Kailash Prajapat's man. It is our group that committed the Vena massacre a few hours ago,' said the man.

'Where are the others? Where is Prajapat?' I asked.

'*Sir, woh toh apne thikane par chale gaye.* They have gone back to their respective homes,' the man replied.

'Then you will take us to their hideouts,' I commanded. My driver Chhotu and the other drivers had also reached the settlement by then. I was impressed by everyone's efficiency. Of course, my bodyguards were constantly in touch with the drivers over the wireless. We loaded Prajapat's guy in my Gypsy immediately.

I was quite tired and dozed off in the vehicle for some time, only to be woken up by the shrill ringtone of my cellphone.

'Sir, I have cracked the case. I have arrested the real culprits,' said an excited Rashid.

I was now awake after my short nap, absolutely fresh, as if I had slept for eight hours.

'Go on,' I said. I had almost forgotten that Rashid was also on the lookout for the murderers.

'My source led me to the den of Kailash Prajapat, a small-time criminal. He was hired by Sukhu to eliminate Kanhaiya's brothers. This fellow Prajapat and his accomplices got heavily drunk. Instead of killing just three people, they killed nine people in a frenzy. I'm reaching the Asthava police station in twenty minutes, Sir. We will wait for you there,' Rashid said.

'Rashid, you are right. Even we have the same information,' I said, apprising him of the turn of events.

Chhotu drove at breakneck speed and we were in Asthava thana soon.

'Get the prime suspect, Prajapat, in front of me,' I ordered the SHO. A constable opened the lock-up and ushered a gruff, bearded man towards me. His eyes were bloodshot, partly due to lack of sleep and partly because he had been drinking. As I looked at him, I wondered how many crimes took place just because the perpetrator was under the influence of alcohol. Perhaps this was why, in 2016, the Bihar government banned liquor in the state. The rate of crime has definitely decreased since.

I saw a number of shady-looking characters hunched in a corner of the lock-up.

After a few questions, we learnt about the conspiracy. Sukhu was indeed behind the murders. Rashid had even recovered a blood-stained sword from Prajapat's house. We carefully preserved it as evidence. I was determined to use forensics this time.

I was glad with the progress we had made. Though we could not prevent the unfortunate killings, we had arrested all the perpetrators that same night.

I checked my cellphone. It was 7 a.m. I decided to go home to take a shower.

My cellphone buzzed just as I reached home. It was Rajshekar Sir, the DIG.

'Amit, the Commissioner Patna and I are about to reach Nalanda. Where are you?'

'Sir, I am at my residence,' I replied.

'What? How come? How is the situation? Should you not have been at the scene of crime?' he said, partly angry and partly surprised.

I explained everything to him in detail.

'That's excellent news. The government was concerned about the situation.'

'Thank you, Sir. We can all have breakfast at my residence and then leave for the village.'

'Sure, Amit,' said Rajshekar Sir.

I entered the bedroom. Tanu turned around and looked at me with a big smile. She was always happy whenever I returned home.

'How are things?' she asked.

'Fine. Absolutely under control,' I said as I hugged her.

'I was confident, like always,' she said.

'*Accha, ye batao, India ke match ka kya hua?* Tell me, what happened in the India–England match?'

'*Jeet gaye.* We won!' replied Tanu with a big smile.

Yuvraj Singh and Mohammad Kaif had led India to one of its finest victories. I never got to see it live, but it was the same match in which Sourav Ganguly famously whipped off his shirt when India managed a glorious victory.

31

Canara Bank

Avi had started becoming more and more independent. He was three years old now. I realized he was quite happy around my staff, particularly my computer operator, Bikramaditya Jha. Apart from Tanu, it was my staff that took care of him. They treated him like family. I was hardly with Avi during his waking hours, away on work most of the time.

Things were going quite well in Nalanda, but I was getting a little bored. It was a quandary any police officer, particularly a young one, faces. It there is a lot of crime, life becomes stressful. It there is no crime, it can feel as though you are unemployed! You are caught between the devil and the deep blue sea.

Unfortunately it seemed the gods had heard my thoughts. One morning, the SHO of the Lahiri police station called me.

'*Sir, Canara Bank loota gaya.* There has been a robbery at Canara Bank,' he said.

'A robbery? How much money?' I asked.

'Sir, Rs 32 lakh been taken from the bank. There were four armed men.'

'Have you alerted all the police stations? Ask them to check all exit points of the state.'

I issued a few standard instructions and left for Canara Bank.

'Shucks, why did I say I was getting bored? *Aur bol!* I cursed myself as I got into the Gypsy.

The bank was located in a crowded area. There were a lot of people waiting for the police to arrive. Earlier I used to get angry or irritated to see people milling around a crime scene because they hampered the investigation. But I soon realized it was inevitable, as most people had a lot of time to kill, and seeing the police in action was high on entertainment value. So I started ignoring them.

My bodyguards made way for me. A visibly shaken man was sitting in a corner, surrounded by media personnel.

'Please, I do not want to answer any questions. Let the police solve the case,' the man was saying to the mediapersons.

'Sir, meet Mr Joshi—he's the bank manager,' said the SHO Lahiri, introducing us to each other.

The moment the press saw me, they forgot the manager and started poking their microphones in my face. And the camera lights started flashing.

'*Jaise hi kuch pataa chalega, aap ko bataa diya jayega.* I will let you know as soon as we know something concrete about the case,' I said confidently. As a senior police officer, one always has to be in charge of the situation—or, at least, appear to be so.

'*Aap please jaiye, humko apna kaam karne dijiye.* Now please leave, let us work.'

After some resistance, the journalists left. I knew the next day's headlines already but I did not bother. The media had to do its job.

'Joshiji, tell me what happened,' I asked.

'Sir, four young men entered the bank as customers. Suddenly, they took out weapons and threatened all of us—the staff and the customers,' Joshi said.

'One of the robbers pinned me down and asked me to open the locker,' he continued.

'And then?'

'Sir, I tried to misguide them. I told them the locker didn't have any money and even if it did, I wouldn't be able to open it. I told them to take some money from the cashier and leave. But a guy who looked like their leader hit me on my head with his gun. He asked me to get the other pair of locker keys from Anand Somani.'

'Who's Anand Somani? Can you please call him?'

Lahiri ushered him in.

'Sir, the locker is opened by a set of two keys. One key stays with the manager and one with any designated staff as per the roster. Today it was with me,' Somani said.

'The robbers pointed their guns at us. We were really scared, so Manager Sir and I used our keys to open the lock. The robbers put all the money in their bags and fled,' he continued, clearly still shaken from the experience.

'Wait . . . wait a minute. How did they know there were two keys? And that you were the one who had the second key today?' I asked, sitting up.

Somani and the manager looked at each other.

'And tell me, don't you have an alarm?'

'Of course, Sir. We tested it just a week ago,' Joshi said.

'They why did you not use it? Show me the location of the alarm.'

We went out to the main room where all the cashiers and bank staff sat. Then Joshi took me behind one of the counters.

'Sir, this is the alarm,' he said.

The alarm was well concealed behind the counter, impossible for anyone to see. A man came forward and introduced himself.

'Sir, I am Ram Avtar Saini. I was behind this counter. I was caught unawares when these robbers entered the branch,' he said. 'I thought of pushing the alarm button but could not get an opportunity to. In fact, one of the robbers came straight at me and threatened me if I did push the alarm button. He pointed his gun at me and made me come out from behind the counter immediately.'

After we had spoken to the people, I searched the bank premises with our forensic team. We had very basic equipment but managed to get a few fingerprints. Those were still not the days of CCTV footage. I went to the Lahiri police station to have a discussion with my team of officers.

'I am convinced that an insider is involved. How can someone possibly know the exact location of the alarm? And that two keys are required to open the locker?' I said.

'Sir, there is one more interesting thing. There was maximum cash in the locker today. This fact also corroborates your doubts,' added DSP Shambhu.

'Good for us that none of the robbers wore masks to cover their faces. They could not have entered the bank without arousing suspicion otherwise,' I said.

'So, now, the team has a few immediate tasks. Shambhu, get an artist from Patna Arts College to make some sketches for us. The bank staff can surely recall the faces of the robbers to help the artists,' I continued.

'Sanjay, make a list of all the employees of the bank, right from the manager to the sweeper. Find out their financial status, whether they are in any debt, whether they have gambling habits . . . Also find out the call details of these people and analyse them. I want all this work done in the next three days.'

I concluded our meeting with a few more instructions.

Three days was too long a period. When the police have to crack a case, they work at lightning speed.

Lahiri was in my office the very next morning.

'Sir, one of the employees, Govardhan, was on leave that day. But, according to my source, he was among the onlookers who had assembled outside the bank after the loot,' said Shivam, the SHO.

'Sir, this Govardhan fellow has a girlfriend who is quite demanding. I have found out that Govardhan keeps gifting her expensive things. He recently gave her a colourscreen cellphone,' he continued.

'Investigate Govardhan deeply. I think he is our man.'

* * *

I had a lovely dinner of my favourite aloo puri. It had been a while that I had last had it.

'*Aaj toh kha lo, par aapka kaafi weight badh raha hain.* Have all this oily, fried food today but you are putting on a lot of weight,' Tanu said.

'*Tanu, yaar, itna fit toh hoon.* I am very fit. Let me enjoy!'

'*Abhi nahin toh jaldi hi mote ho jaaoge.* If not right now, you will become fat soon.'

'*Tanu, ab tumhe toh main hi milunga, koi Hrithik Roshan nahin milega.* You will get only me, no Hrithik Roshan!'

'Even his wife must be saying the same things to him,' replied Tanu. I realized there was no point arguing with her, as I could never win.

My phone rang.

'Sir, SHO Lahiri is here,' said Pavan, the telephone orderly. '*Koi ladies ko lekar aaye hain.* He's come with a lady.'

I went to my residential office to meet them.

'Sir, this is Priyanka, Govardhan's girlfriend,' said Shivam.

Priyanka was a young, good-looking girl. She was wearing expensive jewellery and, more interestingly, a Rado watch, which was extremely rare in a small town such as Nalanda.

'I see Govardhan treats you like a princess,' I said. The lady constable accompanying her gave a faint smile.

'Do you know where he gets all the money from?' I asked.

'Sir, he works for a bank,' she replied softly.

'*Bank mein kaam karta hain toh bank ko hi loot lega?* So he robs the very same bank he works for?' I asked deliberately, arching my eyebrows to show my anger.

Priyanka's faced turned ashen.

My ploy of asking suspects direct questions had worked most of the time. I tried it again.

'Priyanka, I know you are not involved in the robbery. Just tell me the truth,' I said, sounding sympathetic this time.

'*Ji, Sir, Govardhan kal raat ko aaya tha.* He had come to see me last night. *Bola, humara accha time shuru ho gaya hain.* He said that good times have started for us,' Priyanka said. 'He did not divulge any details. *Bas keh raha tha, Canara Bank ne humein lakhpati banaa diya.* He was just saying that Canara Bank has made us millionaires.'

'Shivam, go get Govardhan immediately,' I said.

Govardhan was sitting in front of me in my residential office in an hour.

'*Chalo, jaldi batao, kaise lootwaya bank ko?* Tell me quickly, how did you get the bank robbed?' I asked sternly.

'*Hum kuch nahi kiye hain.* I have done nothing,' replied Govardhan confidently.

We questioned him for quite some time but he did not budge. He was more difficult than many hardened criminals. All our interrogation techniques failed. I sent Govardhan out.

'*Ye toh kuch bataa nahin raha hain.* He's not saying anything. Get me the call details tomorrow morning. Meanwhile, send Priyanka in again,' I said.

'Right, Sir,' Shivam replied.

Now was the time to use another trick of our trade. I called Govardhan into my chamber again. He was shocked to see his girlfriend.

'*Dekh, sab sahi bataa.* Tell us the truth. Your darling has already revealed your grand honeymoon plans,' Shivam said.

Suddenly Govardhan lunged at Priyanka and grabbed her throat.

'You b*$@oh! I loved you so much and you betrayed me! I will make you pay for this,' he snarled.

The policemen pulled him away from Priyanka and restrained him.

Priyanka was in shock. The lady constable escorted her out.

'All this money won't be of any use to you. At least see that you don't go to jail alone. Now tell me the names of all the people involved,' I said, trying to take advantage of Govardhan's rage.

I put my hands on Govardhan's shoulders. He started sobbing. After a few moments, he gathered himself.

'Sir, I needed money to make a new house for Priyanka and me. Priyanka is quite an ambitious woman and loves the good life. She wanted a beautiful house before we got married. I was in heavy debt as I had borrowed a lot of money from my friends,' he said.

'One of my friends, Gulzari, suggested that all my problems would be solved if I robbed the bank I work in. *Toh khud hi bank mein hain, tere ko paise ki kya dikkat honi chahiye?* You work in a bank, why should you have any money problems, he told me.'

Govardhan paused. His throat had gone dry. Shivam got him a glass of water.

'Gulzari introduced me to Shoyeb, a small-time criminal from Nawada. Shoyeb hatched the plan for the robbery. I gave him all the details. Since Shoyeb is not from Nalanda, we were confident no one would recognize him. In fact, he and his accomplices came to the bank as customers twice earlier to do a recce.'

'Yesterday was the best time to execute our plan. After the robbery, Gulzari and I went to the bank just to see what the police were doing. We thought we were smart but got caught,' he said.

'*Beta, police se hoshiyar koi nahin hota.* Nobody is smarter than the police,' Shivam said.

'Where is the money?' I asked.

Shivam's team had already checked Govardhan's house in the meantime and found nothing. We had to race against time not only to arrest the rest of the people involved but also recover the money.

'Sir, Shoyeb has it. We were supposed to divide it after two days,' Govardhan said.

'Govardhan, we will have to fix your meeting with Shoyeb immediately. Tell us where he lives,' I said.

Govardhan was more than happy to tell us about Shoyeb's whereabouts. Obviously, Govardhan did not want to languish in jail alone while Shoyeb enjoyed the Canara Bank money.

By the next afternoon, Shoyeb and his accomplices were produced in my office. Rs 20 lakh had been recovered. A tractor worth Rs 3 lakh, which had been bought by Shoyeb just after the robbery, was also brought to Nalanda.

The police also seized a brand-new TV from his house.

'*Sir, ye toh maine apne paise se khareeda hain.* I have bought this TV with my own money,' Shoyeb said.

All of us burst into laughter. The press had a field day taking pictures of Shoyeb and his tractor.

32

Bhoot Bungalow

It finally happened. I had completed more than three years in Nalanda and got transferred to Muzaffarpur, the biggest town in north Bihar, in 2003. The assembly elections were round the corner. The Election Commission rules are such that all officers who have had a tenure of three years or more at one place have to be transferred.

As it happens in Bihar, I got a rousing farewell. It took me almost four hours to cross Nalanda town. Hundreds of people, particularly the youth, were out on the streets wishing me luck for my next posting. I had mixed feelings. I was overwhelmed by the tremendous love shown by the people but also sad to leave them. It was my first posting and I had many fond memories.

* * *

I reached Muzaffarpur late at night. It felt good to see a flyover, a railway station and some semblance of infrastructure. The SP's bungalow was a colonial structure situated right next to the Gandak river.

* * *

'I am not going by your past performance or reputation. I want to see you work first-hand, so I am giving you one month to deliver results. Dekhiye, I expect all of you to perform your job with full honesty and sincerity. I have faith in you. I won't interfere in your day-to-day working, but remember I will know everything about you. If any complaint against you is proved, I will not spare you. Remember that you need to be accessible to the public,' I said to all my subordinate police officers during the first crime meeting I held in Muzaffarpur.

They were familiar with my work in Nalanda and knew of my priorities when it came to policing.

I had soon established a good rapport with all my subordinates, and they did their job well. Knowing that everything was in control, I could relax a little. I would spend my free time on the worn-out tennis court at Langat Singh College.

Around this time, Tanu got pregnant with our second child. She started having a lot of nausea and mood swings.

'*Chun, mujhe kaafi zor se ulti aa rahi hain. Mera jee ghabra raha hain.* I am nauseous and am not feeling well,' Tanu would tell me every other morning. During her first pregnancy, Tanu had mostly stayed in Jaipur, so I had not been there for the morning sickness the first time. Naturally I did not realize the trouble she had during those times.

'Tanu, you have to be strong. All women go through these phases during pregnancy,' I told her. Instead of being supportive, I used to admonish her. After a few days, she stopped telling me about her problems. Our maid, Manju, used to treat her as a daughter and take care of her.

I soon got busy with the impending assembly elections.

Quite a few senior politicians made a beeline for Muzaffarpur. One powerful leader, who had been at the helm of affairs just a few months earlier, visited the house of a local candidate who was not exactly on good terms with me. The leader called me from his house.

'*SP Saheb, aap se kuch baat karni hain.* I have to discuss something with you. Please come over,' he said.

I had been about to leave to play tennis. I was in no mood to meet anyone. Moreover, it was better not to meet any politician during election time—that, too, at his house.

'*Sir, abhi main kuch vyast hoon.* I am busy right now. Please tell me if there is anything important,' I said.

'*Theek hain, SP Saheb, humara bhi samay aayega, tab dekh lenge.* It's all right, our time will come, we will see then,' said the politician, his tone clearly telling me that he was not happy.

'*Theek hain, Sir.* Okay,' I said and disconnected the call. I did not think about it anymore. But I would pay the price for my attitude later. I could have certainly handled things better, but I had become too cocky since taking up the post at Muzaffarpur to realize and accept my follies.

* * *

My brother Nikky had just finished his B Tech from IIT Mumbai. I invited him over to spend some time with me. Anyway the huge bungalow used to feel empty, with most of the rooms not in use.

Nikky was intrigued by the way we government servants worked.

'*Bhaiyya, aap logo ke paas official cellphone kyun nahin hain?* Why don't you people have official cellphones? That way all of you officers will be accessible to the public. Why can't you instal traffic lights at the busy roads? Why can't people register their complaints online?' Nikky would throw a volley of questions my way every day and I had to manoeuvre my answers. For most of the questions, I had a standard answer that began to sound bureaucratic to my own ears—'It's being processed.'

After a while, I started getting annoyed by his questions. I decided to play a prank on him. My household members, particularly the cook Khatri and Tanu, became my accomplices in the plan to fool Nikky.

There was a rumour that many years ago, an SP had a fling with a woman in Muzaffarpur. The SP would invite her to the bungalow to spend time with him. Unfortunately, one day, there was an altercation between the two. The SP hit her on the head and the woman died on the spot. The SP then took her body to one of the rooms and made it look as if she had died by suicide there. There was no truth to the story, but people loved to believe rumours. In fact, some of the locals and house staff said that they had seen the ghost of the woman in some of the rooms of the bungalow!

One night after dinner, I got a chance to play my prank.

'*Nikky, tere ko pataa hain, iss ghar main ek bhootni ghoomti hain.* Do you know, a ghost roams this house?' I said in all seriousness.

'What nonsense, bhaiyya. You believe in these stories?' said Nikky, mocking me. I looked at Tanu.

'Haan, Nikki, Bhaiyya is telling the truth. In fact, we don't use a few rooms of the house just for this reason,' said Tanu, supporting me. I knew Nikky was putting up a brave face, but in reality he was quite faint-hearted. I had seen his face turn pale whenever he watched a horror movie.

After chatting with us for some time, Nikky went to the guest room to sleep. As he lay down, Khatri entered the room to put a water bottle by his bed. Instead of leaving immediately, Khatri took a round of the room and started chanting some mantras.

A bewildered Nikky asked him what he was doing.

'*Kuch nahin, Saheb, thoda dusht aatma ko bhaga rahe hain.* Nothing, Sir, just warding off the evil spirit. *Iss kamre mein toh kaafi aati hain.* She frequents this room. *Shayad yahin mari thi.* Maybe she died here,' Khatri replied.

Now Nikky got worried.

'*Kya sach mein bhoot hain?* Is there really a ghost?' he asked.

'*Bilkul hain, Sir. Hum kaahe jhooth bolenge?* Of course there is. Why would I lie?' said Khatri solemnly before leaving the room.

Nikky turned over, uneasy that his room was haunted.

It started raining heavily at the same time. And the ever-fickle electricity went off. The house was pitch-dark. We got really lucky that day. Everything was going my way to play the prank.

Nikky got out of bed and started walking around the large colonial bungalow, going through each of the rooms.

'Bhaiyya, Bhaiyya . . . Bhabhi!' he shouted, looking for us desperately. We were hiding in other parts of the house. He panicked when he came to our room and saw no one there.

He went out to the verandah. It was raining heavily. The Budhi Gandak river was swollen and the water gushed loudly. It added to pitch darkness and made the night seem more sinister.

Nikky saw a flicker of light inside the bungalow. He followed it, his heart beating hard. At the end of the long corridor, he saw a woman, her long hair loose and her white dress flowing in the wind. Nikky was terrified now. He started running around the house, shouting hoarsely. He bumped into some furniture, twisted his ankle and tripped.

Tanu finally told me, '*Ab bas karo, bahut daraa diya.* Enough now, you have scared him a lot.'

Then she tied her hair and wore a gown over her white nightie. Both of us burst out laughing.

'*Khatri, generator chala do.* Switch on the generator,' I said.

The lights came on immediately. We saw Nikky crouched in a corner, fear writ large on his face.

'What was the need to invite me to Muzaffarpur? And why the hell did you make me sleep in a haunted room?' he said.

All his fear, rage and other emotions erupted like a volcano. It took him a good ten minutes to calm down. When we finally went off to sleep, we were woken by a knock on our door. It was Nikky.

He entered our bedroom with a pillow and a mattress.

'I'll sleep in your room until I am here,' he said, throwing the mattress on the floor.

'Arre, why are you coming here? We need some privacy,' I protested.

'*Main nahin jaata.* I won't go. *Ab mere ko dar lag raha hain.* Now I am scared,' Nikky said, and sprawled on the mattress.

I had been very pleased with my prank but now I was irritated that Nikky was sleeping in our room. But he didn't budge and continued to drag his mattress to our room every evening, insisting that he had seen the vision of a woman hanging from the fan. I guess I had to pay the price of that prank too.

'*Lo ho gaya aapka honeymoon.* Your honeymoon is over,' said Tanu, laughing like mad, and turned around.

Nikky looked at her and said, '*Kya inme bhoot ki aatma aa gayi hain?* Has the evil spirit entered her?'

33

Who Made You SP?

One day I got a notice from a commission to produce a case diary of an FIR lodged in 1973.

I took the matter as a routine one and directed my staff to search for the case diary. A few days went by and I got another stern notice. My team could not find the diary. I asked the inspector and the SHO of the police station concerned to look for it too. After a few days, they also gave up. I soon got a notice to appear before the commission in Patna.

I got a little wary, as this was going to be my first experience in the commission. There was a big crowd in the room and everyone's attention was focused on me. Most of the people did not know me, so their eyes darted to the name plate on my uniform.

'*Accha, toh ye Amit Lodha hain, SP Muzaffarpur.* So this as Amit Lodha, SP Muzaffarpur!' I could hear the conversation between people.

There was a hushed silence when the chief of the commission entered the chamber.

'So, SP Muzaffarpur, where is the case diary? I have given you two weeks to present it,' said the officer, looking at me with a scowl on his face.

'Sir, we tried our best but could not find it,' I replied.

'"Tried our best?" You can't find one case diary! Produce it in a fortnight, or you've had it,' he said angrily.

I saluted and left the chamber. I felt terrible, as this was the first time I had been shouted at in my career.

I instructed my office to take out all files we had access to and somehow find the required case diary. Every morning, my office staff would take out hundreds of files wrapped in red cloth and spread them out outside my office, as there was not enough space for us to go through them inside any room. Some of the files were moth-eaten and some of the papers had turned yellow with age. Almost all of them smelt really bad because of lizard and rat droppings. In spite of our best effort, there was no sign of the case diary.

The only silver lining was that my office got rid of some utterly useless files. I was appalled to see the unnecessary correspondence of the SP's office. There was a red bundle marked 'Punjab Terrorism Cases'. Intrigued, I opened it to discover that my office had been sending a 'nil' report to the DG's office every day for the past fifteen years! Way back in the early Nineties, a minor terrorist act had been carried out by Punjab militants in Bihar. So the then DG had issued an order for the SP to send him details of 'terrorist acts' daily to him. Now that Punjab militancy was long over, I immediately asked my office to stop the absolutely useless report. And, of course, I stopped all other irrelevant correspondence too.

* * *

I was called to the chief's chamber again. By now, the people there had started to recognize me.

'So, where is it? Don't tell me you could not find it,' the chief snarled.

'Sir, I apologize. I could not find the diary. The file is too old, and we do not have such old records. I was actually not even born then.'

'Not even born then? How dare you talk like that? Who has made such a young boy the SP of a district?' the chief shouted.

'Move heaven and earth, but get the case file, or . . . ' he said with utter contempt.

I left, humiliated.

I returned to Muzaffarpur, worrying about what fate had in store for me. I would sit in my office, trying to work, but could not concentrate. My face started showing the stress, which had never happened before, even during the most difficult situations in my career.

One day, one of the leading doctors of Muzaffarpur, Dr Shyamnandan, came to visit me. Seeing my face, he asked me what the matter was.

I explained the situation to him and said, 'Doctor Saheb, I just cannot find the case diary. I don't know what action will be taken against me for no fault of mine.'

'*Itni si baat!* Such a small issue. We will sort it out,' said Dr Shyamnandan.

'How?' I asked.

'Arre, my best friend is the chief's nephew and he also works in the same commission. I'll ask him to fix up everything for you,' he smiled.

For my next appearance before the commission, the chief's nephew accompanied me.

The chief looked at me with his favourite scowl plastered on his face. He was ready to go after me but stopped when he saw his nephew enter with me.

'Uncle, please pardon Mr Lodha. He's a good officer. This matter pertains to a very old issue and can be closed,' his nephew spoke up.

'Are you sure?' asked the chief.

'Yes, Uncle, absolutely,' replied the nephew.

'Okay, then. Case closed,' said the chief with a big smile. I could not believe that he could use his facial muscles to also smile.

I was grinning ear to ear on my way back. I realized that, even as officers, we needed to have a rapport with people other than our professional colleagues. One never knew who could help us in our difficult times.

34

You Can't Choose Your Boss

My idyllic life in Muzaffarpur was interrupted again by a major incident. A petrol pump had been looted in the wee hours. The SHO Sanjeev sounded worried. He was a brilliant officer and we had good experiences working together.

'Sir, kareeb chaar lakh loota gaya hain. Ek petrol pump wale ko goli bhi lagi hain. About Rs 4 lakh has been looted. An employee of the petrol pump has also been shot. There were six robbers. They came on motorcycles,' he said.

'Will he survive?' I asked.

'Yes, Sir. I have already sent him to the hospital in the vehicle of a passerby.'

'Okay, you follow the trail of those robbers. I will alert all the police stations to put barricades on the roads and check for any suspects,' I said.

I was at home and had just got up to get ready, but was not able to move even an inch. My hip was hurting like hell. It was an attack of ankylosing spondylitis again. It is an autoimmune disease that flares up unexpectedly from time to time. Modern medicine hasn't yet been able to explain why it occurs.

The excruciating pain almost completely immobilized me. I somehow mustered up some strength and managed to make important phone calls to give directions to my officers about the petrol-pump robbery.

Tanu was already up, trying to distract herself from her nausea. Seeing me in trouble, she put aside her uneasiness and started massaging my back.

'Tanu, thank you so much, but this massage won't make any difference. The pain is hurting my bones,' I said, touching her cheeks lovingly.

'*Toh kya hua?* So what? At least I can try,' she replied.

For a moment, I realized how self-centred I was and how loving Tanu was. My thoughts were disturbed by the ringing of my cellphone. It was the ADG.

'Lodha, I have heard that a petrol pump has been looted in your district. And that you have still not reached the PO,' he said rather curtly.

'Sir, I have had an attack of ankylosing spondylitis. I can't move at all,' I replied.

'What is this ankylosing . . . whatever it is?' he replied in an irritated tone.

For some reason, the ADG and I had never got along. I knew that my explanation would not convince him.

'Sir, I have given instructions and I am following up. Even if I were fit right now, I would not go to the petrol pump. My going to the pump will only distract my men. The DSP, the inspector, everyone will wait there for me, giving me the same briefing again and again. I'd rather want them chasing the criminals,' I said in one breath.

Of course the ADG did not like my reasoning and hung up. In our line of work, each case is tackled differently. There are no set theories, no manuals. I wanted my men to be on the job before I showed up. For someone else, it may have worked to go to the petrol pump immediately.

I called Sanjeev again. 'Any progress?'

'*Sir, kuch lead toh mila hain.* I have got a lead from the local people. They have told me the direction in which the robbers went. *Par baarish bahut tez ho rahi hain.* It's raining so hard. It's difficult for us to follow the robbers,' Sanjeev said.

'Sanjeev, it is raining for the robbers too. They must have taken shelter somewhere. After all, they are riding bikes. They can't escape as we have blocked all the exit routes.'

'Yes, Sir. If they are in our district, I promise I'll find them,' Sanjeev said.

I sat in my room, looking at the rain outside. The flowers in my garden were lovely at this time but my pain was too distracting and did not let me soak in the beauty. I could not do anything but wait for news from Sanjeev.

Finally the telephone rang.

'*Sir, SHO Sanjeev Sir ka criminal se encounter ho raha hain.* SHO Sanjeev is having an encounter with the criminals. DSP Saheb is also reaching the spot,' said my telephone orderly.

I waited tensely for good news. I could, of course, not call Sanjeev as he must have been in the middle of the shootout. I called the DSP for more updates.

'Sir, Sanjeev has found the location of the robbers. The police team has encircled the criminals. I am also reaching soon,' said the DSP.

I was confident that my team would be successful.

After half an hour, I got the call I was waiting for. It was Sanjeev.

'*Sir, sab pakda gaya hain—ek ghayal hua hain.* We have caught all of them—one of them has been injured in the shootout,' said Sanjeev excitedly.

'Excellent, Sanjeev. So proud of you!' I said.

Surprisingly, the news acted as a strong painkiller. Though the pain was there, I could ignore it. I somehow got into the Gypsy and reached the encounter site.

DSP Charan, Sanjeev and the entire police team was waiting. Sanjeev and his men were drenched, their clothes full of grime and mud.

I shook hands with all of them and congratulated them.

'*Sir, aap sahi keh rahe the.* You were right. These robbers were finding it difficult to drive fast in the rain. *Bahut zor se baarish thi, Sir.* It was raining heavily. *Inn criminals mein ek ki bike fisal gayi.* The bike of one of the criminals slipped in the sludge. Both the pillion and the driver got injured. The bike also got damaged, so they abandoned it on the main road itself,' said Sanjeev, pausing in between to catch his breath.

'These two criminals also sat on the other two bikes,' he continued.

'Tripling, Sir,' added the DSP.

I nodded.

'*Uske baad ye log Bijnara gaon ki aur mudhe aur wahaan chhup gaye.* They then moved towards Bijnara village and hid there,' Sanjeev said.

'Naturally they could not ride fast in the rain. There were three people sitting on each bike anyway. It was difficult maintaining balance on the muddy, wet, kutcha roads going towards the village. They had no option but to get down and hide near a farm shed,' added Zafar, a brave officer and a close friend of Sanjeev's. He would always accompany Sanjeev on all operations and raids.

'*Hum peechha karte hue aage badhe toh iski bike ko sadak par gira dekhe.* While we were chasing them, we saw the abandoned bike on the road,' Sanjeev said.

'And then we saw the fresh tyre marks of two bikes on the kutcha track. We followed the tracks to the village. A few villagers directed us to their location. Zafar and I split up into two teams and surrounded them,' said Sanjeev, taking his time to narrate the sequence of events. He was visibly exhausted.

Zafar could sense it. So he took over from Sanjeev and continued, 'Before we could plan our next move, the goons started firing at us. Luckily, we had good cover. A farmer was constructing a storehouse in that area, so there were piles of bricks in a number of places. We also fired. One of my bullets hit the abdomen of one of the robbers. In the meantime, the back-up team of DSP Sir also reached to support us. The gunshots made it easy to for them to locate us. Seeing themselves surrounded from all sides, the criminals came out from hiding and surrendered.'

'Excellent work! Wonderful!' I said elatedly. We seized the weapons from the criminals, checked them and sent them to the police station.

I called the ADG and narrated the entire incident.

'Sir, we have recovered the money and arrested all the six robbers,' I said.

'Good,' he said. Much to my surprise, he immediately sent a commendation card to my team and me. Later, I pondered my idiocy. I realized that I had formed a negative bias against ADG Sir purely on the basis of hearsay. My preconceived notions had altered my behaviour with him. Naturally, the ADG was also antagonized. And our dislike for each other had only increased.

But now I changed my attitude. I knew I could not choose my boss, so I just continued working in my own style and stopped complaining about ADG Sir altogether.

A few days later, an IG from Patna came to see me.

'You know, I heard that the ADG was not exactly talking well about you,' said the IG.

'Sir, I just do my work. I can't help what opinion other people have of me. All I know is that he is my senior and might be right about certain things,' I replied.

The IG looked at me and smiled. 'Amit, that is a refreshing change in your attitude. Of course, ADG Sir is quite experienced and well-meaning too. It just sometimes happens that we let our professional disagreements affect our personal relations. I am sure things will be fine between the two of you now,' he said.

From then on, my relations with my superiors were always all right.

35

Poori Zindagi Padhai Ki Hain!

The elections in 2004 had resulted in a hung assembly. We started preparing for the upcoming assembly elections again. Interestingly, crime rates dip around assembly elections. Maybe it is because of an increase in patrolling and number of police personnel deployed, who are ably supported by the paramilitary forces. Or it could be that the criminals are busy rallying for certain candidates. They have 'professional' commitments too!

Since I had already conducted operations for the earlier assembly elections in Muzaffarpur peacefully, I was confident of being able to do so again. But I was in for a shock.

One September evening, around 9 p.m., I got a call from the election commission's office in Patna. It was Deepak Sir, a senior IAS officer who had a wonderful demeanour.

'Amit, you have been transferred to Bhabhua; join immediately. The elections are going to take place there in the first phase.'

'Bhabhua? But why, Sir?' I said, almost stammering.

'It's a general administrative decision,' he replied.

I was silent for some time and then burst out.

'Sir, this is absolutely wrong. I conducted the earlier elections so well. I have been working hard for the past few weeks. Everything is fine in Muzaffarpur. Only a few days are left for the elections to take place. And you expect me to go and start all over again in Bhabhua?' I said angrily.

'Yes, but I am sure you can do it again. You are a young, energetic officer.'

Tanu had just entered the room, listening to me shouting on the phone.

'Sir, my wife is seven months pregnant. It will be very difficult for me to shift now. Who will do the packing? She's not in a condition to do strenuous work and Bhabhua is such a small town, there are hardly any medical facilities there. How will she deliver a child there?'

I was taking full advantage of Sir's kind nature. Otherwise, very few seniors are patient enough to listen to the complaints of a junior officer.

'Oh, I did not know that. But it's too late for any change in decision now. All the best to you,' Deepak Sir said.

I was agitated throughout the day. Tanu also felt dejected. I had worked hard for the elections. She was already tense about her delivery and now this stress. We had settled down well in Muzaffarpur. Avi was going regularly to a playschool. I would play tennis in the evenings, the house was beautiful—life was perfect.

Tanu and I sat holding each other's hands, watching Avi play in the lovely drawing room. I looked at the curtains I had matched with the upholstery, the beautiful pots I had put everywhere in the house.

'Chun, it's part of life. We can't do anything about it. I'll go to Jaipur.'

'You are right, but I'm feeling bad right now,' I said. Transfers and posting are part of every civil servant's career, but an unexpected transfer, that, too, to a nondescript place, does irk.

After two days, I packed up and left for Bhabhua. My friends helped Tanu pack up our furniture and other belongings. A week later, they dropped her to the Patna airport. Later that day, Tanu called me from Jaipur.

'Chun, how are you? I'm missing you,' she said.

'I am missing you too. How's Avi?' I asked.

'He's fine, but he's always looking for you. He has never been away from you, after all.'

We chatted for a little longer before we hung up. I was feeling terrible. My career graph had been going straight up. I was not prepared to be posted to a small, moffusil town.

Bhabhua was the exact opposite of Muzaffarpur. It was very small, the size of a colony in Muzaffarpur. There was no social life. And no challenges for me as a policeman. The house was isolated, located in a corner of the small town. I felt depressed in the lonely environment.

'*Yahaan koi tennis court hain kya?* Is there any tennis court here?' I asked the town SHO.

Initially, the SHO did not understand my question, but I was hopeful that he would bring me some good news soon. After all, there is no question of a 'no' in the police department.

'*Sir, tennis ka khela mil gaya.* I have found a game of tennis.'

I was excited at the news. At least I would have something to do in the evenings. I jumped into my Gypsy and followed the SHO.

'*Bada Babu, kahaan hain court? Ye toh building hain.* Where is the court? This is a building,' I asked, a trifle irritated.

'*Yahi hain, Sir.* This is it. Come inside,' said the SHO with a big smile. He ushered me into the dilapidated hall as if he were taking me to the hallowed courts of Wimbledon.

All my excitement vanished the moment I entered. There was a table somehow managing to stand on two legs—the other end was supported by a column of bricks.

'*Ye toh table tennis hain!* This is table tennis!' I said, dejected.

'*Sir, Bhabhua mein toh yahi wala tennis hain.* There is only this tennis available in Bhabhua,' said the SHO, disappointed that his efforts could not make his 'saheb' happy.

'*Toh phir koi cinema hall hain?* Is there any cinema hall? I have seen the posters of *Spider-Man* on walls,' I asked.

'Sir, there's only one hall—Shyam Talkies—but it's very dirty. *Aapke jaane layak nahin hain.* It's not up to your standards,' the SHO replied.

'Doesn't matter. I need some entertainment!' I replied.

I reached the hall, excited. Undoubtedly, the hall was filthy, with packets of chips, samosas and other things littered on the broken chairs. I did not mind the garbage, for I was about to see the Hollywood blockbuster *Spider-Man*. I adjusted myself on a broken seat. I smiled seeing the towel the hall owner had put on the seat to make me 'comfortable'. My smile vanished and I started cursing the moment I saw the title '*Makad Manav*'. It was a Bhojpuri dubbing!

I exited hastily, to be met by the hall owner outside.

'*Sir, kya koi kaam aa gaya emergency mein?* Is there an emergency at work? Please come next week—we are showing *Eee Naa Ho Payi, Bhaiyya*,' he said, pointing to the poster of *Mission Impossible*!

I resigned myself to my fate. I hung a punching bag in my house and started venting all my frustration on it. In a way, it helped me hone my martial arts skills.

* * *

Tanu gave birth to our second child on 9 October. I was again not with her, as Bhabhua was about to go to polls. I called her late again that night, after she had had a chance to rest.

'Hi, Tanu, how are you? How's the little one? Is she as beautiful as you?'

'Yeah, both of us are fine. But all of us are missing you. You have not been with me for both my deliveries.'

I kept quiet. I had nothing to say to defend myself.

* * *

'Ajit, I have been blessed with a baby girl. Get some boxes of sweets and distribute to our entire staff—the guards, everyone,' I said, managing a smile.

Ajit could understand. He had always been like my shadow. He knew that though I was always happy in my own company, I yearned to be with my family too.

Tanu and I would talk every night, but most of our conversations ended abruptly because of my stupidity. Tanu had had a C-section delivery again and was in a lot of pain.

'Chun, I am not able to sleep properly. These stitches are troubling me a lot. They are very painful. Avi also has fever. I am finding it difficult to take care of Avi, as Aishwarya demands my constant attention. I wish you were here,' Tanu said.

I would listen for some time and then lose patience.

'*Tanu, yaar, thoda sahan karo.* Try to tolerate this. Whenever I call you, you are complaining.'

'Chun, I am not complaining. I am just saying I miss you,' she would say, lowering her voice. I could figure out that she genuinely wanted me by her side, holding her hand, looking into her eyes. But I was being insensitive, taking out my frustration on her for being posted to such a small place. I felt the guilt of not being there for my family but, unfortunately, couldn't show that to her.

The elections in Bhabhua went as uneventfully as possible. Finally, a month after Aishwarya's birth, I went to Jaipur to meet my family. Tanu was overjoyed to see me. Avi kept jumping on me and hugging me. I delicately took Aishwarya in my arms and kissed her. This time I knew how to handle a newborn!

But my visit was abruptly cut short. A couple of days later, I got a call from the ADG headquarters in Patna.

'Amit, Naxals have attacked Jehanabad. This is a serious situation. You are required to be back in Bhabhua at once. Convey my apologies to Tanu,' said the ADG politely but firmly.

I switched on the TV. Every news channel was showing the Naxal attack in Jehanabad. Nearly a thousand Naxalites armed with self-loading rifles and machine guns, and clad in police uniform, had launched simultaneous assaults on the police lines, jail and near a CRPF camp located in the heart of Jehanabad. The magnitude of the attack was unprecedented—341 inmates had escaped from jail that day.

Bhabhua was also a Naxal-prone area. I had no option but to rush back. I left Tanu and the children in Jaipur with a heavy heart.

On reaching Bhabhua, I immediately held a meeting with all the policemen. We fortified our police stations by putting sand bags around the perimeters and stationed sentries on the roofs to be in a better position, in case we needed to fire. We even kept stray dogs in the police stations to bark at unknown persons and alert the jawans.

'*Sir, jila ka toh theek hain, apni kothi ka bhi security dekh lijiye.* It's okay to look out for the district, but do increase the security at your bungalow too,' said Ajit seriously.

'*Theek toh hain.* Isn't the bungalow safe?' I asked.

'*Sir, agar Naxal attack mein SP kothi pe hi hamla kar de toh?* What if the Naxals attack the SP's residence? Who's going to stop them? Any attack on the SP will be a huge setback for the district police and, of course, embolden the Naxals more.'

'You are right,' I said. There were quite a few attacks on even SPs in Bihar and a few young IPS officers had been killed too by the Naxals.

I fortified my house with whatever basic things I had at my disposal. I put sand bags near the sentry post. I put broken glass on the walls to prevent anyone from climbing over. I also got a bulletproof Gypsy and issued AK-47s to my bodyguards. I thought I was well prepared to face any Naxal attack. Fortunately, nothing happened in Bhabhua. Life returned to the usual routine soon enough.

Tanu and the kids came to Bhabhua soon after. I was delighted the house was lively again. I thought that I'd enjoy a lot of quality time with them as I had nothing much to do. I got a collection of film CDs from Patna to watch with Tanu.

'Tanu, I have a few of your favourite black-and-white films of Shammi Kapoor and Dev Anand. I have also got some *Tom & Jerry* cartoons for Avi,' I said, showing off my stack of CDs.

'Chun, you think I'll have time to watch movies? I get too tired taking care of Aishwarya. I would rather catch up on my sleep. As for Avi, we should get him admitted to a school. He is four-and-a-half years old. Let's be serious about his studies,' replied Tanu, surprised that I hadn't thought of all this.

I was disappointed by Tanu's lack of interest in the movies I had got. But she must have been equally disappointed with my lack of interest in Avi's studies.

Tanu was particular about the upbringing of the kids. She would religiously teach Avi for two hours every day and check his work after he came home. And, of course, she was always by little Aishwarya's side. Occasionally, Tanu did complain.

'*Chun, kabhi toh Avi ko padha do.* At least teach Avi sometimes. At least A B C D.'

I did not have the patience to sit with a toddler and teach him. I responded in my typical way.

'*Tanu, yaar, poori zindagi padhai ki hain.* I have studied my whole life—school, IIT, UPSC. *Ab bhi padhaoo?* Now I have to teach too?'

Tanu did not say anything more. She picked up Avi's books and continued teaching him.

Things usually got worse at night.

'*Chun, TV bandh kar do, at least volume bandh kar do.* Switch off the TV, or at least mute the volume. Aishwarya will wake up!' Tanu said.

I would get irritated but say nothing. When I would go to sleep, I would be woken up by Aishwarya's loud crying; she slept in our room.

'*Tanu, isse chup kara do.* Please make her quiet. I am not able to sleep. Should I shift to the other room? I have to get some sleep. I have an important meeting tomorrow,' I used to yell. My frustration with my 'bad' posting was manifesting in the worst possible way.

But it was all soon to change.

I was abruptly transferred to a battalion of BMP that did not yet exist. We shifted to Patna. There was no bungalow, no bodyguards, no cooks and no media to take my interviews. But I got to play tennis!

That was the time I realized that I had had so many fair-weather friends. Everything was ephemeral, postings kept happening, but what was important was your character, when people respected you for what you were and not for your posting.

36

Naxals Ki Aashiqi

From the posting to a non-existent battalion in Patna, I went to Shekhpura, another small, sleepy town. I was fortunate to arrest the biggest gangster of that area and put an end to organized crime there. I was then made the superintendent of police of Begusarai.

Begusarai was a busy town, largely because the Indian Oil Corporation (IOC) had a complex there. A lot of businesses, small and big, had mushroomed to cater to the various requirements of people who were employed by the IOC. We were happy about the posting, particularly as Bhabhua had been tiny and without many facilities.

I used to remain quite busy with work, typical of any district. Once in a while, I used to get some perfunctory messages and alerts from the special branch about the Naxal movement in Begusarai. I delved a little deeper into the issue and realized that the Naxals, particularly a dreaded area commander called Dayanand Malakar, were using certain areas of Begusarai as hideouts and transit routes to the neighbouring districts of Munger and Jamui, which were hotbeds of Naxalism. In 2004, in an unfortunate incident, IPS officer K.C. Surendra Babu and his team were killed in a landmine blast in Munger. Before that incident, Munger had not been known for any incident linked to Naxalism. Not taking stray Naxal-related incidents seriously initially creates a monstrous problem that takes a lot of effort and sacrifice to control later. Begusarai was on the cusp of such a situation.

Interestingly, with the help of our informers, we easily found the mobile numbers of Dayanand Malakar and a few of his accomplices, including a woman named Sheela. She was the chief of the women's wing of CPI Maoists for the region. She was considered quite ruthless and more dangerous than her male counterparts.

I promptly tapped into their numbers and analysed their tower locations. The Maoists were frequenting Begusarai once a month. They followed a particular trail but did not stay in any specific village. Maybe the Naxals did not yet have sufficient support from the locals to take up permanent residence there.

Though the Naxals used their cellphones rarely, they were not exactly cautious. Maybe Malakar and his associates did not expect the police to listen in on their phones. After all, they had been travelling through Begusarai for the past three or four years and had never encountered the police.

I had put two of my best constables on the job of listening to their conversations. I especially got a computer from the police headquarters for logging all the calls and storing the conversations.

After a few days, Mithu Singh, one of the constables listening in on the conversation of Malakar, came to my office with an amused look.

'Sir, this Dayanand fellow doesn't talk much on the phone,' he said.

'Then?' I asked, my eyebrows raised at Mithu's expression. He was usually composed and sombre.

'*Sir, par Maowadi bhi dil rakhte hain. But* even Maoists have hearts,' Mithu said.

'Heart? Dayanand has killed so many people in cold blood. Don't you remember the landmine blast in Pratappur in the Jamui district where we lost six of our brave jawans?' I said sternly.

'*Arre nahin, Sir. Mera matlab hain ki Dayanand ka Sheela se setting hain.* I mean to say that Dayanand is having an affair with Sheela. And he is going to meet her in the coming days in Begusarai,' said Mithu, with a smile.

'Dayanand hardly calls anyone. Except Sheela. And with her there are no code words, just plain romantic talk. *Jaise hero heroinwa karte hain.* Like heroes and heroines do in films,' Mithu continued.

'Excellent. Then we should be hopeful of catching them soon,' I said.

'But Sir, why would they come to Begusarai?'

'Simple. They are area commanders of different districts, and know that the police of their respective districts are constantly after them, waiting for one false move. Begusarai has been a traditional safe haven for them. They assume that Begusarai Police has no priority of catching them. After all, they have never created any problem here,' I explained to Mithu.

'*Baat toh sahi hain, Sir.* You are right. *Aashiqi toh shaant jagah mein fursat se hi ho sakti hain.* One can be romantic only in a relaxed environment, when at peace,' Mithu said.

I gave him a stern look.

Mithu quickly saluted me and left the room. But he saw that I could not resist smiling at his nuggets on romance.

A few weeks passed. I was enjoying a rare lazy Sunday, signing some urgent dak at home, when Mithu called me, 'Sir, Dayanand has come to Virpur village near Ramnagar police station. And Sheela is about to reach the rendezvous.'

I was happy and angry in equal measure. Happy that it was our chance to nab Dayanand, and angry that I was a good 50 km from Virpur. I had no choice but to call DSP Sadar Pankaj immediately.

'Pankaj, there is a group of Naxals in Virpur, Ramnagar. You are quite close to that area. Reach immediately and cordon off the area. Be careful, as the Naxals are being led by their zonal commander. I will try to reach as soon as possible.' I told Pankaj about the operation in as much detail as possible.

I got up, put on my uniform and took out my Glock. Tanu immediately sensed that something serious was going on. As an SP, I rarely carried my pistol, unless there was a crisis. In normal circumstances, not many SPs carried firearms, as they had sufficient security around them. Moreover, it was dangerous to keep pistols or guns on one's person as cases of accidental firing were common. I naturally used to keep my pistol safely, far from the reach of my young children.

Tanu quietly handed my water bottle to the driver.

'*Ramvilas, gaadi dheere chalaana.* Drive slow,' she said.

'*Aaj toh tez chalani padegi, Tanu.* Today we'll have to drive fast,' I said.

'Ajit, get my bulletproof vest. Ask all the bodyguards to carry their BP jackets and sufficient ammunition. Keep an extra magazine,' I commanded. Now Tanu knew for sure that I was going for a major operation.

'*Ajit, Saheb ke saath rehna, unkadhyaan rakhna.* Stay with Sir, take care of him,' said Tanu in hushed tone to Ajit. She did not know that I could hear her.

As I sat in the Sumo, Tanu ran towards me. I asked Ramvilas to stop.

'*Kya hua, Tanuji?* What happened?' I asked.

'What will you have for dinner? Should I make your favourite aloo puri? *Aath baje tak toh aa hi jaaoge?* You'll reach by 8 p.m., dinnertime, right?' she asked.

I just touched her cheek and left. I smiled on the way, thinking about how much she cared for me. When I would be home, on normal days, she would always chide me for having oily, fried food, stuff that I loved, even though it was unhealthy. But today she had herself volunteered to make aloo puri, something fried and fattening! And the 8 p.m. deadline was the hope that her husband would return home by that time. Safely.

I thought about the wives of all the men sitting in my car. Some of the jawans had families in Begusarai. Their wives must have had the same thoughts as Tanu. Some jawans had families who lived in other towns or states. They must not even be aware that their husbands were embarking on a dangerous mission, about to risk their lives. I shuddered as I thought how a policeman's wife found out about her spouse's martyrdom. Her world came crashing down. Everything changed in that one instant.

I focused my thoughts on the mission. I picked up the cellphone to dial Pankaj's number, hoping that he could reach the village and cordon it off before we reached with additional reinforcements. Before I could even dial Pankaj's number, I saw his number flashing on my cellphone.

'*Sir, jaldi pahunchiye.* Come soon. *Hum ghira gaye hain.* We have been surrounded. One of our jawans has been injured in the crossfire. He's losing a lot of blood,' said Pankaj, his voice jittery.

'Oh, shit! I hope the jawan is safe. Ensure that he doesn't lose much blood. I'm reaching in a few minutes. Just hold on till then,' I replied.

Without even waiting for my instruction, Ramvilas pressed down on the accelerator and raced towards Virpur.

After a few minutes, as I looked out of my window, I saw Pankaj and four or five policemen lying in a pit. They were mired in dirt and mud, but it was the least of their problems.

'*Sir, Sir, jaldi se koodiye.* Jump quickly,' said Pankaj in a hushed tone.

I got down from the Sumo and tidied my uniform as a matter of habit. I wondered why Pankaj was asking me to jump into the pit. I thought about it only for a second, because a bullet whizzed past my head. Without any further thought, I jumped into the pit.

'*Ye goli kahaan se chali?* Where did the bullet come from?' I asked incredulously.

'*Sir, saamne ke ghar se.* From the house in front. Just about 50–60 metres away,' Pankaj replied.

I was shocked. As in all operations, I had expected Ramvilas to stop at least 500 metres before Virpur village. From there, we would have cordoned off the village after taking all possible precautions. I wanted to scold Ramvilas for driving straight to the village, that, too, right into the firing zone.

Sensing my surprise, Pankaj said, '*Sir, ye road abhi state fund se bani hain.* This road has just recently been built on state funds. Even we came to know about this road today. That's why we, too, drove straight into the village without realizing we had reached. Both the Naxals and us were in for a surprise. Since the Naxals were safely ensconced in a house, they could fire at us easily. As we were taking our positions, one of the SAP jawans, Bahadur Prasad, got hit in his abdomen.'

I looked up from the pit. The house from where the Naxals were firing was just in front of us. For once, I wished the government had not made a road to the village! A few metres away, the SAP jawan Bahadur Prasad was lying on the ground. He looked as though he was in pain, but from past experience, I estimated that his wound was not fatal. One of the jawans, his partner, was holding a cloth tightly against the wound to prevent further blood loss. Luckily, a few trees were giving them some protection. I had to get Bahadur back to Begusarai town for immediate treatment. To get Bahadur out of the firing line of Malakar and other Naxals, I had to distract the Naxals and give covering fire.

'Chalo, Bhushan, let's go. We'll go from the right flank. Pankaj, you and your team move from the left,' I told Pankaj and Bhushan, one of my bodyguards. As we were about to move out of the pit, I got a call from Nikhil and Santosh, my officers who had reached with additional force.

'*Sir, hum bhi pahuch gaye hain.* We have reached Virpur. We are coming from the back. We can see you,' said SI Santosh.

'Great, let us encircle these Naxals. Be patient, don't lose your cool. Also remember, since we are almost in each other's line of fire, do not shoot indiscriminately. Our own men might get shot in the crossfire,' I told Santosh. Suddenly I realized that none of us were wearing bulletproof jackets.

'Pankaj, put on your bulletproof jacket. Why are all of you not wearing them?' I said angrily to all the policemen in the pit.

'*Sir, bahut wazani hain.* It is too heavy,' Pankaj said. The average bulletproof jacket provided to a jawan or a soldier is almost 7–10 kg. The jacket is basically two plates of steel hanging in two bags that cover the chest and the back of the jawan. Kevlar jackets, which are made of a much lighter fibre, are not common in our country.

Pankaj and his men put on their jackets reluctantly. I gestured to Ajit to get mine from my car. Ajit got himself out of the pit and sprinted to the car, parked next to the pit.

'*Sir, isko pehan ke toh baahar nikalna mushkil ho raha hain.*
It's difficult getting out of the pit wearing this heavy contraption,'
said one of the constables. He was right.

'*Okay, utaar lo.* Take it off,' Pankaj said.

Ajit had got my jacket but even I found it too cumbersome
to wear. I left it in the pit too. We all started crawling towards
the house, intermittently firing in that direction.

On my orders, Pankaj and his men started crawling from
the left flank. After a few moments, one of the constables got up
from the crawling position and started walking. To my horror,
one by one, all the men, including Pankaj, got up and started
walking towards the house.

For a second, even I was tempted to stand up. Why?
Because I did not want to crouch like this in front of my men.
My stupid thought died a natural death in a moment. I heard a
shrill sound. One of the BMP jawans in Pankaj's team had been
shot. The constable fell, grimacing in pain. I saw the silhouette
of a Naxal, with a rifle clearly visible in his hands.

'*Sab ke sab neeche leto!* Get down on the ground! Crawl!'
I shouted at the top of my voice. I got angry with all my men,
and most of all with myself. I was a trained professional. I had to
lead my team by example. And here I was, thinking of emulating
the foolish constable.

Now we had two men down and the Naxals holed up in a
house in front of us.

'*Ruk ruk ke goli chalao.* Shoot in a disciplined manner,'
I shouted. Our teams kept shooting intermittently, but we were
not making much progress. We were out in the open and the
Naxals were well protected inside the house.

I really hoped that Santosh and Nikhil would reach quickly
and fire at the house from the other side. My prayers were
soon answered—I heard a gunshots in the distance. I could tell

from the loudness of the shots that the additional police team was firing at the Naxals about 200 metres from our location.

Malakar and his men got confused. That was enough for Pankaj and his team to rush towards the fallen BMP jawan. One of the jawans on Pankaj's team showed exemplary courage. He lifted the injured BMP jawan on his shoulders and ran as fast as he could towards the pit. It was, of course, very brave of him. And very foolish too. But I guess that was the best thing to do in that situation.

Meanwhile, Ajit got the injured SAP jawan Bahadur Prasad back to the pit. My driver, Ramvilas, immediately got my Gypsy ready and put both the injured men in the back. Much to everyone's relief, the shots on both the jawans were not fatal. The bullets had apparently not hit any vital organ.

Ramvilas drove the Gypsy at top speed towards Begusarai. It was flanked by the Jeep of Inspector, Teghra, Emmanuel Kistopa. Now that the vehicles were out of firing range for the Naxals, I started crawling with renewed vigour.

All the jawans were also charged up. We had managed to encircle the house, and the Naxals had nowhere to go. After some intermittent firing, it went quiet. This was dangerous too. I really did not know if we should move forward. It could have been Malakar's ploy to give us a false sense of victory and shoot at us when we got very close to the house.

We spent a few tense minutes just waiting.

'*Sir, aa jaiye.* Come over. *Hum andar aa gaye.* We are inside,' said a jubilant Nikhil.

Nikhil was one of the most daredevil officers I knew. He had just barged into the house from the back, taking Malakar and his team by surprise.

We all got up from our crouching and lying positions and ran towards the house. I was delighted that the operation was progressing so well. I entered the courtyard and then the storehouse, where all the Naxals were hiding. I saw Malakar standing in front of me with his hands up. A bandolier with a number of cartridges was hanging around his waist. It seemed he had given up. I smiled and sat on the windowsill to relax for a bit.

Suddenly we heard Bhushan shouting.

'*Niklo baahar!* Get out! *Hum batate hain operation kaise hota hain.* I'll tell you how an operation is conducted. After all, I am NSG-trained,' said Bhushan, pointing his bayonet at a young woman. It was Sheela, the chief of the women's wing of Naxals! Three more Naxals had been hiding in the haystacks.

I was a little upset with Bhushan's haughtiness but he deserved to be a bit arrogant. Like a trained commando, Bhushan had started checking the house. While poking his bayonet in the haystacks, it was he who had discovered Sheela and her accomplices.

God, how many mistakes we had made that evening! I realized that I had become complacent a bit too soon. I immediately called the primary medic to ask about the two jawans who had been injured.

'*Sir, dono out of danger hain.* Both are out of danger, but they have been referred to Patna,' said Azam, the town DSP.

It is standard practice for all doctors of small towns to refer serious patients to the nearest big town, and rightly so. The medical facilities, particularly for serious cases, are far better in the bigger towns and cities. This is true for any state, whether it is Bihar or Rajasthan.

Begusarai was not very far from Patna and the roads were excellent.

'Send two escort vehicles with the ambulance. Direct all police stations in the Begusarai district to keep the roads clear until Patna. There should be no traffic jam,' I said.

All the thanas on the highway to Patna sprang into action immediately. The ambulance blared its siren and moved at full speed towards Patna.

I made the next call to Dr John Mukhopadhyay, one of Patna's leading surgeons. I had excellent relations with him, having played squash with him in Patna a long time ago. He was quite a busy doctor and usually did not pick up calls. But it was my lucky day. Not only did he answer my call, but he also had some excellent news.

'Amit, can you believe it? We have an international conference of surgeons tomorrow. And one of the leading surgeons of the world has come here from France. I will ask him to assist us in the surgery of your men,' said Dr Mukhopadhyay amiably.

I could not have been more reassured.

That day we arrested nine Naxals, including Malakar and Sheela. We recovered six looted police rifles and carbines. It was a big achievement for Bihar Police. Begusarai has had no Naxal-related incident ever since.

I reached home much later than 8 p.m.

Tanu was waiting for me and trying to hide the tension she had been through the past few hours under her 'cool' demeanour.

'Did you make aloo puri?' I asked expectantly.

'No, I have made kheere ki sabzi. Aloo is too fattening,' she said.

'Kheera? Cucumber? Chalo, at least you have not made lauki,' I said, all my hopes dashed.

I sat at the table and with great reluctance started eating the kheere ki sabzi.

'Yaar, it's tasting almost like gourd, but tolerable,' I said, disappointedly eating the food. Avi could not control his laughter. He said, '*Papa, lauki hi hain.* It *is* gourd!'

I got up and ran after Tanu. Both of us started running around the dining table. Finally I caught her and playfully pretended to throttle her. I looked at her and embraced her tightly.

* * *

As it often happens, I was suddenly transferred as SP Railways, Muzaffarpur. I was a tad surprised, considering that I had just succeeded with the Naxalite operation in Begusarai. But then, transfers happen in our career when we are least expecting them.

Nevertheless, the new posting, though not important in common parlance, was a blessing in disguise for me. My ankylosing spondylitis had become so excruciating that I could not sleep at all. The moment I lay down, there would be searing pain in my back and buttocks. Since I was largely immobile and my work was definitely less taxing, I spent a lot of time at home with my family. It was a pleasure watching my kids grow. Their laughter would act as balm to my pain. I realized that, ultimately, it is your family that matters the most. I also rekindled my old passions and hobbies. I learnt to sing Kishore Kumar songs. It was a different matter that my family had to suffer the cacophony.

Postings and transfers are an inevitable part of one's career. There is no point thinking about them. And I realized that one should look at the silver linings in the postings that aren't coveted as much.

37

Acche Ghar Ki Ladki

'Sir, some engineer saheb has come to meet you. I told him it's quite late but he is adamant,' said my telephone orderly.

'It's all right. Have him sit in the chamber,' I said.

I had a habit of meeting everyone, even at odd hours, in my house. I knew that nobody would come to meet an SP unnecessarily. Most of the people were anyway too scared of the police. Unfortunately, some policemen are also inaccessible to the public—the very people we are supposed to serve.

'Power should not be construed as keeping someone waiting outside your office for two hours. Power is bringing instant relief to an aggrieved person by your just actions,' my ADG, Shastri Sir, had told me early in my career, and it had stuck.

My easy accessibility to the people helped me a lot in understanding the public's problems first-hand. It also helped me develop a good rapport with the people, which usually came in handy in difficult law-and-order situations.

As I entered the chamber, the engineer got up, folded his hands and started crying.

'What is it, Engineer Saheb? Please calm down.'

'Sir, please see all these e-mails,' he said, handing me a file with hundreds of email printouts.

I started reading the emails. It was a conversation between two people, describing sexual acts in lurid detail. I felt uncomfortable reading them.

'Engineer saheb, the emails are gross. But why are you showing them to me?'

'Sir, these are email conversations between . . .' he seemed to hesitate, 'my daughter Shikha and her college professor. I chanced upon them recently.'

'Really? But why?'

'I don't know, Sir. *Aap hi bula ke poochhiye. Humari toh izzat khatam ho jaayegi.* Please call and ask her. Our dignity is at stake.'

'It's not exactly a police problem. What can I do about it?'

'I know, Sir, but I have great faith in you. Maybe she'll get scared of the police and tell the truth. She's not telling me anything. And please threaten the professor. He should stop all this nonsense,' the engineer pleaded.

I managed a smile. 'Scared of the police? Why? Are we like Gabbar Singh of *Sholay*?' I mused.

I could make out that the engineer would not relent. He had invested great hope in the police.

'Okay, okay, I'll call your daughter right now.' After half an hour, a lady sub-inspector escorted the engineer's daughter, a young girl, to my chamber.

'Namaste, Sir,' she said. She seemed well-mannered and sophisticated. I was surprised that she was the author of all those emails.

'Shikha, can you explain these emails?' I came straight to the point.

The girl hesitated for a few moments. Then she said confidently, '*Sir, ye toh thoda aise hi bas chats hain.* These are just some harmless chats.'

'Harmless chats? This content is so explicit!' I said.

'Sir, to tell you the truth, I was trying to seduce my professor through these messages. I had not studied for the exams. I thought my charms would win over the professor and help me get some good marks. So I sent him some messages initially. But when I started getting a favourable response from him, I got emboldened,' she said.

'So you had physical relations with the teacher, just to get good marks?' I asked angrily.

'No, no, Sir, of course not. My teacher is quite old, almost my father's age. I was just enticing him through my messages. I never had any physical relations with him. Anyway I would have stopped sending these e-mails after the results were declared. *Main acche ghar ki ladki hoon.* I come from a good family.'

I was shocked at Shikha's audacity.

Acche ghar ki ladki, my foot—people could stoop to any level if it benefited them, I thought.

I sent her away and sent an officer to get her teacher. Soon, a bald, haggard man entered my chamber. He stood in front of me, scratching his paunch. I was flabbergasted. How could Shikha write such e-mails to this man?

'Don't you feel ashamed? Look at your age, your profession!' I shouted angrily at the man.

'Sir, I had fallen in love with Shikha,' the teacher replied, his head hanging in shame.

'Love? This is called lust. Keep away from Shikha and mend your ways. A teacher is supposed to be a role model. Please don't denigrate the institution,' I said as I got up from my chair. The professor got really scared, as if I was about to beat him!

'Don't be scared, I am not going to hit you, but remember what I have told you,' I said.

* * *

The engineer thanked me profusely. I saw immense relief in his teary eyes as he turned at the door to thank me again.

Suddenly, the teacher entered the chamber again, trying to hide behind me.

'*Sir, mujhe bachaa lo, mere dono bete aur biwi mujhe maarne aaye hain.* Please save me. Both my sons and my wife have come to thrash me,' he said, frightened.

Before I could react, a lady entered the room. She took out her slippers and started beating the professor.

I just got out of the way. I had had enough of family drama for a day.

'Another day in the life of a police officer,' I thought.

38

Blast Ho Gaya

'*Sir, kya inka har jagah jaana zaroori hain?* Is it necessary that he go for all the Naxal operations?' asked Kranti.

I just could not look her in the eye and tried to evade her question.

'*Sir, aise hi kuch bol deti hain.* She just says anything. Please pardon her,' said Dilbagh, Kranti's husband.

Dilbagh, a young, genial sardar, had been recently posted to Gaya as my city SP. Gaya, a hard-core Naxal-affected district, was one of the toughest areas in the country.

'Kranti has recently conceived, she must be under tremendous stress that her husband has to go for such dangerous assignments. Can't you do something about it? So much tension is not good for a pregnant woman,' said Tanu, on our way back from Dilbagh's house.

'Tanu, a senior police officer has to lead the force in all Naxal-related operations. You know that even I lead the Gaya Police and CRPF teams once a fortnight. We can't expect our subordinate officers and constables to venture out alone in such dangerous areas while we just issue orders from our office,' I replied.

We were quiet for the rest of the journey. I kept thinking about Kranti's request.

Elections were round the corner. The DM and I had planned for every possible contingency months in advance. I had prioritized the polling booths according to their sensitivities and assigned paramilitary forces and local police components as per each booth's threat level. Gaya was given 108 companies of paramilitary forces such as the BSF, the CRPF and the ITBP. It was a difficult task to provide them with adequate accommodation, and that, too, in safe areas. The district administration decided to make the uniformed personnel stay in local schools close to the polling booths. There was a booth in the Dumaria police station that was set up for only the six voters in the district. But we sent a full company of almost eighty BSF men and twenty constables of the state police to ensure that people had the greatest safety while exercising their democratic right.

Dumaria was such an isolated and godforsaken place that only a handful of senior police officers had visited the police station in the past many years. There was only one road, straight to Dumaria, the farthest police station from the district headquarters. After Sherghati was a stretch of 45 kilometres of kutcha road that was ideal for planting landmines. And the hills on both sides of the road were perfect for laying on ambush on any motorcade. Naxals were at a huge advantage in that area because of the ideal topography for any guerrilla warfare.

* * *

One day, a gas cylinder exploded in the vicinity of the Dumaria police station. The police personnel at the station took their positions, thinking that Naxals had attacked. The Dumaria SHO, Arun Pal, got quite unnerved. It was not that he was not brave. In fact, his years of working in Naxal-infested areas had made him paranoid of any suspicious activity, however innocuous.

'*Sir, aap ek baar aa jaiye. Humko Naxal ka bhoot dikh raha hain.* Please come. I am seeing ghosts dressed up as Naxals. I will kill all of them,' said Arun, completely shaken.

'*Relax, Arun, thodi himmat rakhiye.* Be brave,' I said trying to calm him down.

But Arun kept blabbering on the phone. I knew that I had to go immediately to take stock of the situation and motivate the men.

I summoned my driver, Narendra.

'*Gaadi nikalo aur chaar commandos ko taiyyar karo.* Get the civil car ready and ask four of our commandos to come with us,' I said.

* * *

'*Chalo Sherghati ki taraf.* Drive towards Sherghati,' I said as I sat in the car. As the road was quite busy until Sherghati, there was little chance of a landmine blast on that road. The Naxals did not want to have any civilian casualty. They were fighting an ideological war against the Indian state, and the police, being the most visible face of the state authority, were always a target for the Naxals.

'*Sir, Sherghati aa gaye hain.* We have reached Sherghati,' Narendra said.

'Drive straight to Dumaria,' I said grimly.

'*Sir, escort le lete.* We should have taken an escort. Or at least changed the number plates of the car. One of the SPs of Gaya kept many number plates with different registration numbers, and changed them depending on where he went,' said Narendra, his face turning ashen. Narendra was not worried without reason. The stretch was risky as the Naxals had targeted a few police vehicles earlier, causing considerable loss of life.

'Don't worry. First, we have the element of surprise. Nobody, except the six of us, knows that we are going to Dumaria. The Naxals can't put landmines randomly. They can plant landmines on the route only on our way back, when they come to know about us travelling in this area,' I said confidently.

'Moreover, we are moving in an unmarked civil car, without any VIP light or the SP's name plate,' I added.

Nevertheless, all the bodyguards became alert, as our car had entered dangerous territory. Even I felt my stomach tightening. Though we were all tense, we were ready to face any threat. Now Narendra pressed down on the accelerator without any hesitation. When we work as a team, it gives us all courage. Maybe it is the bonding, the esprit de corps. Whether a police team faces a mob or terrorists, all the men come together to do their best. I have never seen any policeman shy away from a crisis.

After almost an hour of travelling on the kutcha road, we reached Dumaria. The thana was almost like a fortress, though not impregnable.

I took a round of the police station and met all the policemen.

'*Bada Babu, ghabrao mat.* Don't worry. We are all with you.' I patted Arun's back. He seemed to be much calmer now.

'I will send you extra force, some more bulletproof jackets and an anti-landmine vehicle,' I continued.

I knew that all these reinforcements would certainly help improve things. But the policemen still lived in mortal danger. Every day.

'Arun, get the elections done. You have been one of the bravest officers of Gaya. You have to lead from the front.'

My words energized Arun. '*Huzoor, badhiya se election ho jayega.* The election will be conducted peacefully,' he said confidently.

I talked to the constables of the police station and was impressed by their high motivation.

'And put some sandbags near the gates. Also deploy a constable on the terrace. That's a vantage point to counter any Naxal attack,' I said, before getting into the car.

This time Narendra started driving much faster. All of us knew that there was a high probability that the Naxals might have come to know about our visit. We were all alert, looking around us. Just after about twenty minutes, our car stopped all of a sudden. Narendra turned on the ignition a number of times but the engine refused to come alive. He got down from the car and opened the bonnet.

'*Sir, gaadi kharab ho gayi hain.* The car has broken down. We will have to tow it,' he said.

All of us got down immediately, the tension palpable. All the bodyguards removed the safety catch of their weapons and cocked them. Everyone's hearts started beating faster.

I looked at the hills around us. If, by any chance, there were even a few Naxals on those hills, we would be sitting ducks for them.

Luckily for us, we saw a Maruti 800 coming towards us. Amod, my bodyguard, immediately stopped the car and asked the driver to get out. We knew that very few vehicles plied on this stretch and we might not get another car for a long time. We had no option but to leave our car there.

We quickly stuffed ourselves into the car, with Narendra at the wheel.

'Wait, make the owner of the car sit with you. We'll return his car at the Sherghati police station,' I said.

I was concerned that the man might tell people about our visit.

For the next half an hour, every moment felt like an eternity. Every time the car bumped over the potholes of the kutcha road, our hearts skipped a beat. Any of those holes could turn into a crater if the Naxals had planted improvised explosive devices or IEDs there.

As we were about to reach Sherghati, I got a call from Dilbagh. I checked my cellphone. Finally we had a signal again.

'Sir, we have just found three IEDs near one of the polling booths,' he said.

'Dilbagh, immediately evacuate the building. Try to surround the IEDs with sandbags. Ask the bomb-disposal squad to defuse them if possible. And you stay away from the site, you hear me!' I told Dilbagh.

'But, Sir, I need to stay and supervise it,' he protested.

'It's an order, Dilbagh. Sanitize the area and leave,' I said sternly.

Our Maruti 800 was about to reach Sherghati. We were all drenched in sweat, particularly the bodyguards sitting at the back. Luckily, the opening of the hatch let in some breeze.

The moment we reached the Sherghati police station, all of us felt immensely relieved. But then I saw the SHO Sherghati, Amjad, running towards me.

'*Sir, Sir, blast ho gaya!* One of the IEDs at the polling booth has exploded. I think there are at least two casualties.'

I stood motionless for a moment. All kinds of thoughts came to my mind.

What will I tell Kranti? How will I face the families of the deceased?

'Sir, Sir . . . ' Amjad tried to talk to me but I was lost in my thoughts. I gathered my composure and frantically tried calling Dilbagh. After a few harrowing minutes, it finally connected.

'Jai Hind, Sir. One of the members of the bomb-disposal squad is no more. One more constable is dead too,' said Dilbagh, his voice quavering.

'Where are you? What exactly happened?' I asked.

'Sir, I had left the area as per your directions. The area had been cleared and made out of bounds for everyone. Our bomb-disposal team got down to work, after taking all precautions. Unfortunately, as our expert was defusing the bomb, something went wrong and the bomb exploded! Everything was over in an instant.'

I closed my eyes and thought about the instant the bomb must have exploded. The bomb expert's body must have been blown to smithereens. But even in his death, he had saved the lives of so many people around him. He had taken the full impact of the IED.

I realized that the Naxals must have put a booby trap in the IED. The bomb-disposal expert must have cut the wrong wire and activated the IED. I felt immensely sad and anguished at the loss of the lives of my jawans. What was their fault? They were just simple people doing their jobs. The jawans also came from rural backgrounds. Many of them were the sole breadwinners of their families. Some of them could have joined the Naxals but chose to serve the country.

I felt extremely sad for the loss of the bomb-disposal expert and the constable. It was the first time in my decade-long career that I had lost some of my men.

I called the DIG Gaya Range and apprised him of the incident.

'I am aware of this accident—very tragic. Amit, it is a difficult time, but you must keep your chin up. You have to conduct the elections. You should not get demoralized,' said Jeet Sahi, the DIG.

* * *

'Major Saheb, arrange for the caskets for the two slain jawans. Also ask all ranks of Gaya to contribute at least a day's salary,

I want to send the money to the families of the martyrs. Let me know when all the arrangements are made,' I instructed the sergeant major.

I reached the police lines. The grounds were teeming with hundreds of policemen who had come to pay their respects to the martyrs. Everyone's uniform was drenched in sweat, their eyes wet with tears.

'*Sir, sab paise ikkathe ho gaye hain.* The money has been collected. Many people have given more than a day's salary,' said the sergeant major somberly.

I nodded. I knew no amount of money could get back the lives of the brave constables, but we could do at least this to pay homage to our martyrs

Soon, I got another call.

'Amit, we have reached Gaya. Where are you?' asked Sharma Sir, IG Operations.

'Sir, come to the police lines. We are about to send the bodies,' I replied.

'Are you sure? Is the situation all right at the police lines? Are the jawans not agitated?' asked the IG.

'Of course, Sir. Why would there be any problem?' I asked.

In fact, he was thinking back to a few years ago, when a similar incident had occurred and some jawans had ransacked the house of a senior officer in protest.

'Good, Amit, always treat the jawans like your family and take care of them. They are the ones who are willing to sacrifice their lives in the line of duty on their senior officer's single command.'

After a few minutes, the IG Ops and other senior officers reached the police lines. All of us saluted the martyrs one last time before putting their bodies in the trucks. The entire police lines reverberated with chants of '*Amar rahe! Zindabad!*'

39

Police Se Toh Sabhi Darte Hain

'Sir, SHO Aamas, Alok Kumar, has come to see you,' said my reader Om Prakash. I was finalizing the plan for the deployment of force for the impending assembly elections.

'Send him in quickly. I have to submit this plan to the observers of the Election Commission of India. I have a busy day ahead,' I said, looking at the reams of paper in front of me.

The SHO Aamas, a smart, young officer, entered my office, accompanied by five people, their faces covered with hoods.

'Sir, I was conducting a drive against criminals in view of the elections. I saw these five people roaming around suspiciously in the market. On rounding them up and checking them, we recovered three country-made pistols and a few looted cellphones. It is the same gang that was robbing people near the Gaya railway station,' the SHO said.

'Well done. Keep it up, Alok,' I said.

'If you permit, can we have a briefing for the media? Most of the press guys are anyway outside your office, covering the police's preparations for the elections,' Alok said.

'Okay, get the mediapersons in. You get your team that arrested these criminals for the photo op. Also give me their names, so I can award commendation certificates to them,' I said.

I had started interacting with the media and organizing press conferences to mark significant achievements by the police. I had learnt from my experience at Begusarai.

'*Sir, Begusarai mein aapka bahut naam nahin ho raha hain.* You are not making a name for yourself in Begusarai,' said Pradeep Tolani, a noted businessman.

'Why, Tolaniji? Things are so much in control here; the crime rate has gone down,' I had replied, disappointed with Tolani's observation.

'*Sir, woh toh theek hain, par police ka kaam logo ko dikh nahin raha hain.* That's all right but the police's work is not visible to the people.'

'What do you mean?' I asked.

'Sir, you do not appear in the newspapers at all. There is hardly any achievement of the police that is highlighted in the press. You have kept too much distance from the press. Without any news, you have kind of become an inactive SP to the public.'

I remembered my trainer Jaishankar Sir's advice too. 'Amit, you have to be visible in the media—appear once in while, so the public knows you are working hard. This instils confidence in the people,' Jaishankar Sir had said.

I then realized my mistake and started organizing press conferences when the police force did good work.

Alok called the press guys and briefed them. I was too busy to interact with the media and hardly even looked at the camera. After the conference, Alok removed the hoods and started ushering the criminals out. Just out of the corner of my eye, I saw a very young boy, barely out of his teens, in the group.

'Hey, you!' I gestured to him.

Alok and everyone else stopped.

'You are so young and seem to be a decent bloke. Why are you spoiling your life by joining criminal gangs?' I asked

'*Sir, hum kahaan crime kiya hain?* I have not committed any crime. I don't even know these people,' said the boy, tearfully looking at the criminals.

"Does this boy work with you?" I asked the arrested robbers.

'*Nahin, Sir.* No. We don't know what he is doing with us in your office,' replied one of the goons.

'Then, Alok? What is this?" I asked the SHO of Aamas.

'*Sir, ye ladka bhi wahi tha. Humein dekhke bhaag raha tha.* This boy was also there. He started running when he saw us. So I arrested him too,' Alok replied.

'*Sir, hum dar gaye the.* I got scared. *Police se toh sabhi darte hain.* Everyone is scared of the police. So I ran,' the boy said.

'Alok, this is not done. Let this boy go immediately,' I said.

'But, Sir, we have had a press conference and I just gave the names of all these people, including the boy's, to the media. Moreover, I have made a challan for the court. How will I remove his name?' Alok asked sheepishly.

'Alok, you can't spoil an innocent boy's life just for some paperwork. Talk to the media. I am sure they will understand. And tear the earlier challan and issue a new one,' I ordered.

'Son, go home. Sorry for the misunderstanding,' I told the boy.

The boy smiled and scampered out of the office as if he had got a new life.

The press was quite understanding and removed the name of the boy from the news article. Two days later, I got a call from the district judge.

'SP Saheb, I must congratulate you on behalf of the judiciary. We are aware of the recent wrongful detention of a young boy and are happy to know that you let him go. Well done!'

I had done nothing great. Instead of following a procedure that would surely have spoiled a young boy's life, I had followed my conscience and taken a decision instantly. It's always necessary to take the right step, even if it is only to correct a wrong one.

40

Jaan Bachegi Toh Naukri Karenge

'*Sir, poora thana jal gaya.* The entire police station has burnt down,' blurted the SHO Dhamdaha.

I had just joined as SSP Gaya.

'What? Really? I hope all the jawans are safe,' I said. I was about to take a slice of bread from the toaster when I received the call. The bread had charred to a dark black, with a little smoke billowing from the corners. I was not amused at the irony.

'No, Sir, everyone's safe,' replied the SHO.

I heaved a sigh of relief. Though an extremely rare incident, this was not the first time a police station had been burnt down. At that point, I was more concerned about the safety of my men and, of course, the law-and-order situation.

'What happened? Tell me in detail,' I said.

'Sir, early in the morning, a body was found floating in the pond next to the police station. Unfortunately, the people thought that the man had been murdered and dumped by the police in the pond. An agitated mob ransacked the police station and burnt it down in a frenzy.'

I immediately understood the situation. My intuition told me that the man must have gotten drunk, fallen into the pond and drowned to death. No policeman would kill a man in cold blood and throw the body in a pond adjacent to the police station. I also knew that one of the local small-time politicians was looking for an excuse to create some kind of ruckus to increase his vote base. And the body of a man from a particular community was the perfect opportunity for him to create a controversy.

I immediately told the DSPs of Sadar and Town to reach the Dhamdaha police station with additional forces. The mob fury had died down for some time after the burning down of the thana but things could flare up again. The DSP Dhamdaha, who had already reached the thana, somehow managed to pacify the mob for some time. I asked my driver and guards to get ready immediately.

'*Sir, aaj hum bhi chalenge.* Today I will also accompany you,' said Ajit, my most trusted and loyal bodyguard, who had been with me for the past ten years. He would usually stay back to take care of my family when I would go out to handle a critical situation.

'*Ajit, tum Madam ka dhyan rakhna.* You take care of Madam,' I told him.

'No, Chun, let Ajit go with you. We'll be fine,' Tanu said.

I could sense the earnestness in Tanu's eyes. A wife somehow develops an intuition when her husband is going to land in trouble. She had been right so many times earlier.

I didn't argue and asked Ajit to jump into the Sumo. The guard commander had already checked the rifles and ammunition. After my earlier experiences, I always kept body protectors, helmets, shields and, of course, lathis in the Gypsy accompanying me.

I kept inquiring about the situation on the wireless throughout the way. After thirty-five minutes, I saw a huge crowd, restive yet somehow in control, on the road close to the pond. I also saw sufficient police force in the area. The police station's burnt facade loomed in front of me. I felt sad as we had recently renovated the premises and made a special visitors' room, that, too, with the public's contribution.

'*Boss, ye toh theek nahin hua.* This is not good,' said the DM M. Muthu, on reaching the spot. This was the third time Muthu and I were working together. We naturally had a good understanding.

'*Ab toh ho gaya.* Whatever had to happen has happened,' I said with a resigned look.

'Let us keep the situation under control and we will take action against the rioters in a day or two,' said Muthu. Many times, the administration deliberately does not take action against troublemakers immediately, as it is impossible to predict how the public will react. As administrators, we also want things to settle down and return to normalcy.

We took a round of the area and talked to a few people. Though I was not happy with the public for burning down the thana, we tried to assuage their feelings.

'Okay, boss. Things seem to be normalizing now. Maybe the rioters have realized that the man must have been drunk and drowned in the pond,' Muthu said.

I partly agreed with him, but the policeman in me was still alert.

'Thakur, please see that the force gets some food. Ask the sergeant major to send some food packets from the police lines,' I ordered the DSP Town.

I knew we still had a long day ahead.

'Come, boss, let us sit in the BDO's office and discuss the next course of action. Ah, and meet Sushant Bajwa, a young probationer. He has joined Purnea for his training,' said the DM.

I looked at the young man, clearly quite ruffled on seeing the mob and a burnt-down police station.

'It's all right, Bajwa. You'll experience many such incidents,' I said, as I patted his back. He just looked down gloomily. Bajwa probably did not know that there were a lot of brickbats in our services. In fact, the brickbats were far more than the bouquets.

We had just settled in at the BDO's office when Ajit came running in. His expression made it instantly clear that something really bad had happened.

'Sir, the mob has gathered again and is coming towards us. *Sir, aap log jaldi yahaan se nikaliye.* Please leave immediately,' said Ajit, visibly tense.

'*Boss, kya ho gaya?* What happened? I thought everything was coming back to normal. I spoke to the local MLA, and other politicians and stakeholders, and they all assured us that there would be no more trouble,' said a bewildered Muthu.

'Let us go quickly. We'll find out soon,' I gestured to Muthu and Bajwa.

The scene we saw the moment we got out of the BDO's office will be permanently etched in my memory. There were hundreds of people baying for our blood.

Swoosh! A bottle flew right past my temple. I instinctively ducked, but there was a hail of stones and bricks coming our way too. I saw the mob getting closer. Quite a few rioters held Molotov cocktails, a crude device of a bottle filled with petrol and a means of ignition. It is also called a poor man's grenade. But, in this case, it was us who were the poor, hapless men. We had nowhere to run as we were surrounded from all sides. If we went back into the BDO's office, there was every chance that we would be burnt alive. We took cover behind the perimeter walls of the BDO's office.

'Where is the force?' I shouted out to Ajit.

Sir, most of the men have gone to eat lunch. Only a handful are here. *Doobke huye hain.* All the men are sacred. They need someone to command them,' replied Ajit.

I cursed. Why the hell did everyone have to go? The sergeant major should have distributed the food packets to the constables at their place of duty itself. Anyway, this was not the time to think about the sergeant major's blunder. I had to save our lives first.

'Ajit, you and Shankar go out and fire in the air. This will scare the mob and we can move to a more secure place,' I commanded Ajit and Shankar.

Shankar was the burly bodyguard of the DM.

Ajit cocked his pistol and ran out, shouting. He looked at Shankar but Shankar had not budged an inch.

'Shankar, what the hell are you doing? *Dimaag kharab ho gaya hain kya?* Have you gone mad?' Ajit shouted at Shankar.

Shankar, for all his size, was a timid policeman. He stood there, petrified.

'Shankar, Shankar,' I kept coaxing him.

'Shankar, you imbecile. Why the hell are you not giving covering fire to Ajit?' shouted the DM.

I realized that Shankar wouldn't be able to go and fire. He was too scared. I had to take matters into my own hands. I snatched his carbine from him and cocked it.

'Where are you going?' the DM asked me incredulously.

'I am going to challenge the mob. You can escape the moment I give you a signal,' I shouted.

'I am not going anywhere,' said Muthu.

Both Ajit and I charged towards the mob, shouting out to our policemen to join us. Ajit fired two shots in the air. The mob did not bother as they knew too well that the police would never normally fire at 'innocent' people. It was true. No administration wants people to be killed in a police action. Even if the people incite violence, it is for the police to show restraint.

But today was different. The DM and I were certain that we would be lynched. To his credit, the DM did not flinch. He was right behind me.

'SP Saheb, if need be, shoot at them. *Nahin toh apan log zinda nahin bachenge.* Otherwise, we will not remain alive,' said Muthu in his sweet Bihari with a distinct south Indian twang. I nodded and fired with the carbine at the wall of a closed shop. The ricochet of the bullets from the wall somehow scared the rioters for a moment. That was all I wanted. I moved forward and looked for policemen. A bunch of constables were hiding behind a *thela*, crouching with rifles in their hands.

'*Arre, utho, fire karo!* Get up and fire! Or all of us will die,' I shouted at the top of my voice.

The constables jolted into action and fired.

'No, no, don't fire at the mob. *Aasmani fire karo!* Fire in the air!' I commanded, realizing that the mob was retreating. A number of policemen started appearing now.

The DSPs of Sadar and Dhamdaha also came. The tables had turned now. We started charging the rioters with our lathis. Hell hath no fury like a woman scorned. Or an angry policeman.

As the police was taking charge, the DM got incessant phone calls from the state capital to show 'restraint'. But he was in no mood to relent.

'*Arre, hum mar jayenge toh kal humari body pe phool chadhayenge.* If we die, we will be cremated with state honours tomorrow. I don't want to be a martyr unnecessarily. Continue with the police action,' said an angry DM.

The police action continued for about two hours. We rounded up at least fifty rioters and sent them to judicial custody. The police made videos of the rioting and had sufficient evidence against all the mischiefmongers. The media was with us, for a change. The mob had torched a few vehicles of the media personnel too, which worked in our favour.

I returned to the BDO's office to take stock of the situation. I was drenched in sweat, my uniform soaked. To my shock, I saw Bajwa standing in his vest, a little torn in places, with his shirt rolled like a turban on his head. Muthu was staring hard at Bajwa.

'Wh—what happened to you?' I asked, worried for the young probationer.

'This guy doesn't deserve to be in the service. You will not believe what he was doing. *Bajwa, tum khud hi kyun nahin batate?* Why don't you tell SP Saheb yourself?' said Muthu angrily.

'Sir, actually I had got really tense. I have never experienced such a nerve-wracking situation in my life. I thought the best way to save myself from being lynched by the mob was to be part of it. *Toh maine apne kapde thode se phaad liye.* I tore my clothes to look like an ordinary civilian. I thought my dishevelled look and the turban would make me look like a labourer and make it easy for me to blend into the crowd. And I would escape. *Jaan bachegi toh hi toh naukri karenge.* I can do my job only if I am alive,' said Bajwa sheepishly.

'*Here, ye patthar bhi le lo.* Take these stones too. Hit us! This will make you a definite part of the mob,' snarled the DM sarcastically.

I remained quiet for a few moments, too shocked to believe what Bajwa had done.

'*Plan toh bura nahin tha.* The plan was not bad,' I told Muthu. Then both of us burst out laughing. At least he had brought some comic relief to a day that was full of tragedy.

41

Sa Re Ga Ma Pa Li'l Champs

'*SP Saheb, aap mein woh baat nahin rahi.* You don't have that fire any more,' said Dr Devi Ram, a reputed doctor of Purnea.

'Why? I am doing my job quite all right. The district is quite peaceful,' I said, surprised.

'No, Sir. You have to be seen by the public. Your work should be publicized, your pictures should come in the media more often,' the good doctor said.

'I have been in the service long enough. I am about to be promoted to the rank of DIG. I am past getting my pictures printed in the newspaper for trivial things. Of course, if something big happens, the media will come itself.'

'Sir, let me suggest another idea. You can stand on the main *chauraha* and keep an eye on any person who breaks the traffic rules. The moment you see somebody not stopping at the signal or people tripling on a bike, take off your belt and give them the thrashing of their lives—in full public view,' Dr Ram said.

I was mortified. Dr Ram was a highly qualified doctor, who had just returned from London. And he was suggesting such stupid things to me!

I politely declined his novel ideas. People in our country still want feudal policing to continue. I have been asked by numerous educated people to interrogate their servants using third-degree methods because they suspect them of stealing. This attitude needs to change, and, as senior police officers, it has to start from us.

In many countries, the police addresses the public as 'Sir' or 'Madam'. I often think that our police should do the same. But then, does the public follow traffic rules? Do people stop at red lights when there is no one to watch? Do we happily pay the fine when we are riding without a helmet or do we try to pressure the constable by saying, '*Jante ho main kaun hoon?* Do you know who I am?' I wish the public's behaviour also evolves enough to warrant being addressed as 'Sir' or 'Ma'am'.

* * *

'*Sir, ek Class XI ka ladka gayab hain.* A Class XI student is missing since yesterday,' said the SHO of the K Serai police station.

'I think he ran away from home. I inquired at the school. His results have not been very good of late,' continued Khalid, the SHO.

'Anything else? The father's financial status? Any family disputes, enmity with someone?' I asked specific questions, a habit developed from tackling so many kidnapping cases over the course of my career.

'Sir, the father is sitting with me right now. I'll get him to your office immediately.'

* * *

Pratap Sahu was a typical middle-class businessman. A simple person, he was remarkably composed for a man whose only son had gone missing. Human beings are programmed to think that no harm will come to them until it actually does. And then they don't know how to react. I talked to him about his family, his financial status and other things. Finally, I asked, 'Did you get any ransom calls? Your son might have been kidnapped.'

'*Sir, hum kamaa ke khaate hain.* We live from one day to another. I have a small everyday *kirana* shop. Why would someone kidnap my son? I don't have any animosity with anyone.' He broke down the moment I mentioned the dreaded 'K' word. His emotions gave way as reality sunk in.

'*Ab toh situation sudhar gayi hain.* Things are much better now. I thought kidnappings were a thing of the past,' he sobbed.

I cursed myself for suspecting that his son had been kidnapped. But as a policeman, I always feared the worst.

'How does he go to school every day?'

'Sir, by a cycle. It was found just about 100 metres from my house. His schoolbag was also on it,' said the father.

'Why would a boy park his cycle so close to the house if he wanted to run away? He might as well have run away on a cycle. And why would a child get ready to go to school if he had planned to run away from home? And, in any case, his results had been declared almost a fortnight ago. There seems to be no apparent reason for him to go missing. He might have been kidnapped,' I said matter-of-factly.

Contrary to popular perception, it is easier to track a kidnapped person than a missing person, for the simple reason that at least someone would call for ransom and give you some clues with which to move forward. But if someone went missing, it was difficult to track them down.

* * *

I remembered a particular incident a few years ago. I had had a very difficult time when I was the SP Begusarai because three children had gone missing. It so happened that the two sons of a renowned doctor had gone missing, along with the son of the compounder working in the doctor's clinic. The town SHO, Arvind, had done a thorough investigation immediately after he had received the news. The classmates of the boys had told him that the children, particularly the elder son of the doctor, were keen to take part in the reality TV show *Sa Re Ga Ma Pa Li'l Champs*, and that the boys had been planning to go to Mumbai for quite some time.

The town SHO had gone to the railway station to find if the children had boarded a train for Mumbai. A rickshawallah had confirmed his doubts.

'*Huzoor, main inn teeno bachchon ko station pe chhoda hoon.* I have dropped these three children at the railway station,' the rickshawallah had confidently said on seeing the pictures.

It was a clear case of the boys running away on their own, apparently to take part in a TV show. But the doctor would have none of it.

'SP Saheb, my sons have been kidnapped by Saurabh, the compounder's son. *Woh bigda hua ladka hain.* He's a juvenile delinquent. Send his father Govardhan to jail. It will put some pressure on Saurabh to release my sons,' the doctor said.

'But Doctor Saheb, the police is investigating the matter seriously. All the evidence is pointing to your children running away of their own accord. I agree that Saurabh must have accompanied your children, but what is Govardhan's fault?' I tried to reason with the doctor.

'Govardhan has links with smugglers in Nepal. He has been to jail earlier too,' said the doctor.

'But Doctor Saheb, all these are rumours. He has never been to Nepal. We have verified all the allegations against

Govardhan. And he was sent to jail a long time ago because of a false complaint by a neighbour. He has already been wronged once. How can I spoil his life on an unsubstantiated accusation? His own son is missing too.'

'I don't know anything. You put Govardhan behind bars.' The doctor was adamant. So was I. There was nothing to suggest that Govardhan was involved in the 'kidnapping'.

Soon, the issue snowballed, and all the doctors of Begusarai were up in arms against me. My effigies were burnt and there were daily protests against my 'inaction'. Even my son was mocked in school.

'*Tere papa kuch nahin karte.* Your father doesn't do anything,' said one of my son's classmates. I used to feel very bad every day. The chief minister also made a rare call to me, asking me to expedite the 'recovery' of the children.

* * *

'Lodha, why don't you send the compounder to jail? It will buy you some peace,' said my ADG earnestly.

'But Sir, he's innocent. You can inquire for yourself,' I replied, steadfast in my resolve to not send an innocent man to jail.

Luckily for me, the ADG was a bold man. Once convinced that the boys had run away by choice, he supported me to the hilt, even against strong opposition.

I was really worried about something untoward happened to the kids. As a police officer and a father, I did not want any harm to come to them. I put out an advertisement in major newspapers, which included my number and an appeal to call me if anyone saw the three boys.

Some politicians I had rubbed the wrong way were baying for my blood.

'*Begusarai mein aag lag jaayegi.* Begusarai will burn if any harm comes to the boys,' they threatened me. I knew they were waiting for an opportunity to ruin my career. I had found no leads to track down the boys. They did not carry cellphones and there wasn't any ransom call either. I hoped for divine intervention. I was under tremendous stress and finding it difficult to sleep.

* * *

'Sir, is it the SP Begusarai? I'm calling from Juhu beach, Mumbai,' said a man with a strong Maharashtrian accent. I checked my watch. It was 4.10 a.m. I had anyway been tossing and turning in bed.

'Yes, I'm the SP Begusarai,' I replied.

'*Sir, abhi mujhe teen bachche mile hain beach pe.* I've found three kids on the beach. It seems they have run away from home. They are quite hungry too. I'm calling you because I saw an ad in the newspaper and I think they are the same children you are looking for,' said the man.

'Please give me your address. Keep the kids safely. You'll be rewarded handsomely. And thank you very much!' I was really excited. My heart was pounding hard. This was unbelievable luck. I immediately called Arvind, the town SHO, and gave him the information.

'Take the first available flight to Mumbai. Once you find the kids, get them back to Begusarai immediately and straight to my office. No need to tell the parents right now,' I instructed the SHO.

I immediately sent some secret service money to the SHO to take care of the expenses.

I also called my batchmate who was posted in Mumbai and apprised him of the news. 'Vishal, just keep the news under wraps.

I do not want anyone to know that the kids have been found,' I requested. He immediately sprang into action and took the children into the Mumbai Police's custody.

I got a call in the evening from Arvind.

'Sir, *bachche mil gaye hain.* I have got the kids,' said an elated Arvind. I took a deep breath and thanked all the gods. My prayers had been answered.

I deliberately did not want the doctor to meet his sons at that point of time. The doctor was a strict father and would have easily forced his sons to concoct a story about their alleged 'kidnapping'.

The next day I met the children, working through a variety of emotions. I was angry at their stupidity, which had made life hell for me, but I was also relieved that they were safe.

I held a press conference soon after. The children answered all the questions of the press confidently.

'*Kyun bhaag gaye the?* Why did you run away?' asked a journalist.

'Li'l Champs *mein gaana tha.* We wanted to sing on *Li'l Champs.* I had stolen some money from home. We could not find the venue for the show and we also ran out of money,' replied the doctor's elder son.

I did not feel any elation but I did feel vindicated. The entire town, which had turned against me, suddenly became apologetic. And the local politicians had to eat their words.

* * *

After a few days, I saw Govardhan, his wife and Saurabh standing outside my residence. The moment I got out of the car, they hugged me and started weeping.

'Sir, we will always remember you. You have saved a family from certain ignominy. And definitely saved our son from being branded a criminal,' said Saurabh's mother. 'Whatever Saurabh becomes in life, we will remember you. You have given him a new lease of life.'

A policeman has to do his duty with utmost dedication, even if he faces a lot of trials and tribulations, and opposition from all quarters on the method of investigation. Those few days were terrible for me, but I was glad it had all ended well.

Ironically, when the organizers of *Sa Re Ga Ma Pa Li'l Champs* came to know of the boys' running away from home for their show, they specially invited them to Mumbai. And the boys were promptly eliminated in the very first round. Their singing was atrocious.

* * *

But, in Pratap Sahu's case, my gut feeling was that the boy had been kidnapped. I put the father's number on call observation purely on a hunch. I started listening in on Sahu's conversations, waiting for a call from the kidnapper. A few days passed, and there was no suspicious activity. I was getting restless. Finally, he got a call.

'*Tera beta mere paas hain.* Your son is with me. If you want him alive, pay Rs 25 lakh as ransom. I know that you have recently got that amount from the sale of your ancestral land. And it will be futile to tell the police. They can't trace me.' The voice was quite commanding.

'So it was someone who knew about Sahu's deals,' I mused.

I felt a little relieved that my hunch about the kidnapping was right. I clandestinely called Sahu to my residential office.

'So the kidnapper called you. That is a good development,' I said. Sahu was shocked that I was aware of the kidnapper's call.

'Sir, how did you know? You will put my son in danger,' he protested.

'Sahu, you will have to trust me and follow my instructions. Next time the kidnapper calls, tell him that you are arranging for the money. But insist that you want to talk to your son. That will ensure that your son remains safe—and alive,' I told him.

I immediately noted the kidnapper's number from Sahu's cellphone and sent it to the home secretary's office for call-observation permission. I ran the IMEI number and found that no other SIM card had been inserted in the kidnapper's cellphone. The call details showed only one call to the father. I concluded that the kidnapper was a professional. He knew well the police's modus operandi of tracking criminals through cellphones. I had to think fast and smartly find the kidnapper.

Three more days passed, and yet there was no activity on the phone of the kidnapper. I had to come up with some out-of-the-box ideas.

'Indu, do something for me. Pose as a call girl and call this number,' I told Indu, a female home guard who worked at my residential office, showing her the kidnapper's number.

'*Sir, kya keh rahe hain?* What are you saying? *Humse nahin hoga.* I can't do this,' Indu protested.

'Indu, a child has been kidnapped. I don't really know if the child will stay alive in the next few days. You have to entice the kidnapper,' I explained the grim situation to her.

'And, yes, you are one of my smartest staff members. You can do it,' I said to instil confidence in Indu.

'Okay, Sir,' she said, a little reluctantly.

'Put the phone on speaker, so I can also hear the conversation,' I said. She dialled the kidnapper's phone and waited with bated breath.

After a few seconds that felt like an eternity, a rough yet controlled voice answered, '*Kaun bol raha hain?* Who's speaking?'

'*Arre, Sir, main aayi thi kal Katihar station pe.* I had come to Katihar railway station yesterday. You had promised to pay me for my services. Why didn't you come? I was wearing a red sari with a sleeveless blouse, as desired by you,' said Indu, in a fake accent.

I smiled at her ingenuity. She was lying so cleverly, making it seem like a normal conversation.

The job of a policeman requires one to become anything according to the situation; a policeman can become a mediator to assuage a mob or an actor to fool a suspect.

'It seems you have dialled the wrong number. Don't call again,' said the kidnapper tersely and disconnected the call.

I was a little disappointed as the criminal had not fallen for our bait.

'Doesn't matter, you keep calling him after every two or three hours. He might get lured,' I said, hoping against hope.

Indu called the number again after sometime. '*Hello, jaaneman. Naraaz ho kya?* Sweetheart, are you angry with me?' said Indu in a sexy voice.

'I told you not to call. It seems you have some confusion,' said the kidnapper angrily.

'No, no, this was the number given to me by my pimp. *Raja, mujhse mil lo.* Meet me, my king. I will make you happy,' Indu said unabashedly.

The phone went silent. Again, no luck.

'Okay, thank you, Indu, for being such a sport. Let me think of some other idea,' I said.

Out of ideas and with no new leads, I tried to sleep for a few hours.

* * *

I was nearly asleep when I heard a loud knock on my door. I cursed and turned in my bed. The banging continued. I was surprised and a little worried. In case of any emergency, which is quite common in my line of work, I usually got a phone call from my telephone orderly or directly on my cellphone. Who would be banging on my door at this hour?

I opened the door and saw a visibly tense Indu in front of me. I just hoped that the kids were all right. On some days Indu took care of my daughter Aishwarya, as she was quite attached to her.

'Sir, the criminal called me a few minutes back,' she said in a hushed tone. I checked the cellphone. It was 3 a.m. Quite an unusual time for a normal person. But then, we were dealing with a criminal.

'What did he say?' I asked.

'Sir, he just asked me my rate. But he called me from another cellphone. The incoming call was not from the number you gave me.'

'Then why did you not talk further?'

'I disconnected the phone saying I would discuss the rates with my boss, the brothel owner. I thought I would talk to him as per your instructions.'

I gave her a wry smile. Indu was indeed a smart policewoman.

'Okay, call him right now and try to decide on a place to meet. Negotiate the rates a bit and agree with his demand.'

Indu redialled the number. Her call was answered immediately.

'*Haan, bolo*. Speak,' said a voice on the other side.

'I'll charge Rs 5000 for a night. Transportation charges extra,' Indu said.

I could immediately sense that the caller was not the kidnapper Indu had talked to in the morning.

'I'll give you Rs 3000. Meet me at the Katihar railway station near Platform No. 2 tomorrow at 11.30 p.m. if you are interested,' the person said.

'*Okay, rate toh kam hain*. The rate is low, but I'll come. I will be wearing a green sari for you to identify me,' Indu said as she looked at me.

I nodded.

'Okay, see you tomorrow.' The line went blank.

'Phew!' Indu took a deep breath.

'Good job, Indu. The guy you talked to just now must be an accomplice of the mastermind, the main kidnapper. He must have overheard your conversation with the mastermind and gotten excited by your proposition,' I spoke, channelling my inner Sherlock Holmes.

I motioned to Indu to rest and waited eagerly for morning to arrive.

By 11 a.m., I had the call details of the kidnapper's accomplice. The SIM card was found to be issued in a fictitious name. The tower location kept changing between Purnea, Katihar and Bhagalpur. I quickly made a list of the most frequent incoming and outgoing calls. By afternoon we had ascertained the identities of two callers who were constantly in touch with the accomplice. I asked Arvind to bring Sahu, the child's father, immediately to my house so I could ask him about the two names, Shyam Kishore and Mafat Lal.

'Sir, Mafat Lal is my neighbour. I have very cordial relations with him,' said Sahu Pratap.

'Can I call him in for questioning? You sure you don't suspect him?' I asked.

'Absolutely, Sir. Mafat Lal is a decent man.'

Mafat Lal was standing in my residential office in half an hour. He was trembling in fear.

'Why are you scared? Are you a criminal?' I asked in a deliberate baritone, glad in this situation that at least some people were still scared of the police.

'Huzoor, I have never talked to a constable and you are the SP, the boss of the district,' said a terrified Mafat Lal.

'I really wish I could be the boss of the district and find the boy,' I thought.

'You have received a call from this number quite a few times. Whose number is this?'

'Oh, this . . . This is Raushan's number. He is the son of Gautam Sahu, our neighbour, though I have not seen him in the last fortnight,' Mafat Lal said.

'Arre, Sir! Raushan has recently been out on bail. He was arrested six months ago for being a suspect in a kidnapping case,' Arvind exclaimed.

'Then why didn't you tell me earlier?' I said, a little upset.

'Sir, I had used an informer to keep tabs on Raushan but he was not seen for quite some time. His father also assured me that Raushan was working in West Bengal and had mended his ways. Since I did not find anything suspicious, I did not tell you about Raushan. Apologies for that, Sir. *Humse galti ho gaya!* I made a mistake!' said the SHO, his head down.

'What did Raushan call you for, Mafat Lal?' I asked.

'Sir, just routine things. And, yes, he did ask me about the sale value of Pratap Sahu's ancestral land,' he replied.

Everything was almost clear now. Raushan must have discussed Sahu's deal with some criminals, whom he must have met in jail. Being a neighbour, he must have easily lured Pappu and then kidnapped him. I just had to find Raushan to get to the boy.

I called Ajit, Parmatma, Indu and two other trusted constables.

I gave them a brief on the kidnapping.

'Indu will pose as a prostitute and all of you will take positions around her at Katihar station. The moment Indu gives you a signal, grab the man.' I gave detailed instructions and sent them off.

* * *

I kept looking at my cellphone. It was well beyond 11.30 p.m. I was a little worried that Ajit had not called yet.

'*Tension mat lo*. Do not worry. Have patience,' said Tanu lovingly. She knew exactly what was going on in my mind.

I got up and switched off the TV. After a few minutes, I got a call from Ajit.

'*Sir, lagtaa hain gadbad ho gaya*. I think something has gone wrong,' he said. I could clearly feel the disappointment in his voice.

'Sir, the man called Indu on her phone and abused her,' he continued.

'Why? Give the phone to Indu,' I said.

'Sir, the man called me and asked if I was wearing a green sari. When I confirmed, he shouted at me and said that I was a middle-aged, rotund and unattractive woman. He said that I had wasted his time and abused me,' Indu said, now in tears.

I cursed myself. Raushan must have seen her from a distance and abandoned the idea of meeting Indu.

'Don't worry. Call the fellow right now and tell him that you are just a *maalkin,* or a supplier of girls. You will provide the girls to him after the deal has been struck.'

Indu immediately called up Raushan.

'Hello, I have a lot of young, beautiful girls. How do you expect me to take them with me everywhere? *Chain se kaam kahaan karne deti hain police?* There's so much police pressure nowadays. I will supply a girl to you once we strike a deal,' she said.

There was a studied silence at the other end. After a long pause, the man answered, 'Okay, bring me a young girl near the Jubilee paan shop, K Hat Market, in Purnea tomorrow at 4 p.m. Ask her to wear a red sari. And make sure you get a good-looking girl.'

'*Bilkul heroine hogi.* She will look like a heroine,' Indu replied.

Indu and the entire team reached early in the morning, looking haggard and tired, yet with hope in their eyes.

I briefed Ajit and the other members of the team about the trap we were laying for the kidnapper's accomplice.

'Call a young lady constable from the police lines—anyone reasonably attractive,' I said to Ajit. It was something that I had to do to nab our man.

After half an hour, a young, smart woman was standing in front of me.

'Constable Reena reporting. Jai Hind, Sir,' she said.

I told her about the operation. 'Please do not mind but please put up some make-up and dress up. We need to entice the kidnapper. *Koi shaq?* Any doubts?' I said.

'No, Sir,' replied Reena confidently.

'Ajit, all of you take positions near different shops in the market. The moment Reena makes contact with the guy, grab him,' I told Ajit.

The plan sounded simple because it was. We just needed to execute it well. And like always, we needed some luck.

Ajit, Indu, Reena and the other policemen saluted me and left for K Hat Market at 3 p.m. Exactly, at 4.30 p.m., an elated Ajit called me.

'Sir, *pakda gaya!* We have caught the guy!'

I was delighted.

Within twenty minutes, Raushan was sitting in front of me with his hands folded. Ajit narrated the exact sequence of the 'successful' operation.

'Sir, we had all spread out around the Jubilee paan shop. Reena and Indu sat on a bench near it. Suddenly I had hunger pangs. I crossed the road to buy some chips. Sorry for that, Sir,' said Ajit sheepishly.

'When I was buying the chips, I saw a "*gunda mawali*"-type boy loitering around. And then suddenly he made a phone call, and said, "*Woh jo ladki lal sari mein, woh toh sundar lag rahi hain.* That girl in the red sari is quite beautiful."

'The moment I heard this statement, I knew he was our man, Raushan. I dropped my packet of chips and grabbed him.'

I laughed, imagining Ajit grabbing the neck of poor Raushan. It's always good to have some burly guys in the police.

'*Jaldi bataa, bachcha kahaan hain?* Tell me, where is the kidnapped boy?' I asked Raushan sternly.

I always believed in cornering a criminal by asking direct questions that implicated them. If you ask a criminal, '*Bataa tune kidnap kiya hain kya?* Are you the kidnapper?', the criminal will never accept it. My ploy almost always works.

'Sir, *bataata hoon.* I'll tell you. I needed some money for my expenses. I came to know about the money Pratap Sahu got from his land sale. So I thought of kidnapping his son. The boy lived in my colony. It was easy for me to lure him on the pretext of showing him a blue film. Santu and his gang members then overpowered him and took him to Bhagalpur Diara area,' blurted out Raushan. 'I know the place. In fact, I saw the boy two days ago. He's doing well. Santu will take care of the boy. I had met Santu in jail and became friends with him. He's a thorough professional.'

'Professional my foot! *Criminals bhi professional ban gaye!* Even criminals are now being called professionals!' shouted Ajit at Raushan.

I asked Arvind, Ajit and Satish, the town DSP, to immediately start for Bhagalpur to recover the boy. Of course, Raushan was also put into the vehicle.

'Satish, when you are about to reach Santu's hideout, ask Raushan to call him. We have to get Santu at any cost.'

After three hours of a tense drive, Satish and the other policemen got out of the car and walked for another hour or so. As they were about to reach the hideout, Satish asked Raushan to make the call to Santu.

'Santu, boss, I have to meet you. I need to discuss something urgently,' Raushan said. We don't know what alerted Santu but he just disconnected the line.

The police team immediately rushed towards the hideout and broke in.

Satish found Pappu in a stupor. It seemed that he was dehydrated. He had been heavily drugged.

'Sir, *Pappu toh mil gaya hain, par Santu nahin.* We have Pappu but Santu has escaped,' Satish said.

At least Pappu was safe. I was relieved. We would get Santu some other time.

It took us a full three months to arrest Santu and all his gang members.

Pratap and Pappu Sahu boldly testified against the dreaded criminals and ensured their conviction.

This was my last case as an SP. A few days after we wrapped it up, I got promoted to the post of DIG.

42

Mere Yahaan Bhi Bijli Nahin Aati

'Sir, we are going to organize a peaceful dharna in front of the power grid premises tomorrow,' said Dr Sripal, as he stood before me with a few other doctors.

'Why, Doctor Saheb?' I asked.

'SP Saheb, the power supply is really bad. We hardly get any electricity, even though the power grid corporation is located in Nalanda, our district,' said another doctor.

'It is so difficult for us to run our clinics. Even otherwise we face so many issues every day because of the erratic power supply,' Dr Roy said.

'The power grid does not generate electricity—it only transmits power. The dharna is not going to solve Nalanda's electricity woes,' I said, trying to reason with them.

'*Sir, ab toh soch liya hain.* We have made our decision,' said the doctors in unison.

'Chalo, let them do whatever they want to,' I thought after the doctors had left. I issued orders to deploy forces near the power grid campus as a precautionary measure. I was hopeful the 'dharna' would be event-free.

* * *

The next day, I brought my son Avi to the office so I could spend time with him and also give Tanu some time to relax. He was happy, playing with the many pens on my table, when I got a call from the DSP Sadar.

'*Sir, jaldi aaiye.* Come soon. The dharna has turned aggressive. They will burn down the power grid campus,' said Paswan, the DSP. He sounded tense.

'Arre, how is it possible? Only a few doctors were supposed to sit on dharna as a peaceful protest against the power supply. How can they try to burn down the power grid office?' I asked.

'Sir, there are hundreds of people who have come out of nowhere. In fact, more people are joining in from other areas as well. Please come with adequate force,' said Paswan.

'Okay, I am on my way. Till then, keep the crowd at bay by using tear gas,' I said.

'Sir, we fired tear gas at the crowd but the people picked up the tear-gas grenades and threw them back at us. Moreover, the wind is in our direction, so the tear gas is blowing towards us,' said the DSP.

I was surprised and worried. I had not received any information on the congregation from the special branch or the local police stations. If the mob did cause damage to the power grid campus, it would be catastrophic and a failure of leadership on my part.

'Ajit, take Avi home immediately. I will go to the power grid with Shukla, Ritesh and other bodyguards. I have also called for additional force from the police lines,' I said, quickly rushing out of the police station.

* * *

When my Gypsy reached the power grid premises, I was shocked to see not hundreds but thousands of people surrounding the area.

'The crowd is not against the police. This is just a protest against the power grid. I should be able to talk to the people,' I thought as I saw a few familiar faces in the crowd. Just as a precaution, I put on a helmet before getting out of the Gypsy.

'*SP Saheb zindabad!* Long live the SP!' Some people suddenly started chanting my name. I knew I was popular with the public, particularly the youth. Emboldened, I took off my helmet and walked towards the crowd.

However, my confidence in my 'popularity' was extremely short-lived. From the corner of my eye, I saw a brick flying towards me. I ducked, but the brick hit me on my cheekbone. In shock, I sat motionless on the street for a few moments. Before I could gather my senses, Ritesh and Shukla cocked their carbines and started shooting in the air. As loyal bodyguards, they were supposed to protect me. Unfortunately, the firing had the opposite effect. The mob got even angrier and started closing in on us from all sides. I got up dazed and looked around.

The force from the police lines had not reached yet. I saw the DSP and his posse of constables valiantly guarding the gates of the power grid campus. There was no way they could come out.

I had to quickly take a decision. The situation could escalate to uncontrollable levels and people could get extremely violent. Heavily outnumbered, we could be lynched and the power grid would most certainly be destroyed. Moreover, I would face a departmental inquiry for not being able to handle the situation.

I mustered up the energy to get up and call out to Shukla and my officer guards.

'*Goli mat chalao.* Don't fire!'

Seeing that the guards were not relenting, I physically started stopping them, asking them to lower their weapons.

Once my team stopped firing, I started waving my arms and gestured to the people to come forward.

'*SP Saheb paglaa gaye hain. Hum sab maare jayenge.* SP Saheb has lost his mind. We will all get killed,' I overheard one of the guards saying.

But I kept waving at the crowd, hoping the people would stop and listen to me.

I noticed a few young men I had spoken to at earlier events and had developed a good rapport with.

'Arre, Ravi, Ashish . . . Why are you throwing stones? Please stop it,' I shouted.

Luckily, the youngsters responded favourably to my call and asked the crowd to cool down. Soon, the people started dropping the bricks and stones they had picked up from the road and walked towards us. By then, Inspector Rajgir P.C. Sinha, an excellent officer, had reached with forces from the police lines.

The mob's fury fizzled out when they saw so many policemen.

Somebody again shouted, '*SP Saheb, humein maaf kar dijiye.* Please forgive us for our unruly behavior.'

A number of people came forward and apologized. Sensing that the tide was turning in our favour, I climbed on to the bonnet of my Gypsy to address the crowd.

'*Bhaiyyo!* Brothers! It is true that the power situation is bad in our town. Even my house does not get sufficient electricity,' I said.

There were loud cheers from the crowd, happy that I was acknowledging their problems and even facing the same issues they were!

'But your protest was not the right way to air your grievances. You could have submitted a memo to the government. Violence does not behove the people of Nalanda, the land of the Buddha and Mahavira,' I continued with my sermon, like a seasoned politician.

The huge crowd listened to me quietly and, when I was done, dissipated, leaving behind a trail of bricks and stones on the road.

DSP Paswan and his men emerged from behind the gates of the power grid complex. All of us heaved a sigh of relief, for we had managed to avert a major disaster without the loss of any life, including ours.

Suddenly, a few doctors came towards me.

'Sir, we are extremely sorry. We do not know how so many people joined our dharna. Before we realized what was happening, the crowd swelled and started becoming restive. We were reduced to mere bystanders,' said Dr Sripal, his eyes filled with guilt.

'SP Saheb, I think this crowd comprised unwanted elements from a local politician's party. The politician must have thought of taking advantage of this mass movement to increase his popularity,' added another doctor.

'Now, please come with us. We should get some tests to ensure your injury is not serious. You are extremely lucky that the brick hit you on your cheekbone and not on your head,' Dr Sripal said.

I had been very fortunate. Just a few months earlier, the DSP Hatia, U.C. Jha, had been hit on the head with a stone while handling a mob. The brave DSP had gotten his head bandaged and returned to duty immediately. Unfortunately, he had later developed complications and passed away. Sometimes, the difference between life and death is just a few inches for a policeman.

As for the power situation, ironically, it became even worse in Nalanda after that day! It is a different matter that Bihar now boasts much better power supply.

Epilogue
Aakhri Goli, Aakhri Dam Tak Ladunga

My camouflage dress was dripping with sweat. I constantly wiped my forehead to avoid the salty sweat from entering my eyes. The hot sand also kept flying into my face as my Gypsy drove over the huge sand dunes.

'*Sir, aaj toh temperature kam hain, nahin to ye 52–53 degree pahuchta hain.* Sir, today the temperature is lower, otherwise it reaches 52–53 degrees,' said Inspector Shyam Kaushal, a veteran of the Border Security Force, or BSF.

'When I joined the BSF almost thirty years ago, we had to ration our water. *Company commander paani ko taale mein rakhte the.* The company commander used to keep the water under lock and key! *Hum ko decide karna padhta tha ki kitna nahaye ya peeye.* We had to decide how much water we would use for a bath and how much we would drink. Water was so limited then,' continued the inspector, recalling his early days.

'Really? And what about desert coolers?' I asked, realizing how absurd my question was.

'*Arre, Saheb, uss waqt toh hum jhopdo mein sote the.* That time we used to sleep in huts. Getting water itself was a luxury—there was no question of a cooler! And, honestly, these things never bothered us. We used to just patrol the borders on our camels, keeping an eye on smugglers and infiltrators. We also had to watch out for scorpions and snakes,' he replied.

I finally reached the border outpost to take a look at the operational procedures of the BSF. I had recently joined the BSF, the world's largest border-guarding force, and had been posted as DIG, Jaisalmer sector. I had done my share of district policing in Bihar and wanted to have a different experience. Moreover, I was lucky to get a posting in my home state of Rajasthan. Though I was still a good 700 kilometres from my parents, it was a big psychological comfort for them to know that I was in the same state.

'Let us take a round of the border fence and interact with the jawans,' I told the inspector.

After sometime, we came across an ACP, or an ambush-cum-patrolling party.

'Sir, main Constable Gurnaam Singh. I am Constable Gurnaam Singh. I have an SLR and two magazines. Aakhri goli, aakhri dam tak ladunga. I will fight until my last bullet, my last breath!' he thundered.

I was impressed by his warrior-like demeanour and steely gaze.

'Gurnaam, tumhe koi taqleef, koi shikayat? Do you have any problem, any complaint?' I asked.

'Nahin, Sir. Kaisi taqleef? Desh ki seva ka mauka mil raha hain. No, Sir. What problem? I am getting a chance to serve my nation,' he replied resolutely.

I met a number of other jawans, but not one of them complained about the sweltering heat or the inhospitable terrain. I admired the dedication of the BSF men I worked with.

A few days later, I met Inspector Shyam Kaushal again.

'Sir, ek dukhad khabar hain. There is sad news,' he said, almost choking with tears.

'Sir, remember Gurnaam, the constable you had met on your last visit to the border?'

'Yes, of course! What happened?'

'Sir, he is no more. He has made the supreme sacrifice of his life for the country,' Shyam said.

'How? I mean, I just met him,' I stammered, shocked to hear the news.

'Sir, his battalion moved to Jammu and was deployed at the LoC. His bunker was attacked and damaged by heavy shelling from across the border. Even then, Gurnaam assumed his duty at the same post. The post came under fire again from the enemy. Without caring for his life, Gurnaam engaged the terrorists and killed them. Unfortunately, a mortar landed exactly at his bunker and killed him.'

I felt extremely sad to hear the news.

A family had lost its son, a breadwinner—and his old parents their support.

I found the number or Gurnaam's parents and called them. I gathered some courage and finally said, '*Maaji, mujhe bahut dukh hain Gurnaam ki shahadat par.* I am very sad to hear about Gurnaam's martyrdom.'

'*Gam kis baat ka, beta?* What is there to feel sad about, son? Gurnaam laid down his life for our country. It's a privilege very few people get.'

I had goosebumps. What a strong and brave woman Gurnaam's mother was.

Whenever I move around the border and meet a jawan or a lady constable, I always hear in the end, '*Aakhri goli, aakhri dam tak ladunga.*'

I feel proud to be a member of the force where everyone is a Gurnaam Singh.

Acknowledgements

First and foremost, I want to like to thank my readers, who loved my first book *Bihar Diaries* so much. I am fortunate to have been motivated by the countless messages from book lovers all over the world, from places as diverse as Vancouver and Dhaka! Milee Ashwarya, my friend and editor-in-chief of Penguin Random House India, almost threatened me into writing my 'memoirs' as a police officer. Not many people can do that with a policeman. Thanks so much, Milee, for getting me out of my comfort zone.

Next, of course, I thank my family, which has always been my biggest pillar of strength. My son Aditya, a voracious reader himself, went through my manuscript countless times. I am impressed with his patience! Lots of love to the two beautiful ladies in my life—my wife Tanu and my daughter Aishwarya. Neither has bothered to read the manuscript, but they don't need to—they have lived every moment of the book.

I want to thank my parents, Dr Narendra Lodha and Asha Lodha, and my father-in-law, Arun Dugar, for always motivating me to try new things. My brother Namit lives in the United States, but his heart beats for us in India.

My friends, who have always stood by me. I know I can count on them anytime.

Superstar and super human being Akshay Kumar, the uber-cool Emraan Hashmi, the incredibly talented Virender Sehwag and the brilliant Neeraj Pandey have encouraged me in all my endeavours. Hussain Zaidi, one of India's most famous crime writers, has been instrumental in introducing me to the world of writing. And a very special thanks to the rock star of Indian writing, Amish Tripathi, for writing such a wonderful foreword to the book.

Special mention to Roshini Dadlani and Ujjaini Dasgupta for going through the manuscript so painstakingly and improving it in every sitting, and my gratitude to Sarthak Sinha for making me look so good in the cover illustration. I express my gratitude to H.C. Bhawani Singh Rathore for typing out reams of my handwritten notes.

This book would not have come into existence had it not been for the extraordinary work of my colleagues in the police. The hard work, dedication and sacrifices of police personnel largely go unnoticed, but they continue to work selflessly. My salute to the Indian police and the paramilitary forces.